Who Knows Tomorrow

Who Knows Tomorrow

*A Memoir of Finding Family
Among the Lost Children of Africa*

Lisa Lovatt-Smith

WEINSTEIN
BOOKS

Printed in the United States of America.
Editorial production by Marrathon Production Services. www.marrathon.net
Book Design by Ellen E. Rosenblatt, SDDesigns LLC

Cataloging-in-Publication data for this book is available from the
Library of Congress.
ISBN: 978-1-60286-270-8 (print)
ISBN: 978-1-60286-271-5 (e-book)

Published by Weinstein Books
A member of the Perseus Books Group
www.weinsteinbooks.com

Weinstein Books are available at special discounts for bulk purchases in the U.S.
by corporations, institutions and other organizations. For more information,
please contact the Special Markets Department at the Perseus Books Group,
2300 Chestnut Street, Suite 200, Philadelphia, PA 19103, call (800) 810–4145,
ext. 5000, or e-mail special.markets@perseusbooks.com.

First edition

10 9 8 7 6 5 4 3 2 1

This book is dedicated to my mother, Margot, who dared to dream of a different existence from the one she was born into—whose bravery, tenacity, and uncompromising honesty I have happily inherited.

I wrote this book for my five children:

Sabrina, her love made me into a mother and the injustices done to her made me into a warrior.

Fatima, who, like me, cares for other people more than she does herself, and finds herself in the process.

Mensah, who has looked after me more than any other man on earth and saved me time and time again, particularly from myself.

Beliratu, my little fighter, an inspiration who turned her life around with sheer willpower, the lulu, our Lulu.

Ernest, my naughty little Buddha, twelve-year-old poet and philosopher; our family's resident wise man and teacher.

I love you so much; you are my whole life.

But don't be satisfied with stories, how things
have gone with others. Unfold
your own myth, without complicated explanation,
so everyone will understand the passage,
We have opened you.

—Rumi

This is a work of nonfiction. I have changed the names of some places and individuals and modified identifying features, including physical descriptions and occupations, in order to preserve their anonymity. Occasionally, timelines have been compressed in order to further preserve privacy and to maintain narrative flow. The goal in all cases was to protect people's privacy without damaging the integrity of the story.

Prologue

*T*he complicated thing about living in the African bush is water—or rather the lack of it. Sure there was a stream, but it was in a snake-prone bamboo grove and the local fetish priest had bewitched the water so that it killed dogs (or so everybody in the village believed), and I wasn't about to chance it. Fortunately we actually had piped, honest-to-goodness government of Ghana water, which was bloody unbelievable considering we lived three miles from the nearest settlement on the main road.

So somehow we got our own tap at home. You turned it on and piped water came out. Sometimes. In the capital city of Accra, three hours' drive and a whole different lifestyle away, the water flowed once or twice a week. Here it arrived maybe once a week and for some unfathomable reason, usually at midnight. "Because you are up a hill," the bespectacled water guy confidently informed me. Anyway, you filled your bucket and took it into the outdoor bathhouse, on your head gracefully and as if you were wearing a particularly odd hat if you were my daughters, or huffing and puffing and poking your arm out lopsidedly if you were me.

Still, we had never thought it was even a remote possibility to have water coming out the tap in our forest home, however intermittently, so whenever it did flow it was a big deal. Which was why I came to be standing in the middle of the tropical night holding a hosepipe thinking about my foster father's death . . . and the flight back from the funeral the day before yesterday . . . and how the flight attendant wouldn't let me sleep on the floor of the airplane, which was the only thing I felt like doing after he was gone.

I was filling the water tank under the tropical night sky, which because we lived so far from any form of electricity was full of the shiniest stars. I was doing all this in the complete darkness and with no shoes on, wrapped in a scrap of African cloth, because that is how we lived. Tanks were assiduously filled up, no matter what time of day or night the water started to flow.

Our tank took a long time to fill. My eyes were itching and the dried sweat on my forehead was irritating. So after a while I jammed the hosepipe into the top of the tank and held it down with a biggish rock, checked on my two children, and snuggled down beside my husband, Kweku, for a rest. I fully expected to get up again to turn the tap off, since after many years of water shortages our ears had become finely attuned to the different water gurgles, especially *the tank is full and precious water is splashing over the top* type of gurgles.

Except that night. Worn out from the week and my daughter's thirteenth birthday party the day before, and the funeral and the flight, I fell sound asleep. With the bedroom door unlocked.

Ɔwɔ foro adɔbɛ.

—Akan proverb of the Ashanti people, Ghana

A snake climbs the raffia palm tree.
(You can achieve the apparently impossible.)

1

 M y story starts with Italian tomatoes; apparently they were directly responsible for my conception. My curvy, tiny English mother, who had dyed her blond pixie cut brown to downplay her gorgeousness, was having trouble getting pregnant. The market women in Lerici made her success their own personal quest.

"*Pomodori, signora, deve mangiare gli pomodori . . . di piu, di piu.*"

The village of Lerici's claim to fame is that the British Romantic poet Percy Shelley drowned there in the blue Mediterranean while returning from a visit to Lord Byron. Sunny, beautiful, Italian, and romantic. And it had tomatoes. So that's where I was conceived while my mum and dad—English like Shelley and his wife Mary, who wrote *Frankenstein*—lived in a rented house. My parents were temporary visitors, just like they were.

Mum and Dad were both from the North of England, and had married in London, where the bride wore a dark-purple mini (it was the sixties, after all). My father's family disapproved, since my mum was a grocer's daughter from Scunthorpe, and thus was considered common. My dad was a lanky blond art student of no fixed ambition who excelled at the Royal College of Art. He was raffish and apparently not common at all.

My mother was determined to see the back of Scunthorpe as soon as she could escape its dreary confines. One can hardly blame her: this was the lackluster industrial North of England. As a child, for six months of the year she had to break the ice in the pail before bathing. She dropped out of school at sixteen and apprenticed to a hairdresser, where she practiced on poodles dying them pink and blue, kick-starting what was to be an illustrious career as a colorist. Not, mind you, before she'd carried off the "Queen of Rock 'n' Roll" title from the local US Marines. My mum loved dancing—she was really good at it—and rockin' and rollin' in the center of an admiring crowd was when she felt most alive.

She bought herself a two-week package tour to Italy, where every good thing she had ever suspected about the south became a certainty. Her tiny waist and lively looks attracted trails of adoring Italian boys. From the day the joyful recipes of Elizabeth David had crossed my mother's path, the notion of the Mediterranean with its sunlight, fresh figs, dark wine, and bare legs descended upon her like a religious experience. When the tour ended, she promised herself she would live there one day.

In the meantime London would have to do and so she moved there, staying at the YMCA. By 1964, the year that Swinging London was invented, my mother had turned twenty-six, rented a flat, changed her name from Margaret-Ann to Margot, and dyed her hair as blond as could be. She had reached the pinnacle of her profession as celebrity colorist at the famous House of Leonard. The salon was a tiny, bright star in the world's hippest city, because in the early 1960s, hairdressers and makeup artists changed the world, and London was the epicenter of the funky new universe.

My mum could pull off any shade of blond from Twiggy to Bardot. She gloried in her talent, partied, and surrounded herself with a lot of nice gay boys. She was hot, sociable, and fun.

London was about to become the swinging belly button of the world, but Mum still aspired to the Mediterranean. Then she met my dad and they made a pact; my mum wanted to get as far away as possible from England, and my dad would tag along for the ride.

So my young soon-to-be parents drove to the South of France in a rented "yogurt pot" of blessed memory, a quintessentially sixties vehicle with three wheels and no balance. Once on the coast, it immediately overturned (with no damage to my parents) and expired on the spot. My parents wafted around by train until the holiday was over.

The following year my father neglected to come home one night and sent a dozen red roses in his stead. My mother shredded them and danced on the ruins of her marriage in the living room, while downing a bottle of red wine. To cap it all, her husband had run away to Italy (*"Italy, my country"*) with a girl named Dorothy (*"Dorothy, what a common name"*). Chain smoking and with only twenty-five British pounds in her pocket, my mum threw in her brilliant career and finally moved, as she had always wanted, to Italy—by bus, and broken-hearted.

Soon, Dorothy exited the picture and my father courted my mum all over again, until she relented and they settled in the Bay of Lerici on the Italian Riviera, where pale-pink and yellow houses tumbled into the sea like pastel baby blocks.

My mother remembers two main things about their crumbling apricot house: the plumbing (lack of) and the wall geckos (abundance of). It was perched on terraces cut into the steep rugged landscape near the top of a cliff and had a wonderful view of the sea. It was the most impractical choice of location, as it was inaccessible by road. In a gray flannel suit, my father commuted weekly to his job at a top-notch, ultra-trendy advertising agency in Milan. Secretaries in heavy black eyeliner and shiny vinyl miniskirts tripped across the white shag carpet in their platform shoes. Knowing my father's roving eye, my mum hated every one of them. During this time she stayed home and lived in a bikini, theoretically nesting but in reality dedicating herself to her lifelong religion: sun worship that involved lashings of tanning oil.

The one time she *was* called upon to entertain, the chic Milanese guests had to kill and pluck the chicken themselves, as my "Made in England" mum hadn't realized it would be delivered from the market alive.

* * *

By New Year's Day 1967, with bright hopes for what turned out to be a seriously turbulent year, all those tomatoes my mum had ingested had paid off: they were about to have me.

It was the year of the Summer of Love, and in a bout of early onset spring fever, my parents, then six months pregnant, blithely decided to leave their pleasant Italian life by the sea and transport themselves to a repressive military dictatorship: Generalissimo Franco's fascist Spain. I still fail to understand the logic; compared to other cities, Barcelona had very little going for it. London was booming, Milan's golden age of design was about to climax, the United States was one big hippie love-in—but Barcelona? Apparently, my parents were once again in search of a blank canvas. This time, though, they were about to get more than they bargained for.

Under dictator Francisco Franco's regime, the capital of Catalonia had been for decades an oppressed and angry city where the people were barely even allowed to speak their own language. Noth-

ing was happening in Barcelona beyond a few strikes and a lot of
resentment. And even if the subtleties of political repression escaped
them, my father was soon to discover there was scarcely any advertising industry to speak of.

They leisurely crossed the Mediterranean from Genoa to Barcelona by boat, my mum with her elegant white coat flying in the wind
and her big belly peeking out. Boy, she must have trusted him, to
prepare to give birth somewhere in a new place where she didn't
even speak a word of the language. Characteristically she hit the
ground dancing; so much so that after a particularly energetic night
on the tiles and a midnight snack of strawberries and cream, I
popped out a month early. It was the fifteenth of April, the day huge
demonstrations were held against the Vietnam War in New York
City and San Francisco. I was a worryingly tiny two-kilogram, or
four-and-a-half-pound, baby. They had been in Spain barely eight
weeks.

My parents took the usual vastly impractical decision and moved
to Sitges, a tiny quiet coastal village forty minutes drive south of
Barcelona. Picturesque scenery, white-washed cobbled alleys ending
in sea views, steeples and churches, women dressed completely in
black . . . *That* apartment was on the top floor in an old fisherman's
house beside a café called Gustavo's, ten feet from the sand. My parents had several cages of singing birds. And they had me, who swam
before I could walk. It was the Mediterranean dream incarnate.

By the time I was two, my young brilliant father with the easy
infectious laugh had become the toast of the elite who dreamed of a
newer, more groovy Barcelona. His ad campaigns were light-hearted
and airy. At the end of the sixties wave, they spoke of a freer era.
He and my mother threw parties on the beach attended by men
with goatees and women whose fringes brushed their eyelashes.
These *yé-yé* boys and girls (the Spanish version of "yeah, yeah!")
were the Gauche Divine, the Catalan intelligentsia who looked to

France for inspiration and were waiting for the old dictator to die. They smuggled porn, rock music, and champagne from France, along with magazines that revealed the latest fashions. The foreign sheen still on him, my dad was their darling. He was a breath of fresh air, and Barcelona loved him.

Our family fortunes picked up. We moved to a splendid art deco apartment overlooking Turó Park in uptown Barcelona. A Portuguese contessa lived next door, and she fed me *perunilla* cookies flavored with cinnamon and lemon, and weak milky tea. Afterward, a governess wheeled me through the park in a navy-blue pushchair. I had white-blond hair and blue, blue eyes. I posed for tons of bonnie-baby commercials that my dad made.

My father was the darling of the incipient advertising and magazine industry, and therefore was never home. My mum was not having as good a time. Also, in the endless Spanish summer, the streets of Barcelona were dusty and gray, and the light was harsh. The city had turned its back on the sea, despite being a port. It was also profoundly conventional; the small freedoms my mum had previously taken for granted were absent. Censorship was everywhere in the form of black squares in every newspaper and magazine. Sex did not exist, and neither did bare breasts or legs. Foreign radio services were blocked. In the butchered movies shown on TV at night, clumsily cut by a censor, the protagonists invariably went straight to breakfast after the first kiss, as empty film slithered across the screen. On Sundays only brass bands and religious services were on TV, and the dictator endlessly pontificated in a language my mother could not understand. If someone invited you to come to their apartment for dinner, you had to stand outside the building and clap, which was the signal for the *sereno*, the night watchman, to open the door. You could not just turn up. The codes of society were strict and hard to crack. Everyone over thirty wore black; married women never wore trousers, and they stayed indoors. On Sundays they wore lace veils to church.

This dark bitter Catalan city was not Mum's idealized southern world. She wore bright-colored mini-shorts and clickity-clackety wooden sandals until November. She was like the Coppertone girl, tan all year round, smelling of coconut and carrot oil. She loved the sun, long white beaches, and the juicy pleasures of eating and cooking. At this point, with her simple zest for life, the stay-at-home wife with peasant tastes might have slightly embarrassed my father, who was now playing a bigger game.

One day she returned from the market to our expensive apartment, only to find that all my father's clothes were gone. He had taken off with a woman named Debbie. There and then, when I was four, he disappeared off the face of my earth.

He left behind

1. Piles of thick, peculiar-smelling storyboard paper, which for the next ten years I would use to draw on. These were a very exotic and inky black, with six white squares that represented TV screens with the space to write the scripts below each screen.
2. One big box of Caran d'Ache colored pencils, arranged by tone like a rainbow.
3. One box of pastels; square ones that left clouds of powdery tint on your fingers.
4. Four postcards from Paris, all identical, all saying the same thing: "I love you, Daddy."

The snapshots from before I was four show a tall slim man; a sharp dresser. I can't remember him at all, not even his smell or his eyes. I can, however, recall the myth of him with outstanding clarity.

My mum was devastated, although she would never show it. Without my dad, my mum felt like a nobody. Instead of damning him for leaving her stranded, she immediately started weaving the fairy tale of him. This was the myth that sustained us both for twenty years. Unbelievably, she never spoke a word against him. She felt they'd had ten good years together and she'd been blissfully happy, which was more than most women got out of marriage, she said. That they never fought. That until it was off, it was always passion-ately *on*. His friends were divided into two opposing camps. The men wanted to sleep with her. The women wanted her to return to England and get welfare and legal aid.

* * *

She had absolutely no money. She had never finished school, had few marketable skills, and could not drive. She could not speak a word of Catalan; only a little Spanish mixed with Italian. *And yet my mother didn't leave fascist Spain, where she had no one, for an easier life in England.* In this solitary fact lies coiled the essence of my profoundly unconventional childhood. She didn't go back to Swinging London, which by 1971 had seen the breakup of the Beatles, the exodus of the Rolling Stones, and the rise of hard drugs, glam rock, and a haircut called the shag. She was plucky and stubborn, and determined not to drop her Mediterranean delusion.

She moved us to a small apartment in Castelldefels on the long beach south of Barcelona. From then on, our apartments would only get tinier and more dismal, and there would be a long succession of them, sometimes two or three a year. These were rundown rooms in buildings slapped together for seasonal holiday makers on the long streets that ran between the pine forest and the endless dunes.

My mum decided not to look for a hairdressing job because it would mean too many long hours away from me. She found a sum-mer job teaching swimming for a few pesetas, but by the time autumn rolled around again we were both very lost. I vaguely remember a boyfriend with a Doberman. That is, I remember long hours playing with a Doberman. And another who bought me a dress that was too small, but I could not tell him so because I was supposed to be nice to him.

Within a few months, when I was five, Paul and Barbara, a very affluent couple also from the North of England who had two children and who had socialized with my parents in better days, offered to take me in.

2

*F*or almost a year, my mother walked up the long road from her tiny flat to Paul and Barbara's sprawling house so she could tuck me in every night. That fostering arrangement saved us both. It gave my mother some respite from looking after a toddler, and gave her time to sort herself out. She got another job teaching kindergarten in an English school, and she went steady with the boyfriend who'd given me the dress, a handsome taciturn electrician named Juan.

Meanwhile, I had found a brother and sister and parents; a family that was warm, stable, prosperous, and loving. Paul was a self-made man with a roar of a laugh; Barbara was a cordon bleu cook who looked after us children full time. She made things like Rice Krispie® treats clusters and no-cook biscuit cake, and we were made to have long hot baths every night. They had a pool with yellow tiles, and toys I never knew existed. I liked the protected feeling of having a dad around (especially when he barbecued spare ribs), and I loved having siblings, especially Jonathan, who was almost exactly my age. We even looked alike.

After about a year Price Waterhouse transferred Paul and Barbara to Italy, so I went back to living with my mother. This was in many ways a much less safe and sunny situation. My mother could be crabby, exhausted, and just plain absent in a way that Barbara, for obvious economic reasons, never was.

Mum had finally gotten a steady job teaching school to kids my age in Barcelona. This meant she had a commute that involved an over-twelve-mile bus ride on bad roads, plus a tube ride with longish walks at each end. Door to door, it took about two hours each way. She was to do this crazy commute for almost ten years, so she could remain living near the beach.

This meant that for much of my childhood I was alone for long periods in the mornings and evenings. It has also translated into a lifelong inability to wait calmly for people, especially at night. Waiting for her to return in the dark early evening of the short Mediterranean autumn days, I was acutely conscious of being alone in the world. With Paul and Barbara gone to Italy, there were no aunties, uncles, or cousins around. No grandparents; no safety net. With a child's perspicacity I realized that, in order to survive, it was essential that my mum not disappear as my father had. I had to look after her.

Eventually, when she had saved up enough, my mum did decide that we should visit England in the summer holidays. She wanted me to meet my father's family and her parents, and I'm sure she was hoping to get news of him.

There are photos to prove that I met my grandparents on my mother's side, and also Grandma Jay, my father's mother, a tall elegant woman with white hair. She was unable to provide information on my father's whereabouts, but gave us the family Bible as a kind of consolation. It was too heavy to carry all the way back to Castelldefels, so my mum left it somewhere. And that was that for my birthright.

It was inconceivable that my dad had cut all family ties, and yet that was the case. My dad never even knew when his mum passed away a year later.

* * *

The next big adventure was school. A group of "concerned individuals" had approached Pedro de Verda, the headmaster of the Anglo-American School, a small school originally built for the children of soldiers on local army bases. They explained my predicament and made a strong case for my mum. Mr. de Verda agreed to take me in for free as long as I kept up good grades and behavior. I was to stay until I was eighteen, providing some much-needed permanence as well as a decent education. That man's kindness, along with that of Paul and Barbara's, helped to define the course of my life.

"The Anglo," as we called it, was a haphazard mix of thirty nationalities and four hundred kids: hippy-dippy kids, embassy kids, rich expats, and exotic refugees all thrown together, with the occasional lost local child. I was consistently brilliant in class, and consistently miserable out of it.

The seventies were in full swing. The main fun activities at my school were four-square and table tennis. Oh, and bullying, mostly of me. I was the perfect candidate. My need to please (and keep my scholarship) meant that I was a teacher's pet. I had thick glasses, I was plump, and I was poor. So poor that while the other kids wore jeans and sneakers, I wore my mother's hand-me-downs.

I didn't have jeans or sneakers. Or snacks at break, or a car. Or a dad. So I made the most of my differences. I excelled academically. During every recess, I sat on the green baize sofa in the entrance opposite the secretary's office and read every single book in the library. To me, it was quite simply the greatest place on earth; a treasure trove of stories.

I collected a band of stray dogs dumped by the vacationers that infested our village in the summer months. I roamed alone with up to eight dogs at a time, feeling protected in their numbers. I saved my scarce pocket money to feed them, and tried not to mind that I did not have any friends. Instead I had the mutts, and miles of pinewoods and coastline to roam unsupervised. I would talk only to the dogs, because no one wanted to talk to me. It was a strange, lonely childhood.

The only kids who were sometimes nice to me were the clappy-happy churchy ones. I knew why: they were taught they had to be nice in the endless Bible lessons they listened to. One of the evangelicals was bookish, like me. His name was Andrew Reid, and he was as skinny as his name implied. The Agatha Christie he lent me was a bit beyond me but, still, I signed up for Bible club.

High expectations at school accompanied the overriding need to keep Mum on track, especially in light of the quantities of red wine she was consuming. Every weekend morning, I made her breakfast in bed. Every Saturday I cleaned the house. My life revolved around the need to behave well, get the grades, keep the scholarship. I couldn't let anyone down.

When I was eight Francisco Franco, the dictator who'd held Spain in the palm of his hand like a little dove for thirty-nine years, nearly squishing the life out of it, lingered close to death for weeks, monopolizing everyone's attention. Daily life slowed down to the rhythm of his belabored breathing. They played only military music on the TV.

When he finally made up his mind to die on November 20, 1975, the whole of Catalonia exploded in a massive vice-fest. All the stashed porn was taken out and displayed defiantly on the newsstands; Juan the electrician went on a drunken spree that lasted three days. What was happening on the streets was in stark contrast to the twenty-four-hour TV coverage in its ultra-dreary real-time reportage of mourners filing past the open coffin.

Spain threw off its lethargy like a dog shaking its pelt. The old ways changed remarkably fast. Up until I was about nine, the standard Saturday night fare was outdated musicals: *Singin' in the Rain, An American in Paris, The King and I,* and the whole of Esther Williams's back catalogue. Everything more modern was sliced up by the censor's scissors. By 1976, however, wearing a leotard and holding a giant calculator, Victoria Abril had made her appearance in the first locally made hit variety show. She was the pinup of the new order; a sequined revolutionary. In many ways, it seemed that modernity was about the amount of flesh on view.

In my little seaside town, Catalan could now be heard spoken openly on the street. In a burst of nostalgia, Juan began dragging me on strenuous and sweaty hikes through the woods to visit the caves where he and his family had hidden out when he was a boy during the time of resistance to Franco. On Sundays, in the time-honored tradition of Catalan men, he cooked the sacrosanct paella. By three o'clock the group that congregated around the *sofrito* was chattering in a mix of Catalan and Spanish. In our deeply left-wing household, politics and food and wine were all mixed up in the Sunday sunlight.

The memory of those slow Spanish weekends is engraved on my soul. After lunch, the red wine would prevail and the adults would sink into a heavy sleep until dusk. I'd wander off with the dogs.

* * *

Despite the crippling dyslexia that held me back in early primary, by the time I was ten I was doing really well. Nobody ever came to pick me up or came to the school, so the teachers felt protective of me; divorce was still a rarity at that time. I learned a lot because those teachers cared.

The summer I was twelve, Mum and I set out on what was to be our last expedition to England together. Mercifully, this time we were not following the ever-fainter traces of my father, who was obviously fully intent on staying "missing." It was the late seventies and the "whole earth" thing was in the air. We spent time with Mum's communist cousin Peter and his wife Norma in big bohemian London. They had a brood of children and a big house. Everything about their eccentric household was deeply intriguing. First of all, they were the Meacock-Fryers, not just the Fryers, and that seemed very unusual. Even more strange, I was supposed to call them Peter and Norma, not auntie and uncle. Norma Meacock was tall and rangy with lots of frizzy black hair and long skirts and jangly earrings, and she intimidated me. I was a dedicated reader, but I had never met a real live writer before.

Then there was Peter, Mum's second cousin. He was shorter than Norma, and roundish like Mum. I didn't have much experience with dads, but this one seemed widely eccentric; smoking pot, playing blues on the piano at all hours, and storming about the house on occasion. None of this seemed to perturb his children. Male outbursts have always alarmed me disproportionally, probably because I never had a proper dad-in-residence. Peter got particularly tetchy if he was disturbed during his writing.

Peter had a round face and a goatee, and he wore modern heavy glasses with rims at the top but not at the bottom. He was something called a Marxist. Considering that I had lived my whole life under a fascist dictator, I thought that was kind of cool.

He was writing another book, about black people. They visited him at all hours, sometimes to play or listen to music. I had never met a black person before, and I was instantly attracted. Spain in the seventies was still very insular and there were very few non-Caucasians, apart from those in my school, and certainly no black people. He had lots of writer visitors too; such as a man with a name like a song: Sal-man Rush-die.

Peter and Norma's children were James, Frances, and Emily. James was a very tall redhead. Frances was interested in teen things, but Emily, two years younger than me, was amazing. She was tall, messy, and very straightforward, with a strawberries-and-cream complexion and clothes from jumble sales. For the first time, I felt I had found a soul mate; a sister, a best friend. We chose clothes out of the riot of her closet, ate together, played music, and rolled around on the lawn like puppies. For the first time in my life, I felt fully accepted by a girl nearly my age.

In that house it was normal to read all day. After all, had Norma herself not been made famous by a book she wrote called *Thinking Girl?* That household taught me not to be ashamed of my mind. From that family, aside from vegetarianism, I took away the idea that writing could be a respected profession.

The children had visitors too; particularly Hamish and Sarah Bowles who were family friends. Hamish was four years older than me; tall, thin, and flamboyant. He was to play a part in my life forever.

3

*T*hat summer we took the boat to visit Paul and Barbara (my foster parents, whom I now called my godparents) in Turin. Mum had been going on about Italian food, Italian light, Italian men, and Italian shoes for so long that her excitement was infectious.

In Genoa, there were men pinching her bottom and whispering, *"Ciao, bella."* Mum flushed with delight as she peeled off loads of lire, big sheetlike banknotes, to pay for a genuine plate of *pasta al pesto* among the sailors and prostitutes of the country's biggest port. As introductions to vice go, it was pretty okay. We devoured little volcanoes of impossibly flavorful Parmesan atop the oily misshapen *trofie,* and then we walked around the streets eating *gelato.* I will never forget that meal; as far as I was concerned, Italy *was* heaven. In particular, the Italian teens looked so slick that they expanded my fashion references beyond the weekly gypsy market at home.

I was thrilled to see Paul and Barbara again. Although I barely remembered them, I remembered the *feeling* of them: safety and plenty. I was used to our cramped quarters, so the double-height living room, the TV room, and the bar seemed majestic; like something out of a film. Their huge fridge was full of the most delicious things to eat, and everything revolved around food. Jonathan and I spent hours building dens in the garden and hanging out.

* * *

The summer when I was fourteen, Mum and I both worked for a month at a camp in the Pyrénées. She taught English, and I was a sports prefect and general dogsbody. It was my first job. With our pesetas jingling in our pockets, we then traveled to Italy to visit Paul and Barbara again.

They were in Rome now, and I birthed a strong affection for that lovely mysterious city where the past erupts out of the ground on every street corner. Barbara would make *pasta alle noci* or *alla salvia*. My mum would try to grow tomatoes in their garden while I shared Jonty's *motorino* and hung out at the pool and the tennis courts with his friends. Every few days, Paul would pile us into his giant cream-colored Mercedes-Benz and drive us off to some leafy candlelit garden restaurant along the *via Cassia*. In the cool of the Roman evening, we would eat wonderful antipasti and inevitably finish up with *frutti di bosco*. Those are the best memories I have of growing up; the most carefree, the most innocent, a whole sea's-width away from the bullies at school.

That year my mum finally tired of the commute and took the monumental decision of moving to Barcelona. Juan did not move with us, but I didn't miss him too much. We had never been close, although he had always been perfectly kind to me. My mum found an apartment, the fourteenth one I had lived in since my birth (a rate of about one per year).

This apartment was a whole new kind of tiny; only about forty square meters, and perched on the flat roof of an uptown Barcelona block. The building belonged to a widowed marchioness who had built herself a fabulous sky-garden floating seven stories above the road. She had a cloistered patio as well as a lawn and proper-sized trees, including cypresses. Just off this garden and separated by a high wall was the *terrado*, a flat red-tiled roof for drying the wash. The *marquesa*'s defunct husband had built himself a chic shack on the roof; a miniature artist's studio with tall paneled windows and a sheltered patio. The two small rooms were converted into bed–living rooms, one for me and one for my mum, and we slept on sofa beds. Each room had a quirky fireplace, as there was no heating or air conditioning. All my schoolmates lived in sprawling suburban houses or the fashionable luxurious high-rises that contractors were throwing up overnight in the boom brought on by the still-fragile democracy; our new home was—well, different.

My mum was determined to get herself a new life: she sold the bicycle, shook off the beach blues, started going to the opera, wearing makeup, and buying better clothes; even some for me. Occasionally she would buy British *Vogue*, as foreign magazines, films, and books were mercifully no longer censored and now allowed to flow freely into the eager Spanish market.

These were the very first years of the radical youth-quake that was the Spanish *movida*, a delayed post-Franco cultural flowering. Suddenly school and its preoccupations seemed a tiny bit provincial. My mum got me involved in the theater club, which eventually had the intended effect: being onstage made me less insecure in every way. I began to think that maybe the bullies at school were just plain wrong. After all, if I played the lead in Cinderella, with a proper pumpkin-shaped carriage made of cardboard and gold paper, I couldn't be all *that* fat and ugly, could I?

When I was fifteen, we spent the summer in Paris in a tiny *chambre de bonne* in the fifth arrondissement, up eight flights of spiral stairs and with a view of Notre Dame. Mum borrowed it from a glam Parisian writer friend. The one-room studio was ingeniously built like the inside of a ship; everything folded in and out, and the kitchen was in a cupboard. I had never seen anything like it; it seemed so sophisticated. Actually, the whole city did. Mum had not been here since my dad overturned the three-wheeler in the early sixties, and she was thrilled too.

We got by on a shoestring, spending as little as possible. We walked everywhere, ate in the cheap Algerian restaurants, and explored massively. I loved it, and swore I would live there someday, knowing that eventually Price Waterhouse was due to relocate Paul and Barbara there. The French language, however, resisted me. I spoke to everyone in a mix of Spanish and English, with a smile.

My mum and I got close on that trip. She was single for the first time I could remember, and I was growing up. One day we sat in the Tuileries and talked about the fact that I was interested in becoming a vet, or perhaps a writer. We also talked about university. We'd visited the British consulate and spoken to the teachers, but it seemed there were no government grants for people who were not "ordinarily resident" in the United Kingdom. We should have been paying taxes in the UK for the last couple of years in order for me to qualify for free university education. I'd never asked my mum to return to England, since I knew she wouldn't. It was not clear how I could afford to go at all.

Although my further education was up in the air, my mum had always made it clear to me that, to her, I was the most beautiful and talented child in the world. Through her confidence in me came the buoyancy and resilience that would support me in life. Her unconditional love convinced me that I could succeed, whatever the situation. Despite all the moving around, and the poverty and the changes, I was safe in that love. But I also knew that she was very lonely, and that soon my life was going to spin me very far away. She was my heroine, even as I worried that she would fall apart. From that day forward, whenever I got the long bit of the wishbone, I whispered the same thing: "Happiness for Mummy. Happiness for Mummy."

* * *

That September when I was sixteen, I got a steady gig teaching English three times a week to a little Chinese boy. From that moment on, Mum never had to shell out for me again. Downtown Barcelona between the port and the cathedral was dark and dusky, and had definitely not yet been gentrified. Yet on Mondays, Wednesdays, and Fridays I got off the noisy, smelly old bus and religiously tramped down the Ramblas to tutor Dar-Wah in his family's restaurant.

First there was the Ramblas itself, built over the bed of an ancient river, carving through the medieval city to the port. The wide promenade was like a litmus stick of the human experience. At the top there were the noisy, cheerful pet stalls with canaries, budgies, turtles, hamsters, and the occasional monkeys or pythons. Then came a few hundred yards of insanely bright flower stalls, with hundreds of bouquets to give to your mother, wife, girlfriend, or lover. The promenade wound its way, sloping slightly toward the sea, to the main market, *la Boqueria,* with its luscious, almost obscene displays of fruits. Around the opera, the flamenco *tavernas,* the *Grand Hotel del Oriente,* and superbly *modernista Hotel España* gave way to cheaper hotels around patios, with rooms that could be hired by the hour. Lower still, almost within hearing distance of the waves, were the police station, the all-night bakery, and the bars that still sold absinthe, as in Jean Genet's time. This area sheltered the money changers, the gamblers, the prostitutes, the cross-dressers, and the tired-looking transsexuals in their tawdry glittery shoes.

Since it was right after school, I'd stop off in the *Boqueria* to buy a snack. The riotous market extended far beyond its stained-glass façade, and was a paradise for a hungry kid. There were fresh fruits

I had never tried, such as mangos; different cheeses; mounds of gemlike candied fruits; and piping hot *churros con chocolate,* long fingers of deep-fried sugar-dusted batter that I dipped into thick rich chocolate. My turnoff from the loud, busy Ramblas into the maze of tiny streets was just after the market. I veered to the left into the medieval area around the cathedral; never to the right, which led to the drug-addled *Raval.* Everywhere men whispered the soundtrack of my adolescence: *"Rubia!" "Guapa!" "Hermosa!"* ("Blondie!" "Pretty!" "Beauty!")

The predatory looks on the street didn't bother me; that was just the way it had always been. My hair was white-gold, and among that southern race it shone brighter than I did. As a teenager I was prone to severe introspection, and I didn't see the need for boys. I was much more interested in dogs.

That summer I got my fourteen levels, was officially branded a star pupil, and given extra leeway by the teachers. I began modeling in earnest, in particular for Helena Curtis, the Spanish arm of L'Oréal hair products. They shot me in a ton of makeup and with elaborately styled and colored hair. I did a few catwalk shows, doing my own makeup (as was the norm then). I used tips from the transvestites I met with my gay friends from the theater group as we trawled the drag clubs. My gay friends were the most fun because they never gave me any pressure. They wanted to look like me, not seduce me, so we were cool.

I had done a few TV adverts, even starring in a low-budget TV series, and did a radio course on how to learn Spanish. But my forte was always going to be my hair, and so one day I went to a go-see for a shampoo advert with a famous Italian photographer called Gianni Ruggiero. He was graying at the temples and spoke perfect Spanish with a strong Italian accent. After a few awkward stares, I suddenly realized that he had probably been part of Mum and Dad's arty-farty sixties Gauche Divine crowd.

After he had taken the shots, I changed into my own clothes and sauntered over to him casually.

"Hi, Gianni," I said to him in Italian. He looked up sharply; not many models in Barcelona spoke Italian.

"Ciao, bella." His eyes took me in. He didn't recognize me, since I was a child the last time he'd seen me.

"I wanted to ask you if you know an art director called David Lovatt-Smith."

"*Certo*, that crazy guy. Yes, I like him. But I haven't seen him for a long time."

"How long?" I asked.

"*Eee, no lo so—*" he grunted, distracted. He was looking through the camera at the next girl, and I had lost his attention.

"Please, it's important," I said urgently.

Gianni turned around and looked at me straight in the eye. He started laughing. "Why? Has he left you pregnant?"

In that moment, the floor seemed to rise up and hit me in the face. I literally recoiled, as if slapped. Tears filled my eyes.

"No," I said softly. "He's my father." I turned on my heel and left the studio, shaken to the core.

I never told my mother.

* * *

Peter and his youngest daughter, Emily, came to visit. He came for the jazz and blues, and the extreme left-wing politics. Emily came for the sunshine, and to see me. In the early evening, cool after the oppressive heat of the Barcelona day, we went to the Zurich. The ancient sprawling café had a view straight down the Ramblas, and was a rallying point for militant students who believed in Catalan independence. We would sip frozen tiger nut milk, *horchata de chufa,* while Peter talked politics until late into the night.

Barcelona had not yet been "discovered." The recent coup had put casual tourists off, and the city was still mean and gritty, infested with sailors fresh off the hundreds of ships in the industrial port. The musicians in town were mostly American, like the antinuclear activist Jackson Browne. The musicians stayed in cheap *pensiones* and lived on a dollar a day. Peter dragged me to all the nightclubs to be his translator and, as he was an authority on the blues, I learned a lot from him.

After finding out the evening's lineup we would take Emily home, since she was only fourteen, and eat some of my mum's mouth-watering Italian cooking. Then Peter and I would head off again to the jazz joints, which opened at eleven. I was dragged into one smoky underground den after another, surrounded by musicians, cigarettes, alcohol, and drugs. I floated through it protected, I suppose, by an aura of total innocence. I was there for the music, and to learn from Peter, whom I really admired.

A drummer from the Bronx called Alvin Queen saw me watching the show one night, and within half an hour asked me to go live in Switzerland with him. I vaguely entertained the idea, but even that failed to alert my mum that perhaps spending my nights in smoky jazz holes was not ideal for a teenager. He had just brought out a record call *Ashanti*, which he told me was the name of an ancient tribe in West Africa. "They produce gold," he said, looking deep into my eyes and squeezing my little hand in his black one. That was the first time I heard of Ghana.

4

*I*n March 1984, when I was sixteen, I picked up a copy of *Vogue* that my mother had left lying around the house. I knew she'd only bought it because it was a tenuous link to my father; she was more of a *Cosmo* girl. But the heavy glossy pages of *Vogue* reminded her of the luxury my dad loved. Even thirteen years after his complete disappearance, she still wanted to remind herself of her past life. The February issue was a half page dedicated to the *Vogue* talent competition. It quickly caught my eye. Hamish Bowles had done it a few years before; the prize was a fortune, £500, and a job at *Vogue* for a year.

I read the ad again. *Vogue* wanted four pieces of writing, of which the main one should be an autobiography. I got butterflies in my stomach. I decided that I was going to do this.

Over the next few days I mulled it over. My odd lineage—born in Spain but Italian at heart and English by blood—might be peculiar enough to attract the judge's attention. You were supposed to be younger than twenty-five to enter, but it didn't say anything about having to be over eighteen. Hamish had been under eighteen too.

A few weeks after I submitted my entry, I had just reached home after my two-hour commute from school. I was exhausted; in addition to classes, I was in a play and was teaching every night. I had researched my options in terms of grants and universities and decided to apply to Cambridge, even though I had no idea how I would pay for it. I'd been feeling depressed about my lack of funds for university.

I took the service elevator to our little rooftop shack. I rested my cheek against the glass door as the ancient lift proceeded at its usual leisurely pace, juddering and clanking at every floor. I came out of the dark stairwell into the soft light of the early evening. Barcelona spread out below me like a carpet. My mum ran out of the house, waving an envelope madly like a woman possessed, so full of glee that she seemed to be levitating.

I dropped my school bag and hugged her back, although I wasn't sure what was happening. She had of course *not* resisted the urge to open the envelope before me. I looked at the letter; I was invited for lunch at Vogue House, Hanover Square, London, in four weeks' time. I was so excited, and somehow vindicated: miracles *could* happen, it seemed. I could not believe my luck; I rushed to call Emily to tell Hamish. The next day I told my teachers. Everyone was surprised; I was only sixteen, and *Vogue* and London seemed very far away indeed. Mum's main concern was what I should wear.

My previous visits to England had served me well, not only providing fodder for my travel essay, one of the required pieces for *Vogue,* but also preparing me for the intricacies of London transport. Days after my seventeenth birthday I flew alone to Vogue House. I was staying at Peter and Emily's. Peter was vaguely supportive, but mostly locked up in his room working on the publication of his magnum opus, *Staying Power: The History of Blacks in Britain.*

I took the tube to Oxford Street station, pondering the fact that Hamish had done this too. I studied the map in the station for ages, and eventually emerged from the crowds of shoppers on Regent Street into the austerity of Hanover Square. I looked straight down the pavement and saw VOGUE HOUSE, written in discreet gold letters across the lintel of the revolving door of a seven-story redbrick corner building. There was a bright red phone box right in front of the door. The moment felt charged with significance, and my stomach contracted nervously. Suddenly I realized that the made-in-Spain high street clothes I was wearing were all wrong.

I navigated the revolving door. Eventually I was herded, with a few other contestants, up the stairs to be introduced to the formidable Miss Miller of fashion legend; she had been editor of the magazine since 1964. Miss Miller was intimidatingly tall, but she said nice things. Then we met the managing editor, Georgina Boosey, a stout matronly lady in her fifties with short white hair.

At the lunch itself, as I tried to remember which knife and fork to use, I looked around at all the artistically dressed beautiful people. Unexpectedly, I had an odd feeling that I was in the right place. I quizzed Georgina Boosey, whom I liked instantly. She did not look *Vogue*ish; she looked as if she would be happier tending highbred horses than highly strung models. We chatted about books and authors. I told her the Andrew Reid Agatha Christie story. She bestowed an earth-shaking fact: Agatha Christie was her godmother. Someone related to *Agatha Christie*? I couldn't believe it. Finally, after a long and intriguing conversation, I plucked up the courage to ask an important question. "If I don't win," I said with wide eyes, "well . . . could I have the job anyway?"

She looked at me sharply. She was in charge of the sacrosanct talent competition, and had been instrumental in recognizing flair that would fit in at the magazine. There was a longish silence as I fidgeted with my bread knife. If I got special mention, I could come for a summer, she said kindly. "Would I be paid?" I asked. "Yes, sixty pounds a week, but only if you get a mention. I got an honorable mention when I started here," she told me, and very nearly winked. Or it could have been dust in her eye; she did not look like a person who winked. I realized that my future lay with her; to all intents and purposes, Georgina Boosey *was* the talent competition.

When I left the lunch I felt weak at the knees, literally; my legs felt as if they were made of marshmallows. I had actually asked for a job at *Vogue*.

Three weeks later when I got out of the old lift on our rooftop, my mum was even more excited than the first time. This time she held a telegraph on filmy blue paper. She had spread issues of *Vogue* all over the terrace like stepping stones. I had gotten it—my special mention; I had my job at *Vogue*. I was to report in late June 1985. In the meantime they would send me a free one-year's subscription.

That summer I discovered men. They had discovered me a long time ago, I realized, with my curtain of blond hair and my curves. Now I became interested in them too; well, in one of them. His name was Lorenzo. He was Italian, of course. My mum was a hell of a lot more efficient than Cinecittà's entire PR team at making me feel that Italians were the sexiest people on earth. Lorenzo was a pinup boy for her imagined utopia. He was blatantly, obviously gorgeous—tall, muscular, very blond, and a few years older than me. He was more beautiful than was normal, even for a Florentine; and he was a chef, so he knew how to cook. He was very tanned, the fuzz on his arms golden against his brown skin.

His family owned a farm in the Florentine hills, and he had made the twelve-hour trip on his motorbike to holiday in Spain for a few weeks. We met on the beach when I took Dar-Wah, my Chinese student, out on an end-of-year excursion. Very self confident, he just strode up to me and, delighted to see I could speak Italian, invited me out. He cooked delicious food for my mum in our cramped kitchen, and when he left it was amid protestations of eternal love. I told him that I would be seeing him very soon.

And that year Emily pitched up for the usual hanging out over the summer. It was easy to forget she was only fifteen, as she seemed so much older. Peter and Norma had always spoken to their children as if they were adults, as far as I could see. Her parents had separated and Emily wanted to forget all the tension at home. She had come to the right place. That summer the city was awash in Italians and Emily and I had loads of fun. When she left I hitched a ride to Rome with three gorgeous boys who wrote poetry, played the guitar, and were generally charming.

Yes, I hopped into a car with three sexy strangers and drove down the French Riviera to Italy. When I called Mum at work, she just told me to be careful, to have a lovely time, and to come back in time for school in September. Maybe she was living vicariously through me.

We drew up in front of their family home in Virterbo, a magnificent stone city, just in time for lunch. Tommaso and Angelo were brothers; their mum and dad owned the local hardware store, and they all lived together in happy familiarity. That was where I was billeted.

A few weeks passed in delicious self-indulgence as the boys and their *mamma* looked after me. Almost every day we drove to some beautiful spot or another—Rome, of course, but also the *lago di Braciano, lago di Bolsena, lago di Vico, Orvieto, Tarquinia.* The elaborate mating ritual of rural Italian youth involved tons of fresh creamy *gelato* and jumping into the car at any viable opportunity and driving to a dot on the map, the smaller the better; especially at night. Once there you parked, went for perfunctory walk around the local beauty spots near the lakes, and then settled into the car to listen to cassettes of Dire Straits, Vasco Rossi, or Fabio Concato.

Occasionally I remembered to seek out the boiling hot phone booth to call my mum or Lorenzo, shouting at the top of my voice over a fuzzy connection. After three weeks of this Lorenzo said that if I didn't come to Florence, he was going to ride down on his chopper and get me. I said that I would come. Tommaso and his friend Luigi drove me there.

* * *

The winding road from Florence traced graceful curves along the contours of the rolling hills, and boasted some of the best views in the world. I held tight to Lorenzo's leather jacket and marveled as we rode to his home. I had a distinct impression that there was nothing ugly about this city.

The farmhouse in the hills was long and low, made of caramel-colored stone. It sheltered in a lee under Monte Senario, the thirteenth-century abbey where the monks made a famous honey liqueur. As we walked in, I felt as if I was living my mum's Italian dream. I made myself at home. Lorenzo owned only one record, a vinyl of dreamy classical music, and he played it really loud. The master bedroom was full of heavy antique Italian country furniture, and the kitchen was the scene for Lorenzo's repertoire of fantastic Italian dishes. He had no neighbors, so we rarely saw anyone; just his parents for lunch when we made the trip into town once a week. As an introduction to romance it was as fine as you could get. The music wafted through the empty stone rooms when Lorenzo went off to work at Sabatini's, the famous Florentine restaurant. I played house and wandered about the meadows with the dog until he came back.

Lorenzo had it all figured out: we would set up home here in this rural paradise, with a vegetable garden to tend and log fires in the winter. He wanted to start his own company making Tuscan specialties for export, and I would use my language skills to help him. We would make blond babies. I reminded him gently that, no, I was going to go work for *Vogue*. It sounded laughable out there in the

Tuscan hills, but it was already decided. So I returned to Barcelona at the end of the summer.

Preparing for my A levels that year was a bit anticlimactic, as my life had just gotten so much more interesting than my textbooks. For starters, I had written couple of articles, and one about my trip to Paris had been published as a double-page spread in a local magazine. I also had a season ticket to the opera, was working three jobs teaching English, and was staying up late to rehearse in the two theater groups I belonged to. Lorenzo came to visit me once in a while, and drove me to school on his motorcycle. My modeling photos were in the magazines. The bullies had finally laid off.

I finished my A levels on the last Friday in June in Castelldefels, and the following Monday I started work at *Vogue*.

5

On my first day of work at my first proper job, I wore a cheap long black-acrylic skirt, a long shapeless jumper in electric blue, and one of Lorenzo's thick Italian belts. I thought I looked great. I walked along the now familiar pavement and looked up at the façade with the gold letters, but this time there was a swing in my step. Georgina Boosey met me at the door and took me upstairs to show me the office on the fifth floor.

As we exited the lift, we walked into a wide corridor. On my right was a big open space where the art directors and two retouchers worked all day with tiny pots of paint and miniature brushes on big photographic prints. On the left was the fashion room, full of endless racks of clothes, skinny overdressed girls, and large floor-length mirrors. We continued on to features, Georgina's office, and finally through cubicles of secretaries in front of Beatrix Miller's office at the end of the corridor. After Georgina introduced me to everyone, we went into a tiny room squished in between art and features, with three desks lined up next to each other. It was the smallest and shabbiest office on the floor.

I had never used a computer before, and here were three enormous beige ones crouching massively on the desks. Two were being used by two young men, who turned to see who was visiting them in their cave. "This," Georgina announced, waving her hand grandly, "is the copy room."

The copy chief, Richard Askwith, said a perfunctory hello and gestured to the empty desk. Georgina left and I sat down at my new desk, twirling on my seat and then staring at the giant machine on my desk, which glowed dimly. Richard looked me over without saying a word. He was young and serious, and seemed quite unfriendly. He got up to get himself a cup of tea, and then started to explain my job. First, there were big sheets of paper with the text of the coming issue. I had to read them and correct the mistakes, like so. He showed me some odd little scribbly symbols that I was to use.

Georgina had started her career at *Vogue* in the copy room all those years before, and having a soft spot for me already, had wanted to start me out right. But where she was precise, detail-oriented, and organized, I was impulsive, fast, and . . . err . . . severely dyslexic. I could not tell the difference between *from* and *form*, for example; or even spell *Askwith*. I told Richard my secret. This was never going to work.

"Well, you're here now," he said.

"All right," I said out loud while thinking, *Oh, no.*

I stayed in the copy room but I was totally unable to do the work, as letters danced for me the way they always had. I did enjoy seeing the magazine before anyone else did, though. As I became more comfortable, I met the rest of the staff, bit by bit. But I hadn't made any friends yet, and for Richard, I was obviously a waste of time and a liability.

My entire experience of English people had been of two distinct tribes: the expats in Spain and the left-wing bohemians in England, such as Peter and Norma. I was completely unprepared for people

who were close to my age, the so-called Voguettes; a cluster of privileged young women who had been born into the landed gentry and
were whiling away the time between finishing school and marriage.
They all ignored me. While Richard was not exactly friendly, at
least he knew I existed since he occasionally sent me to get him tea,
and he was about to become much more important to me.

At Peter's two-room flat in North London, things reached an
unhappy climax. It was overcrowded, and that resulted in my having
to leave. So now I was homeless. Norma was in Wales; Hamish was
traveling around Europe covering the fashion collections for *Harpers
& Queen* magazine. For the first time in my life, I had no one.

The next day I turned up in Richard's cubbyhole with my suitcase. I literally had nowhere to sleep that night. I looked at him, my
eyes filled with tears. I had just turned eighteen, and did not know
anyone else in London. I left Richard with no option, really. After
work that day, he took me home.

Richard let me burrow into his big house in South London, living quite happily in my new rent-free life. We coordinated showing
up at work at different times so nobody would guess I was living
with him. However chaste our friendship was, Richard was one of
the few men on staff, and neither of us needed the gossip. We decided
that the most productive thing I could do in the copy room was learn
to use the computer, and to this I applied myself with gusto. There I
discovered the miracle of spell-check, which for anyone with dyslexia is like Christmases and birthdays rolled into one.

One month after starting at *Vogue*, much to Richard's relief,
Georgina put me out of my misery and slid me into the comforting
arms of features. Drusilla Beyfus was my new boss. Dru had clipped
tones and a regal manner. The first task she gave me was to type a
letter. *Great*, I thought, thinking of the computers I had just spent
three weeks learning how to use with those incredible spell-check
powers. "No," Dru pointed out, "there are no computers here."

I looked around and realized it was true. The large open-plan room, with its mismatched white desks and shabby gray carpeting, featured piles of paper on every surface. From beneath one of them she unearthed a mammoth Olivetti typewriter—my worst nightmare. Dru made me type that letter seven times until it was perfect. I was in tears by the time I was done. The other assistant looked at me with nothing but pity, not daring to say a word.

I had left everything I knew back home, had been booted out by my only family, and now was required to do things I didn't know how to do, among people who were strangers to me. I didn't even have a desk of my own, let alone an office I could find refuge in. I felt very sorry for myself.

I met Hamish at his office at *Harpers & Queen*, five minutes' walk by Carnaby Street, which looked tacky in the midday sun. We went to Cranks, the sixties relic, for lunch. I was lonely; in contrast, Hamish was on top of the world, having just been promoted to fashion editor. At that point he was the nearest I had to family, so I poured my heart out to him.

He encouraged me to start hunting for a room in a shared flat. I sighed at the thought, but I hadn't really made any English friends yet and I earned only £60 a week. In any case, I didn't know how seriously I should take the advice of a grown man wearing a pink Chanel jacket and pearls.

Drusilla was a fine editor and fantastic teacher, and so was Georgina. But it wasn't until Patrick Kinmonth, wearing corduroys and a baggy cashmere sweater, swanned into the office that my being at *Vogue* finally began to make sense. His humor, his intellect, his understanding of people—here was one man who could knock the socks off the myth of my creative father. I instantly adored Patrick, like a puppy might adore his master. I attached myself to him like a limpet. When I worked with him, I felt like I was home. Even though my official title was features assistant, I invented a role for myself as his personal assistant by simply stopping doing things for other people and doing everything I possibly could for him.

To accomplish this, I planned my first move carefully. When he was off to Paris for the couture collections, I went through everything on his desk and sorted it. This might sound like a simple morning's work, but I assure you it was not. Patrick's modus operandi was to turn up in the morning with a crumpled plastic bag of ideas and inspiration mixed in dry cleaning receipts, ticket stubs, half-eaten sandwiches, and £5 notes. He then turned the bag upside down on the mound of similar items on his desk, which turned the space into an organic installation that overflowed onto the surrounding carpet, other desks, and his chair. It looked like an artwork by Tracey Emin.

What to throw away was the problem. Obviously not the forty-year-old bottle of Schiaparelli's Shocking, its contents thick and yellow. Even I knew that the perfume was precious. Definitely not the original drawings by Craigie Aitchison, or the illustrated letter from artist Patrick Procktor. I sorted through invitations past, invitations present, and invitations future. What about the lone cashmere sock and the broken sunglasses? For these I created a plastic bag of "maybes." When he came back from his trip, everything was in its own pile. I had also taken the receipts to the cashier and painstakingly written them up on detailed petty cash forms. Some were almost a year old, so I had almost £300 to give him too.

Whether because he was flattered by my attention or because he felt sorry for me—or whether it was because he actually needed an assistant, as he was always working on several concurrent projects— my scheme worked. Patrick annexed me, and in the process became my Professor Higgins. When he swooped me up into his world of opera, paintings, fashion, and high and low art, I was a polyglot beach babe from Barcelona. When he had finished with me I was front row center at fashion shows, had dined with duchesses, and had met more stars and divas of both sexes than you could count on both hands—and, maybe more importantly, had learned how to handle them. If *Vogue* was my university, then Patrick was the professor in charge.

For the time being, however, the most pressing need was to find me a place to sleep. Patrick knew every artist in London, and was great friends with many of them. He asked his famous friends to put me up, so I spent a few nights at his house, a few days at the home of Philip Core (whose house was painted entirely black), a few weeks at the home of André Dubreuil, a few more with set designer Robert Carsen, and with the young Peruvian photographer Mario Testino.

Patrick took me everywhere he went—and I mean *everywhere*—before, during, and after work. He would walk into a room and announce, "Here WE are!" Patrick was generous with his time, and took pride in teaching me everything he knew. I drank it all in: the culture, the manners, the fashion, and the beat of London in the eighties. One night it would be VIP seats at a Madonna concert; the next, a grand opening at the opera; the night after that, private viewings at art galleries. I went to editing studios and film sets, viewings and press screenings, backstage at fashion shoots. I accompanied him to transvestite clubs with live performances by the gay icon Leigh Bowery, and to private gentlemen's clubs where you needed a password to get in. London with Patrick became my playing field, with acres of endless possibility.

Patrick was about ten years older than me, and his position was that of arts editor, which had been especially created for him. As I had learned early on, his desk was piled high with invitations and press releases. He had two main jobs under Beatrix Miller: one was to write the Notices section, which was mostly short news items on trends, exhibitions, and the like; the other was to style, commission, and direct all the portraits, food pictures, and still lifes in the magazine. Basically, he was responsible for all the photos in *Vogue* that were not fashion.

My job was to sort out incredible accumulations of raw material that was delivered to Patrick. The guy in the mailroom quickly became one of my best friends. Patrick received the most and the oddest posts, parcels, objects, and telegrams. I was also responsible for booking the photographers, locations, studios, makeup artists, hairdressers, set designers, decorators, cars, and anything else needed for the shoots, which were called "sittings."

At least that is what my job consisted of on paper.

In reality, my fashion and cultural education was so far away from Patrick's exacting level that much of what he said made no sense at all to me.

"Get me Princess Michael on the phone, darling, would you?"

This seemed easy enough. Tentatively I began poking through Patrick's exploding Rolodex, our bible. Would she be under "Michael"? Or "princess"? Or even her nickname, "Pushy"?

As it turned out, she was under "Kent." As in, Princess Michael of———.

As soon as he was off the phone with her, Patrick had another request.

"Can you call Herb Ritts and tell him the sitting with Alaia and Brigitte Nielsen is off?"

What sitting? With *who*? I looked at him blankly, thinking, *He deserves better than this.* Patrick was sorting through random piles while on the phone, and before I could confess my ignorance, he dashed off to see "B," as everyone called Miss Miller. That morphed into lunch since she was about to retire, and there were lots of teary goodbyes around that time. June was to be her last issue.

Adventurously, I crossed the corridor into the fashion room. Although it was less than twelve feet away from my desk, this was another world to me. They were putting together a rail of Catherine Walker and Versace, as Princess Diana was due in at any moment for a consultation with Anna Harvey, her personal style advisor. The already panicked fashion room became visibly more tense as everyone waited for Her Royal Highness's arrival, the air throbbing with anticipation.

I put my head around the door and asked lovely Jo, the booker who sat just to the left of the door, who Herb Ritts was. "He's a photographer from LA; the one who works with Madonna and Naomi a lot."

I knew Naomi Campbell, a beautiful, skinny black kid. She was in the office practically every other day. Jo showed me some pictures; wow, this guy was good. Although the whole time difference thing was still unfamiliar to me, I knew it was five in the morning in LA.

The next time I saw Patrick it was late afternoon, and he was with Sophie Hicks from the fashion room. "Err . . . Patrick," I said quietly, since I didn't want to interrupt them. Sophie had incredible style, mannish and minimal, which intimidated me greatly.

"No one picked up the phone at Herb Ritts's studio, but it's still early there."

Patrick looked at me as if I was crackers. "Darling, Herb is at the Ritz, around the corner," he said, as if everyone knew this. He had this way of looking at me quizzically and raising one eyebrow.

I rushed to make the call. Unexpectedly, Herbs Ritts's voice paralyzed me. I was star-stuck for the first time in my life. I was speaking to a real superstar; Jo had made that clear. Anyway, I had finally got him on the line. I turned around to pass the phone to Patrick, but he was gone. I'd been too slow for my boss. Again.

Thus was my apprenticeship; I got a lot of things wrong and some right. But the main thing was, I stayed. With a few trips to Italy to see Lorenzo scattered in, I survived my first British winter, and I was now living in a squat in Camden.

Very early in December 1985, I was tapping on one of the new computers trying to decipher Patrick's flamboyant scrawl. Personal computers had finally been issued to the features department, and were now obligatory for submissions if you did not want to face Georgina's wrath. A stir in the corridor made me turn around. A hugely pregnant but tiny woman in a white skintight Alaia minidress was walking down the corridor with S. I. Newhouse, the owner of Condé Nast.

British *Vogue* was the stomping ground for women who were slightly frumpy, very eccentric, or deliberately styled, like Grace Coddington and Sophie Hicks. *We did not do sexy*; at least not in the office. And definitely not sexy and pregnant.

I had just caught my first glimpse of Anna Wintour. We were all very worried about her rumored arrival, as she came from New York City, that mad, bad, dangerous city of crazy efficiency. British *Vogue* was about art and style and had other more eternal values, did it not?

The next thing we knew the decorators were in, tearing out all the moldy gray carpeting, installing wide pale-wood floorboards, painting everything a bright white, creating a minimalist glass box for Georgina to work in. She looked slightly ridiculous, like a thoroughbred horse in a stable designed by I. M. Pei. We called her office "the fishbowl," but she looked like a fish out of water. Yet she was the one who held it all together as we panicked, *en masse*.

The highly strung fashion department and the art department were the first to be revamped. Then came our turn. I found antiquities of Patrick's that had been buried under the carpet for the best part of the decade, and we took refuge in a corner. The whole magazine was on edge. Finally, just after the painters and carpenters and electrician had departed, early one Monday morning in April we heard the click-clack of high heels on the new wooden corridor. It was Anna Wintour, the new editor of British *Vogue*. Overnight, all the rules changed.

6

*A*nna's vision for British *Vogue* was fresh and dynamic. Instinctively I liked what she was doing. Her stories featured laughing models (not smiling serenely or gazing tragically, as had been the prevailing trend) with their hair in the wind, like mine, and wearing wearable clothes, even (*shock! horror!*) jeans! But everybody with whom I had begun to weave a tenuous friendship, every person I admired, was part of the old guard.

Anna's reputation preceded her; of the fifty people credited on the masthead for Beatrix Miller's last issue, a dozen had gone by the time Anna sat down behind her Buchsbaum desk, shipped from New York. A year later, out of the original editorial staff when I joined the magazine, a full thirty-five had left or been fired. By any reckoning, it was a mass exodus. Drusilla, who had always been so kind to me and educated me on the hoof, was gone; and so was Richard, who had sheltered me in my first traumatic days. These were people whom I had admired from my lowly position of dogsbody; they had given me my first breaks, my first mention on the contents page, my first article that was published in Beatrix's last issue.

Even still, I felt that my fate was linked to Patrick. As long as he was there, I could stay. And Anna, always quick to recognize talent and very inclusive of gifted eccentrics, liked him a lot; he made her laugh. I limited myself to keeping out of Anna's way, having been influenced by the prevailing fear and gossip (the period was famously dubbed "the Wintour of our Discontent"). Anna had overhauled the entire magazine, and Patrick's pages were also revamped; they had always been very arts focused with a major amount of excellent editorial devoted to theater, books, film, dance, painters, and exhibitions. Now we were asked to shoot more portraits, which were run bigger, and Anna wanted more and more young people. In her second issue, with her first "celebrity cover" of actress Amanda Pays, she ran my article on classical Spanish actress Núria Espert, with a very modern pared-down portrait. I was thrilled. Overall the magazine looked sexy; the fashion pages featured real locations and models that looked like real girls. However delightful the cocktail, the massive exodus of staff still unsettled me.

I started helping Patrick with his freelance work for magazines run by Italian Condé Nast, often working with the young up-and-coming photographer Mario Testino. One of the main reasons Patrick accepted my assistance, I suspected, was my capacity to chatter away in Italian and Spanish. This same capacity attracted two new editors who seemed to swan in and out of my office requesting off-the-cuff translations every few days: Michael Roberts and André Leon Talley. Michael Roberts was one of Anna's first imports from *Tatler* magazine. He was black, immensely talented, and could draw and paint fabulously. I really liked him, and was a frequent visitor to his arty, outrageous office downstairs. He had a fearful reputation and could be haughty, even colder than Anna when he wanted to be; but he was always kind to me, recognizing my appreciation of all things beautiful.

André, a huge man, flew in occasionally from New York. I would walk in to find him dwarfing my desk, booming on the phone and guffawing across the room. He was also black, and divine with the most incredible flamboyant clothes. In that very British office, he seemed to have arrived from another planet; you could almost hear the sharp collective intake of breath as he sashayed into the room. He spoke in quotation marks, spouting pithy sayings such as "You can never have too many black pumps. *Never!*" And that, darling, was that.

The Italian office began giving me tons of freelance work too, which I needed since *Vogue* still paid me only about $100 a week. The wages were so low because the magazine was often perceived in British society circles as being a kind of finishing school for young ladies after their first "debut season," in the (hopefully) short interval before they found a suitable marriage. It was taken for granted that these young ladies were issue of the landed gentry and supported by Mummy and Daddy, which was not my case, to say the least.

I became interested in the work of the Italian artist Fornasetti, and started working with a Peruvian friend of Mario's called Roberto Cilloniz to produce a book proposal for Thames & Hudson. Eventually we became close friends. Soon I requested to work at *Vogue* only part-time. In particular, the unpleasant atmosphere emanating from the fashion room, where everyone was at loggerheads, was toxic to me. The first agreeable surprise was that Anna not only agreed to my being part-time, but also doubled my salary. *Doubled my salary for half the time?* I looked at her with new admiration.

With more free time I tended to put Patrick's needs before mine, and as we removed ourselves from the Hanover Square office and did more freelance work, we often worked nights and weekends. I was permanently on call, usually to do the "street castings" that involved stopping hot young boys in the street and asking them to model for the Italian magazine *Per Lui*, brilliantly run by fashion priestess Franca Sozzani at Italian Condé Nast. As Lorenzo was in Italy, and seemed to be giving up on me, I basically had no one else to occupy my time with. Patrick and work were my whole life.

That changed on my nineteenth birthday. I was walking down the street in Soho in a bright-blue coat in the rain, trying to be discreet as I cried my eyes out after having just heard that I was going to be homeless again, after being a couch surfer for the last nine months. I was cold and lonely and decidedly missing the Mediterranean, so I decided to seek solace in a double espresso at Bar Italia, an ancient Italian outpost in Soho. The tears blinded me as I walked straight into a very tall and very good-looking young man.

Paul was an architect who worked at the Spitalfields Trust, an organization that preserved Georgian houses in London's East End. He recognized me vaguely from a private view and immediately offered me a hanky. He watched me as I sobbed my story out. Being South African and another unwilling émigré from sunnier climes, he either understood or felt sorry for me and invited me to stay with him. We had a light-hearted, platonic friendship cloaked in crazy domesticity where party followed party in the rather grand, crumbling wooden Huguenot house. This led me to meet a whole different group of people, mostly the artists and bohemians who flocked to beautiful decaying homes.

My other new friend was an Italian journalist named Carlo Ducci. I could not write Italian, only speak it; so we made quite a team as I styled the pictures for Italian Condé Nast and he wrote the content. Both were beautiful friendships that have lasted until this day.

At *Vogue* things were heating up. Influenced by the mass exodus and the fact that he had so many other prospects, Patrick had decided to leave. One day he disappeared into Anna's office at the end of the long open-plan room. After about thirty minutes I walked up to Gabé Doppelt, an efficient and funky South African who was Anna's assistant and credited near the top of the masthead (to everyone's horror). She was a valiant foot soldier of the new regime, but she was young and different. I liked her. A lot. I felt that she cared for Anna in a similar way that I cared for Patrick: with a protective adoration that allowed the geniuses to get things done. It was just as well, because we were about to have a lot more to do with each other.

"What is he doing in there?" I hissed as I perched on her desk.

"I don't know." She raised her eyebrows at me. "But they're laughing."

The door opened and Patrick strode out. "Darling, come with me, I need to talk to you," he said. "I have *news*."

The way he said it, mischievously with one raised eyebrow and the emphasis on *news*, sent a chill down my spine. He shepherded me out into the square. It was late fall and chilly; I didn't know what we were doing there.

Patrick looked straight at me. "Darling, I have resigned."

My heart stopped beating for an eternal second and my face crumpled.

"Don't do that, silly. You're one of the world's beautiful women. It doesn't suit you. Buck up, darling. Anna asked me who could do the job, and I told her you would."

"I . . . what?"

"Yes, darling."

"I can't!" I said, stating the obvious.

"Yes, you absolutely can," he said firmly. "You can manage Tony and Bailey and Donovan, and that is really all the job is. You will be with Tony two days a week, and the rest will be a doddle. Bailey adores you, and so does Donovan. You'll be fine."

Tony was the photographer Lord Snowdon, the ex-husband of Princess Margaret, and we spent a lot of time with him since he was on contract to *Vogue*. Bailey and Donovan were the big names in UK photography, famous East End boys made good. So famous, in fact, that they were tricky to handle; they were the Rolling Stones of photography.

"I bet she'll double your salary," he continued, "and you can get a flat."

It sounded terrifying. And terrific.

"Thank you," I said. We did not have a very physical relationship, so I didn't hug him. But I felt like it.

"Don't thank me, darling." he said. "You were in the room. That was the main thing." And he winked.

And thus it played out. I was nineteen years and eight months old when Anna made me picture editor of UK *Vogue*, a position she created just for me. I was now earning what seemed to me a princely sum, and the first thing I did was buy a flat. It was a revolt against the nomadic lifestyle of my parents and the couch-and-floor regime of my life in London to date. By the time I moved into my little duplex in Battersea, near Carlo, I had lived in thirteen different flats in London in the short space of two years.

But now I was a *Vogue* editor with my name on the masthead, and I owned my own place (albeit with a terribly expensive mortgage). I had a big black car and driver to send me anywhere I wanted to go on *Vogue* time. I went to all the galleries and private views in town. I had my two friends, Paul and Carlo, and lots of acquaintances. My new job, however, meant that there was one person I was going to be spending a lot more time with.

From the beginning I reported directly to Anna, whom the British tabloids had started calling "Nuclear Wintour." To me, the hatred she inspired always seemed over the top; Anna was always perfectly polite and encouraging. The woman had practically doubled my salary twice in six months and made me the youngest full editor at Condé Nast anywhere in the world; a record that I still hold. She simply did not feel the need to play the friendly card, to be simpering and feminine. She did not ask permission to be brilliant. She just was.

Plus she liked the off-the-wall geniuses that I admired, like Patrick and Michael Roberts and André Leon Talley, and she gave them the space to be crazy. She did not like boring people, and she definitely raised the bar. Anna was interested in powerful and intriguing women, even if they weren't necessarily part of the fashion world. She was a fan of in-depth articles on, say, AIDS or philanthropy. She was extremely encouraging of young designers and photographers and, of course, of me.

What made us tick, though, was that she loved pictures, and she commissioned many more than there had ever been in the features section of the magazine. This meant working with me, since my job was to produce all the original photos in *Vogue* (except, obviously, the fashion pages). We did a huge spread appropriately titled "The Risk of the New." We did dancers, actors, the duchess of Devonshire, art collector Doris Saatchi, and the French ambassador's wife. We did painters and galleries, and in the July 1987 issue I had to style a grand total of eleven portraits. For one issue! I was working like mad and usually had only one brief from Anna: "Give me *hope*, Lisa," she said. "Nothing dreary. I want *hope*."

Anna regularly asked my opinion on the covers, which was incredibly flattering. I later found out that she also asked the cleaning ladies for their opinion, as she wanted the cover to have a popular touch (something that drove the fashion editors insane). She also, sweetly, asked my opinion on photographers. Anna had a healthy respect for the greats like Snowdon and Bailey and Horst, as did I, and a lot of my time was spent with these older photographers, who taught me much of what I know, but she also asked me to bring in new, hot talent, sending me off to source them. She asked me to do other things for Michael and André; even to track down attractive young men for a cocktail party to celebrate Warhol's exhibition of self-portraits. "He likes to see lovely boys at his parties," she said dryly.

One night I ran into her office. We were the only two there; even Gabé had left. "What is it, Lisa? It's late." She raised her head for a moment from the light box.

"I really want to go home. I want to see my baby," she said. She had tears in her eyes.

I stood frozen in shock, almost forgetting what I wanted to ask her. Anna was human too, I suddenly realized; she was worried about her kid, like any mother. I stumbled out of the room and went back to my office. After that I felt more comfortable around her.

Anna could be intensely protective of her people, of which I was now one. I had a big job to do for her for the April 1987 issue that featured the new movie *Prick Up Your Ears*. It was a group picture, which was always complicated. This one included Gary Oldman, always a wild card and known for being temperamental. Most important for me, though, was that this was my first major shoot with David Bailey for the main pages of the magazine. Previously I had always worked with him on smaller pictures, so this was a big deal. Bailey was outrageous, a huge celebrity, foul mouthed, bossy, and unpredictable.

Anna called me into her office. Most of our conversations took place standing over the light box that ran down the far wall. This time, however, she asked me to sit down. She was dressed as usual impeccably, in Alaia. In contrast, I felt disorganized and out of breath, as she had me rushing from one shoot to another.

"Can you manage Bailey?" she said in her usual blunt nature.

"Yes, of course," I said. "I've shot with him loads of times."

"Don't let him bully you," she continued. "If he gives you the least bit of trouble, just call me." Then, as I stared at her in disbelief, she gave me *her home number*. Whereas I hadn't been at all worried about the shoot, I was now terrified.

Bailey called me at home that night. He seemed to have a soft spot for me and we had always gotten along really well, despite his terrifying reputation.

His Cockney voice floated down the line. "Why is Anna so worried about this shoot, babe?"

"I don't know, Bailey, are you?"

"No, just wondering why everyone's so bloody worked up about it." He rang off, and I anxiously awaited the next day.

When I walked into the studio, Bailey hugged me closely. "You look good. Where are your glasses? I like you better in your glasses."

"I'm wearing contacts," I said firmly.

"Go home, baby, and get your glasses. You look sexier in your glasses."

He means it, I thought. Sighing, I hopped into the waiting car, drove across London to the other side of the river, and got my glasses.

"Good," Bailey beamed when I finally got back to the studio. "Now we can begin . . . Who's fucking you anyway, then?" he asked conversationally as he lined up the actors and started shooting. I could only sigh in response.

The photos were great. Anna loved them. It was a triumph.

* * *

Lord Snowdon did not bully me, but he could be naughty. As my relationship with Lorenzo was on the rocks, mostly due to Anna keeping me too busy to visit him, Snowdon kept asking me sarcastically when I was getting married. That rather hurt.

The plus side to the naughtiness was that he was a wonderful gossip, and all the rumpus at Vogue House fueled hours of piquant chat. He was used to the family politics of that other great house, Buckingham Palace, so he was an expert at intrigue. I learned a lot from him, photographically speaking, and we ended up quite fond of each other—the scrappy penniless teenager from Barcelona and the fifty-seven-year-old earl, a master photographer, which was how I always regarded him. Anna was very keen on him too, so we worked together quite often. He had me wade up to my thighs in muddy Thames water to photograph Michael Gambon one day, and up a ladder in the East End to reflect the light the next. He and his tiny studio, with its painted backdrops and draped couch, were a huge part of my job, which had now taken over my life.

In April 1987 I had a huge twentieth birthday party, at the infamous transvestite club in Soho called Madame JoJo's. Everybody came, including Carlo, Paul, Patrick, and Hamish, and many of the younger photographers. John Galliano was there, along with Leigh Bowery, Tom Dixon, and Mario Testino, sitting next to all the best drag queens in town. In party terms, it was a low-world-meets-high-society coup. It ended up being my adieu to London.

Thames & Hudson Publishers offered me a contract to write a book on Italian interior designer Piero Fornasetti, commissioned by its legendary head of design, Jamie Camplin. Books: now that was something I aspired to. Fornasetti lived in Milan, and if I accepted the job I would have to live in Italy. Italy meant living close to the sun and my boyfriend, and the Mediterranean way of life. I took the crazy, but oddly easy, decision to leave *Vogue*. But of course it also meant leaving Anna, which I felt terrible about. In some ways I still do. After all, she had given me the biggest opportunity of my life.

7

I rented my flat out and packed up, leaving from Paul's with a huge assortment of bags. Mick Jagger's office sent a white limo to take me to the airport, as I had helped out his assistant with a few translations. Typically used to rock stars, I'm sure the driver had never seen such a scrappy assortment of luggage. On the flight I gazed out of my window, looking forward to a slower pace and a proper relationship.

In Italy everything went very wrong, very fast. First, Lorenzo had another girlfriend, which was understandable due to my complete unavailability, although upsetting nonetheless. Then Fornasetti passed away shortly thereafter, making it impossible to do the book as planned. Then I heard that my friend Roberto had AIDS. He was the first of my close friends to be diagnosed, and was too weak to continue with any kind of project. His sickness profoundly upset me. Before AIDS struck, we just did not lose friends in the prime of life.

My Italian Condé Nast pals who had given me freelance work in London had nothing for me to do in Milan, although Franca Sozzani was always charming and encouraging. I did not know anyone except for Marzio and Laura, a couple of artists I had met in London. I could not write the language, and in a few short months I was penniless. In addition, Milan was not Rome or Florence, and its more discreet charms weren't as alluring to me as those of the southern cities.

I called Anna from a phone box in Milan in the sweltering July sun, and Gabé put me through at once. I nonchalantly asked her for a reference letter, and of course she asked why. Had I not left to write a book? I told her it had all been a mistake and apologized for ever leaving her. As expected, she was noncommittal; she didn't say the magic words I was waiting to hear: "Come back." I did not know, of course, that she was herself about to announce her departure to New York. When I hung up, I was crying.

I had a hell of a hard summer in Italy. Although I was thrilled to be in the country, I don't think I had ever felt so alone. In August everything shut down and the Milanese, in time-honored tradition, set out to the seaside. Everyone left Milan. Franca's fashion director Sciascia Gambaccini was extremely kind to me, even lending me her house while she was away on holiday. Still totally broke, I lived off water and flour, rolling my own pasta in her beautiful home. Luckily for me it was summer; I made my pasta sauce out of the abundant produce in the generous kitchen garden, and survived very nicely. She only had one vinyl record, I remember, full of haunting soul vocals and songs that still remind me of that lonely summer.

By the fall my friend Laura had procured me a job as press attaché with Fiorucci, the legendary poppy, always-on-trend iconic seventies brand that people seemed to just adore. Founded by Elio Fiorucci the year I was born, it epitomized funky fashion. The shop was known as the "Daytime Studio 54," after the New York City nightclub. Elio's favorite thing was to go out to dinner in expensive restaurants. I liked to eat, so we always got along well.

I usually modeled whatever his latest creation was, and that fall Elio was big into a daring new line of latex dresses. Skin tight, they were supposed to be worn with no underwear. One night I was wearing a prototype to showcase to some buyers during a dinner with Elio. I wolfed down a divine risotto Milanese at one of my favorite restaurants, the Locanda Solferino. Of course the inevitable happened—it split. Vertically, neckline to hemline, right down the front. Elio had to cover me with his coat to get me out of there, and the latex line was shelved. Mostly though, it was just another regular day *chez* Fiorucci, where stalkers and obscene callers attracted by the label's sexy attire were a constant feature.

Fiorucci pioneered the globalization of fashion, and that is where I came in. It was a very fun gig; we even had the Gypsy Kings, a gypsy rock band, play at all of our flamenco-themed parties to promote a collection called Gypsy Jeans. My artistic side was fulfilled too, since I was able to take a few days off to curate a design show called *l'Amorosa Immago* during Milan's Furniture Fair, and received rave reviews. It opened in mid-October, and a few days later entirely unexpectedly Prince Giovanni de Bourbon Deux-Siciles, a Spanish-Italian nobleman and a *Vogue* envoy, came to call on me in the gallery.

I had never met him, but I knew of him as a writer and style philosopher. It was unthinkable that he had come to Milan to find *me*. But there he was, impeccably dressed in a three-piece suit, along with Luis Carta, the man behind *Vogue* Brazil and a polyglot global nomad who had the license to open Spanish *Vogue*. *Vogue* had a proposal for me, Giovanni said. And it was one hell of a proposal. It was a seven-figure offer (in pesetas) to become the fashion director of the new Spanish *Vogue*, which was due to launch with huge fanfare in Madrid in April 1988, around my twenty-first birthday. It was Jonathan Newhouse's pet project. I could hardly say no, as they pointed out how uniquely qualified I was, having being born there. But I did.

I explained carefully that I would rather take a pay cut and head up the Barcelona office, since I was not a pure fashion person. The Barcelona post would allow me to continue having an input into features: the arts, lifestyle, culture—everything that interested me.

And so I packed up my Italian life after only seven short months and headed back to the city of my birth, as my father and mother had done twenty-one years before. In Barcelona celebrated architect Oscar Tusquets created a divine chocolate box of an office on the city's most exclusive street, Paseo de Gracia, and painted it in pearly lilac. My mom was thrilled; to her this was the return of the prodigal child. I had never been affluent in my own hometown, and so now I was able to discover a whole series of new delights. I dined in all the best restaurants, took my mom everywhere, showered her with gifts, and even had my clothes made to measure. I rented a rabbit warren of an old apartment in the Gothic Quarter, and dug in.

The Barcelona interlude did not last long. The fashion director they had hired in Madrid didn't work out. "Please come!" begged Luis, Giovanni, and the charming art director, Francisco Rodriguez. I liked these persuasive men so much that by May I was whisked off to Madrid to become fashion director of *Vogue*. At the age of twenty-one I had broken another Condé Nast record, that of youngest ever fashion director.

In the late eighties the city was living through the tail end of the *movida* and was, in many ways, very rough and blatant. Much of the time it teetered between brash and obscene, à la Almodóvar. There was another side to it of course; Giovanni's side: the hermetic world of old money, royalty, and privilege. The restaurants I preferred had yellowing bullfighting posters and *castizo* cooking and seemed set in aspic, as if Ava Gardner and Ernest Hemingway had just walked out of the room. Because I was from Barcelona, it was considered normal that I could not "get" Madrid, since there was a long historical rivalry between the two cities. It was complex and difficult for me to infiltrate, but a wave of interest in fashion and design was starting to emerge. *Vogue* contributed to that in a very big way and nursed it, collaborating with the government to create a fashion council to encourage talent development, catwalk shows, and a fashion industry in general.

The magazine set me up to meet Manuel Piña, a legendary designer who had shown in Germany and Italy the previous year. He designed for the royal family and was middle-aged, so I imagined him to be a courtly old-school gentleman. I started back to the hotel to get ready for this important meeting, fully aware that a lot would hang on having strong relationships with the established designers. When I reached my room in the grand Palace Hotel, I suddenly realized that I had no appropriate clothes in my overnight bag to meet a captain of the fashion industry; dressmaker to the queen. I completely panicked as I realized the only thing I had with me, apart from the sweaty suit on my back, was a floor-length navy-blue and white spotted nightgown from Marks and Spencer's.

Well, it would have to do, since it was already too late to go shopping. In my best Scarlett O'Hara mode, I tied a knot in the back of the "dress" and took a taxi to the designer's home overlooking the aristocratic lake in the Parque del Retiro. A handsome muscular man with two days' stubble, wearing only black leather trousers and an undershirt, opened the door. A model, I presumed. Or the funky butler? In Madrid with its wacky mores, you just never knew.

Without much of a greeting I walked right in and sat down on the sofa to await the arrival of the Very Important Designer. I was attempting to be grand, as I imagined he would be somewhat pompous. Needless to say, he never arrived. Manuel was that rock-and-roll pinup, the handsome gay man who had opened the door. We laughed at the misunderstanding and quickly became firm friends. Manuel guided me by the hand for years, always ready to dole out sartorial advice, boyfriend guidance, and general life philosophy in equal measure. For years after that first meeting, we laughed about my turning up at his front door in my M&S nightie.

Giovanni was in charge of finding me a flat. I was determined not to live in a gated compound outside the city, so Giovanni found me a giant apartment on Madrid's iconic Plaza Mayor. It had the wonderful luxury of sixteen windows that made the rooms look massive, a huge dressing room, a four-poster bed, and a cavernous kitchen built for servants. Giovanni got me one of those too; a homely housekeeper called Carmen who took perfect care of me. I never bothered to decorate or cook; I never had time and reasoned that empty space was perfect for *Vogue* parties. I had ten staffers at the office, most considerably older than I was. I started to wear glasses in order to look more grown up, but I don't think it worked. I also tried to put on the aloof demeanor of Anna Wintour, which had more of an effect; all my fashion editors feared me except for Sara and Beatriz, who booked the models.

As I settled into my new position, I quickly realized that getting good models was going to be one of our biggest challenges. A few, such as Yasmin Le Bon, agreed to work with me because of my history at British *Vogue*; but otherwise nobody was interested in the new magazine from Spain. I decided that our only chance of getting the best girls was to catch them on the way up. The bookers crafted a strategy of identifying promising girls. This tactic served us well; the modeling agencies counted on us to give up-and-coming girls a chance, with the understanding that if they made it big, they would continue to work for us. The July 1988 edition, for example, was Carla Bruni's first major cover; shortly thereafter she became a highly sought-after supermodel. She continued to work with me regularly until the end of her modeling career (before she became a pop star and later married the French president). It was a huge learning curve, but I was on it.

Working with Luis Carta, with Anna Puertolas the features director who was also an eminent author, and with Francisco the art director was pure delight. The rest of the staff (apart from the bookers) was more difficult to stomach. After the American professionalism of Anna, the ambience in Madrid came as an incredible shock to me. Nobody turned up before ten in the morning. Everyone went out for long lunches and siestas, resuming work at around five o'clock. They then worked late into the night—except in summer, when everyone worked from eight to three with only a sandwich break, and then never came back at all. On one memorable occasion none of the fashion editors appeared for three days, nor did they pick up their phones at home.

"Oh, it is San Isidro, the bull festival; there are *corridas* every day," Francisco cheerily informed me. Although he was from Puerto Rico, he had been in Madrid far longer than I had and so had a better understanding of these things. The fashion staff would be back to normal next week, he added. *The fashion editors had gone to the bullfights? For a week?* Well, I would have loved to see how Anna Wintour would have reacted to that.

Luis Carta gave me carte blanche, and I took advantage of it fully. I brought over Horst, one of the world's most famous photographers. At age eighty-two, he did a spectacular black-and-white twenty-page spread on Spanish fashion. He shot in the Gaudi building in Barcelona and at locations in Madrid and Sitges. He also did a black-and-white cover, my first *Vogue* cover, for which under normal circumstances I should have been fired. Black and white was a huge no-no I had been taught, since "they don't sell." Instead Luis praised my "wonderfully eclectic eye."

In July I attended the haute couture shows in Paris for the first time. Couture is made-to-measure extremely expensive fashion, created by only a handful of the top designers; a carryover from the days when the aristocracy custom-ordered everything. For a fashion director it is a must-do, since these shows often serve as labs where designers test out their ideas. Also the lack of restraints on cost means, quite simply, beautiful clothes.

I was given a front-row center seat at the Christian Lacroix couture show in the historical gilded salons of the InterContinental Hôtel, probably because he favored all things Spanish. As became usual for me at the end of Christian's shows, I wiped away a tear. It was here that I saw my first Chanel couture show and experienced the Yves Saint Laurent couture show. This one took place with no music; instead the soundtrack was the clicking of the hundreds of photographers snapping away as each model walked out regally onto the runway. This sound was only interrupted by the announcer, who declared the number and name of each dress; first in French, then in heavily accented English.

These were the last of the old-style shows where outfits were shown on "house models" who worked with the designers in their studios, having the clothes literally made on their bodies. This was before the supermodels exploded on the scene and took over the catwalks and the fashion world, which in a sense would never recover. By the time Claudia Schiffer stepped onto the Chanel couture catwalk with her loping gait a few seasons later, despite the fact that the clothes had not been made on her and she didn't know how to do the proper model walk, it was all over. From then on the "photo" girls, the beauties in the magazines, took over and the "runway" girls, who until then had been a very specialized race, essentially ceased to exist. Then the photo girls became full-blown celebrities, and the supermodel phenomenon was born.

* * *

I worked hard, met advertisers and ad agency account execs (including, weirdly, some who had known my dad in the late sixties), held parties, hung out with local designers—Manuel, Jesús del Pozo, Adolfo Domínguez, Pedro del Hierro, the secretive Sybilla, and Roberto Verino. I often had lunch with Luis and Giovanni, and occasionally with Jonathan Newhouse whenever he visited Spain. I carted the prettiest Spanish model I could find to London and presented her to Bailey to experiment with, and he came up with the goods. I booked radical newcomers such as photographer Max Vadukul, and we did a shoot in a bullring (sans the bulls). I booked Michael Roberts, and he came to Madrid and did some amazing photographs.

Fashion was not really my thing. I had always been more interested in art and culture, but I was trying hard. Even still, when the show lights had gone down and the last photographer and model had gotten on their plane, I had no friends in Madrid except Manuel. My position made it hard for me to socialize, since all the people I bumped into were dying to be in the magazine, and it made real friendships difficult. I spent some weekends in the little Castilian village in the Mancha where Manuel was born, and a few evenings out with his friends, including the new Almodóvar stars Rossy de Palma and Antonio Banderas; even the gloriously transgender icon Bibí Andersen. The *Madrileños* were warm and welcoming (if a bit haphazard in their attitude to work), but I was still lonely.

* * *

Luis had decided to replace himself and bring in an editor in chief, which would free him up to work on two of the new Condé Nast international magazines that he was thinking of launching: *GQ* for men's fashion and *Casa Vogue* for interiors. I knew that after the freedom he had given me, it would be difficult to work under someone else. Luis and I got along brilliantly; he was international in his outlook and completely sophisticated. The new editor was someone local, and we did not get on. I began to think of other options, as my great position, big salary, and grand flat (that I still never even cooked in) had started to feel like a gilded cage.

On a shoot on the Isle of Skye in the fall of 1988, I met a rather special photographer's assistant. Eric Adjani was pale and pouting, and very reserved, very French. I don't know why I fell for him quite so hard, but by the following March I had thrown in the towel in Madrid and left for Paris with him.

For Spanish *Vogue*, having me in Paris was an ideal situation; the Spanish market was still undeveloped, and being in the fashion capital would allow me to source clothes, photographers, and models much more easily. Plus I could contribute international material to the two new magazines. It was the perfect setup; I was far away enough to have some freedom, and I could supply the magazines with endless world-class material. It was a job that I was blissfully happy in, and I stayed there for almost ten years. After such hard stints in London and Madrid, I was excited about being in my beloved Paris, particularly since Paul and Barbara still lived there.

Giovanni emphatically agreed. I realized that he actually had a hidden agenda. He was dying to introduce me to his nephew Charles-Henri, one of Europe's most eligible bachelors. When Charlie and I met, we realized right away (to Giovanni's disappointment) that this was not going to be a romance. Instead we began a powerful friendship that has lasted until this day.

Anyway, I was with Eric. On the surface, shacking up him with was not a wise idea. Eric was an ex-bisexual, ex-heroin addict, ex-jailbird who had appeared in a few films and now decided to become a photographer. He had not a penny to his name, but since his sister was the French film star Isabelle Adjani, he lived the life of a celebrity. This included all of the disadvantages like stalkers and tabloids, but none of the advantages like a big steady paycheck.

And yet I loved him. In fact our reality was quite domestic. After a stint in prison, Eric had turned his back on drugs and guns, he assured me. Half Algerian and half Swiss German, Eric was the perfect expression of a certain type of "rebel without a cause" French style; in the vein of Alain Delon in his youth. Ten years older than me, he always wore a Perfecto leather motorcycle jacket, and taught me how to live in France. I learned French (and French cooking), he dealt with the labyrinthine French bureaucracy so I didn't have to, and he brought home his Persian cat named Mozart (in memory of the Joseph Losey movie *Don Giovanni* that he had acted in). We furnished our apartment at charming flea markets, had weekends away in the lovely French countryside, and spent holidays in Tuscany.

* * *

After we had been in Paris for nearly a year, I had a miscarriage while viewing Versace's collection in the hotel Le Meurice and was rushed to the hospital by ambulance, wrapped in a Versace bathrobe. I was devastated, and it marked the start of a painfully tragic series of health issues that had me in and out of hospitals, and eventually spending nearly six months in bed. It was not until Isabelle Adjani stepped in, in true sister-in-law-to-be fashion, and sent me to her doctor that I got a proper diagnosis and had two major surgeries.

Vogue was incredibly supportive during my illness, and I did my best to work though it. The clinic was conveniently situated on chic Avenue Montaigne, Paris's fashion avenue, and I did model casting from my hospital bed. Eric was amazing throughout and eventually I was declared well, but it was unlikely that I would be able to have children. So we bought a dog, the chestnut-colored spaniel Brioche. The French take their dogs everywhere—restaurants, the metro, the office—so I did too. Her preferred activity, however, was running away, and she used to take the metro by herself to the farthest reaches of Paris. One time she ended up getting lost in the Grand Hôtel and they kept her for the weekend, the chef feeding her steak tartare and *pur beurre* croissants. She was a very *Parisienne* dog.

8

*T*hen a child literally ran into my life. Her name was Sabrina, and I met her in early 1991 in Paris, when she was five. At twenty-three, I had been in Paris for two years and had finally learned enough French to feel truly confident. I had a wonderful career, a cozy domesticity with my sloe-eyed celebrity boyfriend, and a killer wardrobe. It was a charmed time in my life, full of love and glamour and an intoxicating feeling of existing at the beating heart of contemporary culture. Flowers sent by Karl Lagerfeld, front-row center seats at fashion shows, highbrow conversation about the newest trends— I loved it all. Becoming the guardian of a little girl wasn't part of the plan.

I first noticed Sabrina one chilly March morning while waiting for a taxi to sweep me off to the *Vogue* office on the sumptuous Rue St-Dominique. The chic little three-story house that I had just renovated took up most of the courtyard of my building, but there was some social housing mixed into the block, inevitably in the way of well-worn French cities where the luxurious and the miserable knock elbows. Sabrina was playing outside my door, and I was struck by her luminous smile. She seemed about five years old, had skinny legs, a dirty face, and tangled hair. She was in a lightweight dress, not at all turned out for the weather.

I looked up and down the street for the adult who should have been supervising her.

"Hello," I said tentatively. "Where's your mummy?"

She smiled shyly and looked away.

"Why aren't you in school?"

She stared down at her shoes, twisting the hem of her dress in her hands.

Something was clearly amiss. I crouched down beside her so we were at eye level, my red Dior coat brushing against the dirty pavement.

"Are you hungry?" I asked.

She nodded.

By the time the taxi arrived, Sabrina and I were sitting together companionably on the step, sharing a bowl of early strawberries with Brioche snuggled between us. I waved the driver off.

By that summer we were spending every afternoon together. In those early days of getting to know each other, Brioche provided a lot of the glue. Sometimes we'd just sit quietly, me reading copy in the courtyard while Sabrina stroked Brioche's soft ears.

One June day as I was walking past her flat, a small TV soared out of the window and shattered on the cobblestones in front of me. A woman screamed. At that moment Sabrina ran out the front door, practically into my arms. I held tight to her and quickly ushered her off the street into my home. I was much more frightened than she was, and alarmed that the violence might have been directed at her. Would her family storm in and demand her return?

A few days later a social worker arrived and filled me in. Sabrina's Moroccan mother had passed away, and her Algerian father was an alcoholic of no fixed abode. It was another relative who had flung the TV out the window. Furthermore, the social worker explained, the family was chronically late with the rent and was due to be evicted. However, when hauled into court for the eviction proceedings, a family member had testified that the child was so attached to me that to remove Sabrina from my vicinity would cause the kid permanent psychological damage.

"Is this true?" the social worker asked gingerly.

The housing board was obliged to investigate the truth of the statement, but had made it clear they were unhappy with the delay it had caused in the eviction. I sat there looking at her with my mouth open. I was completely stunned. This was a degree of manipulation I had never been subjected to. Sabrina's family was exploiting a casual friendship between me and this neglected little girl in order to keep their grip on a cheap flat. I swallowed hard.

"What can I do?"

The social worker, obviously realizing I had been put upon, asked gently, "What do you want to do?"

I looked at her blankly. "What do you mean?"

"Well, if you go to the housing committee and tell them it's not true, the family will be evicted and the problem will be resolved. But—"

"But I won't see Sabrina again," I finished her sentence.

She nodded. "She will go into state care. The family has been judged not suitable to raise her, but they will have visiting rights."

Seeing that I had become uncomfortable, she added, "If the housing board doesn't believe the story, they won't expect you to take responsibility."

"What are the alternatives?" I asked.

"Well, you could tell me that it's true, that there is a bond. Then perhaps we would ask you to consider legally fostering Sabrina. If the judge allows it."

It took me few minutes, but I slowly began to realize that this imaginary bond, conjured up by the family, just might be real. I didn't want Sabrina to end up in care. As I child I had been fostered for a year, so I knew how loved and secure it can make you feel. Furthermore, it was unlikely that I would ever be able to have biological children. And I knew I could not abandon Sabrina.

Once I'd made that decision, it all moved very fast. By August, at age twenty-three, I had become Sabrina's official foster mother, and she had moved in with me full time. Eric was not exactly approving, but accepting. In any case, he was a man who had faced many unusual situations in his life and he was generous, being of the opinion that since life was so hard, it was good to be as kind as possible. But he was straightforward with me: this kid was my idea, and I was to take full responsibility. *He'll come around*, I thought, and he did.

My fashion friends were not as understanding. They didn't think taking on Sabrina was a good idea. Many of them, particularly my editor in chief at the time, argued strongly against it. The phrase "you're ruining your life" became a mantra around me. They joked that no one would ever marry me now; not with a skinny dark-skinned child with a horrific background in tow.

My mum didn't understand it either. She hardly spoke to me for a year, and refused to have much at all to do with Sabrina until she was almost ten. She felt that it was very limiting for me to saddle myself with a totally dependent child; she must have remembered how hard things were for her when I was about Sabrina's age. Although eventually she did teach her to swim.

Despite all of this opposition, I became more and more determined to do the right thing by this little girl. She had known such misery in her early life, and I wanted to make things right for her. I had always gathered vulnerable creatures around me: as a child, stray dogs I found on the street; as a young woman, photographers and models with fragile egos; as an adult, a needy man like Eric whom I could mother. It seems to be in my nature to step in and take control of situations that need righting—a skill that was invaluable in my time at *Vogue*. I could provide Sabrina with a loving home. So I did, and I never regretted it. Sabrina, after all, gave me a very great gift: she made me a mother.

Now we were three. Eric's sister Isabelle loaned us her huge rambling country farmhouse in Normandy that had been beautifully decorated by the illustrious Jacques Grange. We spent our weekends and holidays there, and her son Barnabé sometimes came along too. He was a couple of years older than Sabrina, but they got on. To get there, Eric had bought a majestic Citroön DS, iron-gray with black leather upholstery. To me it looked like a sea monster, so we called it Nessie.

* * *

The house in Normandy was a magnet for our friends: a German-Chilean couple named Eduardo and Gerlinde; Patricia, who had been to school with me at the Anglo and was now working with me; and photographer Michael Roberts, who was now living in Paris and with whom I still shot often. One Christmas we celebrated with Eric Wright from Karl Lagerfeld's, Angela Missoni from the famous knitwear family, and her three children, Margherita, Francesco, and Theresa. Margherita, at eleven or so, was a quiet intelligent girl, and I liked her at once. Isabelle herself never came, although she would occasionally visit us in the Paris house. Once she came with Daniel Day-Lewis, her partner at the time, and when she left I found three pairs of sunglasses down the sides of the leather armchair. Poor Isabelle; she could not go anywhere without being recognized, and had to spend her life hiding away. That was the awful price of celebrity.

When Sabrina was eight, Eric and I split up. He still did not have a job, and was dosing up on over-the-counter drugs like codeine. This made him strangely unresponsive and dull, and after a certain point I could not take it anymore. Sabrina and I deserved someone more present. I've often thought back to this decision. I had accepted him at his word when he told me he was off heroin, but perhaps he was not. In any case, a few months later he attempted to put a bullet through his head, and luckily missed. Still, I was glad Sabrina was not exposed to that situation. I've missed Eric every day since, though; our easy domestic life was something I loved and have never quite recaptured. Society tends to classify addicts, labeling them as evil and dangerous, but Eric was always kind and loving to me; just often absent while being present. At that time of my life I could not live with that.

I focused on being a mum, which I adored. It seemed that I had found my vocation. I told *Vogue* I was no longer available for international assignments, and I focused on packing picnics, singing songs, and reading stories. I was fascinated with anything Sabrina liked. I saw *Beauty and the Beast* seven times; I made pancake batter; I decorated her room so it looked like a ship; I went swimming with her in the local pool. In the summers we had endless sorties to the parks, and I helped her with her homework (a lot, as Sabrina was struggling school). I shepherded her to the Louvre for the weekly children's art class.

I also devised a new professional venture: writing books. This worked out so well that by the time I was done I had edited and written thirteen big glossy coffee table books on decoration, architecture, and contemporary fashion photography. Although they had sold well over a million copies, the publisher of the first three did not pay me any royalties, so I started a process to sue. It boiled away on the back burner for years. My eminent Parisian lawyer, Narboni, was so sure I would win that he provided his services for free. The books gave me unbelievable notoriety, and I stepped down my involvement at *Vogue* to a part-time freelance contract. As a single mum, I appreciated the flexibility.

For Sabrina and me, the most important book of all was the one on Morocco. Since she had come to live with me, I had felt a compulsion to get to know her roots. I also wanted her to be familiar with her origins. This idea assumed vital importance for me, and very soon we were spending every holiday together there. I was even learning Moroccan Arabic. I loved it so much—the beauty of the country, the deep ochre of the wall of Marrakesh, the red mountains, the surprising fresh green of the spring. It was a magical place with a fascinating culture, and I felt deeply at home. Eventually we tracked down Sabrina's birth family, and visited them several times over the years. Sometimes in the summer I would send her there for a couple of weeks alone so she could bond with them.

I worked hard during this period, but my secretary had her alarm set for 5:00 p.m. and she would shoo me out the door at not a minute past, so I was sure to spend the evening at home with Sabrina. I wrote all my books late into the night when she had gone to bed. For exercise, I walked everywhere from her school.

* * *

I was fond of a lot of the designers; in particular Christian Lacroix, who wrote the introduction to my book on Provence. We had a voluminous correspondence, his curly handwriting spreading over sheets of his signature beige paper. I was also friends with the entourage around Monsieur Saint Laurent: the *haute bohème* Loulou de la Falaise and her family; YSL co-founder Pierre Bergé, who included me in all the press calls; and Clara Saint, the queen of the press attachés at YSL. I styled Monsieur Saint Laurent's yearly portrait on several occasions. Once I even ran into Patrick Kinmonth, my erstwhile

Svengali, and Mario Testino, there, much to my joy. Of the Italian designers, Versace seemed to adore me the most, ever since our first meeting when he insisted on doing an interview perching on his bed (which completely intimidated me). Valentino, one of the first designers to be as grand as his clients, was also kind, and his partner Giancarlo Giammetti invited me to their parties.

The craziest moments of the year were the biannual *prêt-à-porter* catwalk shows, satirized in the 1994 Robert Altman film that I had a crowd part in. The capital of the fashion world may have had the most powerful magazine editors arranged on rickety metal seats in tents, but that first row was the most coveted position in the industry, and gate-crashers were legion. The designers' press attachés decided who got the tickets, depending on whether your magazine was considered trendy or popular enough to be accorded a seat. The exclusive front row was something you had to earn, either by having a powerful consumer base or by having featured the designer often the previous year. It was a precise science, and the seats were accorded rigorously on merit. Spain was a new territory for many of the fashion houses, and for the first few years we at Spanish *Vogue* were given lousy positions in the outer reaches. It was very satisfying when I finally made it into the front rows (where you could actually see the clothes) of the hottest designer shows.

The whole thing was kept in order by a battalion of impossibly good-looking stern young male ushers who were easily distinguishable by their red-tie uniforms, which earned them the nickname *cravats rouges*. None of them spoke any English it seemed, while very few of the international fashion press spoke French. I was thus often called in to translate for this or that distraught editor who had misplaced their invitation. I was younger than most of the ushers, and younger than most of the models too, and they were kind to me. Eventually the *cravats rouges*—who were experts at spotting the fans who attempted to squeeze under the ropes, through the tent flaps, or in with the caterers—allowed me to occasionally smuggle someone in, with a wink. These stowaways were usually young designers or photographers, hungry for inspiration and to sit at the table (or catwalk) of the greats. That was how I met Ozwald.

Ozwald Boateng was a very tall, very well-built, and very dark-skinned young Ghanaian menswear designer with a fabulous sense of color, a rainbow palette of suits, and an urgent need to get into the shows. He was, however, not easy to hide, arrayed as he usually was in fuchsia, violet, lime green, and canary yellow, often all at once. Yet for a whole season I managed to squeeze this tall, impossibly flamboyant person around the *cravats rouges* and into every show he wanted to see, cementing a long friendly acquaintance that persisted even when he became hugely famous.

In fact many friendships were made in the hours while one waited for the shows to start. I would chat with Michael Roberts, Hamish, André, and the editors I had known at British *Vogue* (possibly these long waits gave birth to the expression "fashionably late"). Anna Wintour's arrival would mean that there were not usually more than thirty minutes to wait. I always nodded at her, and she nodded back.

Booking the models was another awful matter. When we were just starting the magazine, the bookers refused to give us the famous, hot girls. Some of them had become personal chums of mine, such as Carla Bruni, Yasmin Le Bon, Helena Christensen, and Lucie de la Falaise. I could count on their accepting to shoot with me. Lucie even had her signature long strawberry-blond hair cut into a pixie in my office. A radical hair cut was a big deal in our world, and it if happened on your shoot, it was kudos to you.

Some models, like Kate Moss, with whom I did a poetic little shoot in an artist's atelier, I had to be plugged in enough to spot on the way up, and book them before they became big stars.

The conversation would go something like this:

I would say to the booker, "I have a shoot with—" and mention the name of a reasonably famous photographer. "Can I have—?" I'd mention the name of hugely famous model.

"No," the booker would reply, literally laughing in my face, "but you have to see this great new girl who's going to be *sooo* big." And into my office on the Rue St-Dominique would troop a collection of shy, lost, frightened, and often anorexic teenagers from Arizona or Anchorage or Vladivostok who were looking to make it into *Vogue.* It was heartbreaking; a rough business.

I soon acquired the reputation of being the kind of adventurous editor who could build up photographers' careers. For this reason, I always got very lucky with hair and makeup artists. Sam Mc-Knight and Mary Greenwell, one of the world's most famous duos, often worked with me, as did a young Tom Pecheux, who later became the absolute superstar of dewy foundation. Tom was on permanent call with me; he was a magician with his brushes. I also became popular with the photographers, as they knew that I respected their vision and would fight for it, whatever happened. Having said that, one of the biggest challenges was to make sure that the photographers kept the clothes in the pictures. After all, *Vogue* was about the clothes! It was difficult for me to defend photos, however great and artistic, if they only showed sexy naked flesh, however beautiful it was.

The number of times the models ended up naked in the shots, or occluded by some nubile young thing in a birthday suit, was amazing. Scantily dressed was also a favorite thing; shoots for brides' dresses often seemed to degenerate into shoots for bridal lingerie.

I did a fair amount of underwear work with Mark Wahlberg (who started out as the pop star Marky Mark). This involved arranging his boxer shorts in order to best show off his six-pack. My lowest moment, however, was on a shoot with one of the buff male actors from *Baywatch.* I stuffed a sock into his Y-fronts to make him look more . . . impressive. Then I mistakenly clamped the skin on his bum with a photo clamp as I attempted to make his underwear fit more snugly for the picture. It left a big weal on his expensive rump, and I was mortified. Underwear shoots are stressful work!

Of all the designers, I became closest to Karl Lagerfeld. My office was only a few minutes from his sumptuous home on Rue de l'Université, to which I was summoned at random times: for lunch in his townhouse, or *hôtel particulier*; for a teatime excursion to the Flore; to give opinions at couture fittings at Chanel; or to be fitted with jewelry for his own label, Lagerfeld. I don't know why Karl was so fond of me; maybe because it was the age of "grunge" and my resolutely street style as a working mum included a lot of vintage clothes that appealed to him. In any case, he delighted in the fact that I was not a fashion plate, although he never stopped trying to make me into a little more of one with his generous gifts. A truly multitalented genius, Karl could design, draw, paint, and write with complete mastery of each medium. His all-consuming interest, along with the nine fashion collections he designed every year, was photography.

With Karl, vaguely planned excursions always turned out to be monumental. "Lisa, let's go and buy books on Saturday. It will be *amusant*," he would say to me at lunch with a group of friends.

"Right," I said. "Where shall I meet you?"

"At the airport." Karl then turned to speak in rapid-fire German to model Claudia Schiffer, his current favorite.

"At the airport?" I asked.

"He means to go buy books in Hamburg," hissed my friend Eric Wright, who was Karl's right hand.

Ah, well, then. I had to think again. I had promised to take Sabrina to the zoo.

* * *

Shoots with Karl were major productions. His exquisite taste meant that we often had to source very special things. If we had real jewels, two security guards from each jewelry firm had to guard the boxes; therefore if we were shooting jewelry from five different jewelers, there were ten extra people standing around. If we were shooting something sumptuous like a handmade Valentino couture dress, the dress had its own minder who took it back to Valentino after the picture. Couture shoots always took place at night because during the day the houses needed the clothing to show to private clients.

Once we shot at his gorgeous country house in Le Mée-sur-Seine. At this point, Karl was experimenting with shooting through a translucent sheet of plastic that gave a soft focus filter to the images. This meant that he carted a piece of plastic the size of a Ping-Pong table everywhere we went. This huge piece of equipment added two more photographic assistants to his already considerable entourage. So by the time we were ready to take the picture, twelve people were clustered around Karl, who often had to shoot off a stepladder to get an angle without reflection off the plastic.

Because this was cumbersome, in order to plan the shoot Karl and I decided to do a Polaroid of every possible pose. While the female model was having her makeup done, we enacted the photos with the male model, Madonna's then-boyfriend Tony Ward. First Karl took me all around the beautiful but muddy garden and posed me, standing in for the female model in various languorous reclining positions. Tony loomed over me in the guise of a sexy faun.

The whole pre-shoot shoot was turning into a very long muddy process, and Tony was getting closer and closer. I was terrified of being beheaded by Madonna when she saw the picture of me being embraced by her boyfriend. Eric pointed out to me that the real point behind the whole process was that Karl could not stand my cheap flowing grungy look that day, and was hoping that if my clothes got muddy enough I would change into some Chanel, *pronto!*

Out of all the things that Karl gave me, my favorite was some Chanel leather knee-high motorbike boots, which I wore with plastic trousers from the trashy bondage shops that littered the city. Karl complained about it, but he must have liked the high-fashion, high-street appeal that defined my dressing, because he eventually offered me a job at Chanel. I refused, as I still thought of myself as an arts person more than a fashion maven. But I appreciated his gesture.

One of our most successful shoots was with the model Helena Christiansen. Karl covered her in metallic paint, and she looked like an angel though the gauzy filter of the plastic sheet. As usual with Karl, we worked through the night (fashion, he joked, was his "day" job), and at three in the morning Helena's boyfriend, INXS singer Michael Hutchence, turned up and hung out until we finished. That's how rock and roll Karl's shoots were.

Just before packing up around five that morning, Karl wanted to take a few shots of me.

"Lisa, don't ever have your nose operated on," he said casually, as he snapped.

"Operate?" I looked at him blankly. *What on earth was wrong with my nose?*

I had, he informed me, a curious bump on the bridge; imperfect, he declared, but no matter, it was very aristocratic. It gave me great charm, and I should never have it removed. I looked at him as if he was absolutely bonkers; it would never have occurred to me to redo my nose.

I became very close to Karl, receiving letters and flowers and fabulous photos from him on a weekly basis. We did many shoots together, and one of the photos I styled even made it to the cover of his first exhibition catalogue. He began to design special silver-chained (the usual ones were gold) Chanel bags for me, and would send them to me every year. Every season he insisted I go to the Chanel boutique at 31 Rue Cambon, and pick out a few things, and so my wardrobe went from fabulous to extravagant.

* * *

I worked with the great photographers: Jeanloup Sieff, Alice Springs, Michael Roberts, and younger cutting-edge photographers such as Steven Klein. I was photographed by Karl Lagerfeld and Édouard Boubat, a classic French reportage photographer. For years my "official" author's portrait was a pretty, bleached-out image done by André Rau, a German photographer who was then all the rage with celebrities.

My most enduring relationship as a model-muse, though, was with Henri Cartier-Bresson, the man who was considered the father of photojournalism. He was born in 1908, but in spite of (or perhaps due to) his great age, he still had a wicked sense of humor. In his twilight years he had taken to making line drawings, and one day after interviewing him for Italian *Vogue* he asked me if I would like to pose for him. I guess when you're that old, you don't lose any time beating about the bush! Time, I always felt with Henri, was of the essence.

I was flattered and quickly said yes, which led to numerous long days in his studio off Place des Victoires. The hours of posing went by very quickly, as Henri used to keep me amused by telling me true stories. We played a kind of game: I would evoke one of his famous photos and then he would grin and tell me what had led up to the shooting; how exactly he'd chanced upon the "decisive moment" that made the image a masterpiece.

For example, his iconography includes a famous photo of two women entwined on a bed. Henri told me that the picture was taken in 1934 when, bored at grand party in Mexico, he had left the hulla-baloo below and wandered off to explore the house. Pushing open a door, he chanced on the two women in their (presumably illicit) erotic embrace. Without thinking, he snapped only one frame, and then closed the door quietly. They never even knew he had been there. The picture is unforgettable. Another suggestive photo showed a naked woman floating in the sea, lying back, her breast a perfect orb, with her legs tightly wrapped around a man's waist, her face hidden from the viewer by the back of the man's head. The picture is very revealing, but conceals the identities of the two people involved. The woman, Cartier whispered, the secret from 1933 echoing in his voice, was the surrealist painter Leonor Fini. From his stories, I was transported to the thirties and forties. I came to know the dead artists, revolutionaries, and socialites in his lost world almost as well as I knew him.

At lunchtime, we would take a break and he would take me to the little restaurant in the Gallerie Vivienne, where I would wolf down a big lunch. The drawings Henri did of me were nudes. In the mornings he would usually do portraits naked only to the waist, but after the wine at lunch the eighty-six-year-old would get quite a twinkle in his eye as he asked me, *"Et maintenant, on enlève le bas?"* (And now we will remove the panties?)

I learned a lot from the famous, celebrated, and skillful artists I was meeting. *Vogue* had turned out to be my grad school and I was very grateful. A lot of my work had to do with celebrities, many of them Spanish, because the magazine had to appeal to a Spanish audience: Rossy de Palma, who now lived in Paris; Pedro Almodóvar and Antonio Banderas, who were headed for Hollywood fame. I even got to meet Victoria Abril, the superstar in the mini-shorts on the TV program *123* that I had watched as a child, and who had symbolized the new freedoms after Franco. Victoria was now a huge movie star, and Spanish *Vogue*'s appetite for her seemed insatiable.

In 1992 the shock of my pal Manuel's diagnosis of HIV led me to become heavily involved with "The Love Ball"—a benefit dance and vogueing catwalk show inspired by drag balls, introduced to Paris by demimonde icon Susanne Bartsch to raise funds for AIDS—and I persuaded Condé Nast to print the catalogue and organized a huge exhibit of images of black-and-white photographs of people kissing at the Musée des Arts Décoratifs in the Louvre. It was only my second experience at curating, but I loved it, and some of the world's most famous photographers contributed. Most of all, it provided relief; we were actually *doing* something as more and more people around us started to die of AIDS, which at the time seemed to be a hundred percent fatal and so fast that often it left you no chance to say goodbye. The stigma was terrible, and that was what I was fighting when I showed kisses. "To kiss is to care." I wrote in the preface.

* * *

One day the phone rang in my office in the middle of the afternoon. When I answered, there was pause on the line. "*Allo, allo?*" I said in French and then, "Hello?" Still nothing. Now thinking it was someone at the magazine calling over a bad international connection, in a louder voice I said, "*HOLA?*"

"Hello." An English voice was on the line. "You may not believe this," the voice said, "but I think I'm your father."

I looked at the receiver in my hand and sat down at my mirrored table. The flowers Karl had sent me the day before smiled back at me. I had always hoped this would happen, but only because I wanted to punch him in the face for what he had done to my mum.

"I don't believe you." I replied after a few more moments of silence. "What was my mother's maiden name? What is my date of birth? Where were we living when you left? Where you born? Where did you study?"

He got all the answers right.

"I want to see you, Lisa," he said urgently.

I continued to ask him questions; how he got my number, and how he knew where I was. Apparently he had run into my agent, Randall Walker, at an advertising agency and because we had the same name, our portfolios had gotten mixed up. He was a photographer and filmmaker now, he told me. He'd had the shock of his life when he learned I was in Paris, and then sat down with my agent over a beer to decide what to do. My agent, an enthusiastic Australian, had persuaded him to call. It was the most difficult thing he had ever done, my father added.

I so wanted to say, "Unlike abandoning my mum and me," but I bit my lip instead.

"Where can I see you?" he asked again, more gently.

"The Café de Flore on the Boulevard St-Germain," I responded. I wanted a public place where I could be protected if this guy was a psycho. I knew all the waiters there, as it was Karl's favorite hangout.

Right, he said with a sigh of relief. I have a gray beard and I'm wearing a yellow T-shirt. A gray beard? I could not imagine my father as an older man, since in all the photos I had seen of him he was in his twenties. A gray beard seemed an affront to me.

The first thing I did was to call my good friend Charles-Henri, Giovanni's nephew. I explained my anger, fear, and anticipation all mixed into one, and he tried to calm me down. We talked for a long time, especially about the possibility of the whole thing being an elaborate hoax, and we made a plan. He would get to the Flore before I did and find a place to sit. When I arrived I would head to the table closest to him, so he could eavesdrop and keep his eye on the situation. Feeling relieved that he had my back, I called my agent and checked his side of the story.

It all seemed to be true. Randall was almost as emotional as I was, and he urged me to be kind; after all, twenty years had gone by.

But I still burned with anger. I told my secretary what was happening, called the au pair to say I might miss Sabrina's suppertime, and headed out. It was a short walk to the heart of the left bank, but I was so nervous that I seemed to fly. I got there early and winked at Charlie, who was pretending to read the paper, just like in a B movie. Then I started to scrutinize the passersby. "Gray beard, yellow T-shirt," I repeated over and over to myself. Suddenly the boulevard seemed to fill up with people who either had gray beards or were wearing yellow T-shirts.

When he walked up to me, my heart started beating very rapidly. The first thing I noticed about him was that he was not that tall; my mother had always said he was tall. But I suppose she meant in comparison to her.

The second thing I noticed was that he was as nervous as I was, spraying breath freshener, his hands a little unsteady.

As Charlie observed us, I asked a few questions and then my father began to talk. There were things in him that I recognized in myself: a quick wit, literary sensibility, an artistic eye. But my hard-work ethic—that I got from my mum.

We talked for long time. He wove a tale of a rollicking life with different wives and lots of travel from the Caribbean to Canada. As I listened to him sharing his life's adventures, I suddenly realized what he was: an irresponsible bon vivant who had probably hardly given my mum and me a second thought after he left us.

I should not have been surprised. It was only my mum's enchanted memory of him that had made him anything other than a man who had abandoned his wife and child, never to be heard from again. There was no secret narrative of suffering or loss. It had been his choice to just walk out of my life without so much as a look over his shoulder. Until today.

My father stayed in Paris. We saw each other about once a week. My mum was initially forgiving, but later extremely and rightly annoyed. My father spoke to her on the phone once though, and thanked her for the "marvelous job" she had done with me. He was proud of my career that had followed so closely in his footsteps. He met Sabrina, and I met my two adorable blond half-siblings and his new wife, who seemed the earthy, solid type and might be able to keep him on the straight and narrow, I surmised. I hoped these children wouldn't have to go through what I'd gone through.

One day my father phoned my house while I was at work. He left a message on the answering machine saying, "Lisa, actually Paris is expensive, and I'm not getting work here, so we are off to Canada for a bit. I'll stay in touch. Bye for now."

And that was that. In the same way he appeared, with a phone call, he vanished. I have never heard from him again.

9

*I*t was while preparing for the publication of my third big fat illustrated book, the one on Provence, that I met Olivier Gagnère. Olivier was fifteen years older than me and very much the trendy French gentleman. He was divorced, a designer and decorator, and had impeccable taste; for instance, a Moroccan carpet juxtaposed with a leopard-print chair, and an Indian throw over a table with a simple sculptural vase of his own design. He had recently finished designing the ultra-trendy Café Marly inside the Louvre, and had produced a whole series of china cups and vases. It seemed as if you could not open an interiors magazine without stumbling upon his creations.

Olivier courted me assiduously, and the proposal was tempting. Here was a man who was charming, handsome, and debonair. He was wonderfully funny, and seemed to make my life glamorous and easy. In addition, he was ready to take on Sabrina. At twenty-eight, I had been a single mother for the last two years, and it was tough. Olivier was a dream come true. I had spent my twenties working several jobs, raising my child, taking care of Eric, trying to take care of myself, in and out of the hospital, spending my free time on my books. Sometimes it seemed as if my whole life was work (however glamorous) and parenting. Surely there was more to life than this? Now I would marry a sophisticated man who would be an incredible father figure for Sabrina and could provide for us both. I would have liked to ask Manuel's advice, but he had finally, painfully died of AIDS the year before. I dutifully introduced Olivier to all my friends, and they unanimously approved.

How could I say no to this life? It was so easy to fall in love with him. Then it happened; Olivier was down on one knee in middle of the night asking me to spend the rest of my life with him. Completely swept up in the romance of it all, I said yes. I was blissfully happy, and we set the date for September 16, 1995.

Charles-Henri wanted us to get married in his château where Sabrina and I had spent a lot of weekends and holidays, but Olivier wanted a small urban wedding. And so we tied the knot in the *grand Mairie* of the seventh arrondissement. I wore a tiny white devoré velvet minidress and pastel-pink glitter platforms. Paul Duncan, my friend from my London days, gave me away, and then we had everyone to my friend Hervé's for a relaxed wedding lunch. Hervé was an incredibly talented jewelry designer and artist who was one of my best buddies. He also hosted the hen party—for girls or men in drag only. The catering at the wedding was Moroccan, and it was absolutely perfect. Olivier and I went for our wedding night in what is now the incredibly trendy Hôtel Costes on the Rue du Faubourg St-Honoré, but at that time was still a few weeks away from its opening date. It belonged to Olivier's friends, the Costes brothers, and we slept in the only room that was completely finished. There was plastic sheeting on the carpet in the corridors, the odd workman in the lift, and the impossible romance of a huge luxury hotel just for us. That Christmas my mum came, and we all stayed in Charles-Henri's château.

The Château de Botz was a typical nineteenth-century pile in the Bourbonnais, a region of central France that had been associated with Charles-Henri's family for generations. His intention was to restore the much older and prettier ruin on the grounds, but in the meantime we made do with the nineteenth-century version. In the winter he heated only one wing, since the cost of heating the whole thing was prohibitive. A sprinkling of snow lay on the vast grounds and Sabrina, my mum, and I pottered around taking walks, cooking, and in Sabrina's case admiring the cows and having adventures in the wonderful third-floor attic: the abandoned servants' quarters and her personal fiefdom. Olivier, however, seemed withdrawn. My mum got worried for me, I got worried for him, and even Sabrina asked me what was wrong with him.

There were other troubles in my life. Sabrina, who was now ten, had started getting bad grades, lying compulsively, forging teacher's notes, and generally acting out. Olivier moved her into a stricter school: a small private Catholic school near his studio, so he could take her and pick her up every day. They bonded on the car rides, and Sabrina loved it. She responded well to the more structured environment, but it became clear that the endless problems at her biological family's new home, where she was still required by the judge in charge of her case to spend a weekend every two weeks, were severely affecting her. Sometimes they didn't turn up to collect her; sometimes they came late; sometimes they did not bring her back.

Every time the pickup or drop-off time approached, I would start to get sweaty palms and a ball in my stomach. Every cell in my body rebelled at the idea of sending her to an unsafe environment, even just for the weekend; but legally I had no choice. Sabrina reported beatings, violence, and the door being kicked in, all of which the social workers had on file. I found an incredible psychologist and we started, slowly, working together. Sabrina loved her, and after a few months the shrink called me in. I sat there in her office, slightly intimated.

"The atmosphere in that family is not conducive to Sabrina's thriving. There is little regard for the truth, there is violence, there is manipulation. . . . My advice is that you should cut all ties. That is what would be in the best interest of the child. You have to be in your role as a mother and protect her." She advised me to go ahead and request an adoption from the judge, and have the visits to her biological family stopped.

I looked at her in amazement, explaining that my instinct had always been to preserve her links to her family. "Yes," she said, "that would be the usual choice, but in extreme cases and if the family is unsuitable, then you have to create a full attachment with the new family, which is you."

I had been wrong all along. I asked to see the judge to make a request for adoption, and we started working to ensure Sabrina's safety. It was not going to be easy but I knew Sabrina should not go back to that environment. The courts were set up to fight for biological family rights, which they should be, in normal circumstances. They were unlikely to choose an affluent single British woman over a large extended family unless we could prove abuse. However, I did have three strong arguments: the family's unsuitability, the fact that they had given up custody voluntarily six years earlier, and the fact Sabrina had been with me ever since. I also had one trump card up my otherwise empty sleeve—her father.

It took me ages to pin him down, and when I did it was like a scene from a movie. He was jailbird and an alcoholic, living in a hostel in Clichy. When he saw me walk in the front door, he dashed out the back, so I chased after him. Eventually I caught up two blocks away, puffing and out of breath, and explained my predicament. I loved his daughter, and if the family obtained a custody ruling Sabrina would be taken away from me. In an instant the man transformed from a fleeing ex-con to a proud dad. He puffed out his chest and invited me to sit down for a glass of wine. It was ten in the morning so I declined the wine, but we did sit down for a talk.

"I don't want her to live with them—she is unstable." he said. "What can I do?"

"We would have to go to a notary and you would have to declare that you give up your parental rights and recommend she be adopted by me."

"Right, I would like to do that," he said. "I'll be there."

A few days later, I waited anxiously in the street for the short Algerian man who held my baby's life chances in his hands. He was late, and I panicked. Had he bolted? But just when I was about to give up, he arrived, signed the papers, and even insisted on paying the notary, a very grand gesture on his part. When I thanked him, he stopped me.

"I have to do the right thing." he said. "I should be thanking you." He shook my hand, shyly and formally, and walked off back down the street with his head held high.

* * *

In early 1996 Olivier left me. We had been married less than five months. Since Christmas he had been distant and withdrawn. He seemed out of love with me. In parting he said that my life was too harsh, referring to the terrible stress I was under with Sabrina's family. The sadness and shock I felt were beyond description. My heart was broken. The whole situation reminded me of my own father's abandonment. Although Olivier and I ended up as friends, at the time I was frozen in pain, and it was a very long time before I could trust again.

Sabrina was in school at the opposite side of Paris next to Olivier's studio. Then began a nightmare period when I had to pick her up and drop her off on the metro with more than an hour's commute each way. It was unbelievably time consuming and tiring. However, if there was one thing I had learned from years of working with drama-queen photographers and editorial dragons, it was how to wing it. Photo shoots may look luxurious, but they're not easy to run: models get love sick; photographers want to put naked girls (or boys) front and center instead of the advertiser's frocks; heels break; makeup melts; people spill the most appalling things; dresses are torn; colors run; people miss planes. On one shoot, the French actress Béatrice Dalle threw a pair of Harry Winston diamond earrings clear across the studio. On another shoot, a photographer left $10,000 in cash on a car rental counter. Once a shoot in LA was delayed due to unexpected heavy rainfall, so I flew the crew to New Orleans to find the sun. I then had to fly them all back the next morning because suddenly the sun had come out in California. Everybody is always inevitably late, for everything. Even still, shirts must be crisply ironed, photos must be perfect, and you yourself must always, in every circumstance, be perfectly well dressed and pulled together. So even though Olivier's abandonment was very brusque and very public, I soldiered on.

I made a weekly appointment with Sabrina's shrink. The first day I went to see her, I looked down across the Esplanade des Invalides and noticed that the trees were skeletal, leafless. I have no memory of the next six months; just that one day I was standing at her window in the waiting room looking at the same trees and they were all in full leaf. That image finally penetrated the fog of self-pity. *To hell with this*, I thought. *To hell with him. I've got to move on.* A few days later Olivier called and took me to lunch.

"Don't give up on us," he said, "this is not final. I'm beginning to think I made a mistake."

"A mistake?" I nearly threw my *steak frites* at him. "Forget it," I said. "I want a divorce, and I'm moving back to Spain."

I don't know why I said that, but the moment I did it became the obvious thing to do. My old chum Patricia had recently moved back, and she loved it. Barcelona was cheaper and sunnier, and Sabrina could spend time with my mum. More than anything else, it was 650 miles from both Sabrina's family and Olivier. However, I could not move for a few more months until Sabrina was twelve, the magic age when according to French family law she would finally be able to testify that she wanted to be adopted by me.

By June 1997, Sabrina and I were packed up to go. Olivier took us, Brioche, and Mozart to the train for Spain. "You'll be back," he said. "You, *especially* you, can't live anywhere except Paris."

"We will see about that," I said.

In Spain I purchased a rambling, charming old house from the 1910s on the outskirts of Barcelona. It was in ruins (literally; its roof was caving in), and I began the massive task of restoring it. Sabrina went to the French lycée, and I set up a company with Josh, another Condé Nast colleague, to syndicate my work from the books. I had more work than I needed, including writing for *Vogue* and still occasionally shooting covers for them, and I finally had a lovely house of my own. The only real worry was Sabrina. Although we had cut off contact with the part of her family who lived in France, she was still acting out big time. The adoption was, however, finally done. It was classified as *reconnaissance des faits*, a recognition that the child had been with me since age five, and that French law had formalized it.

* * *

On one notable occasion when Sabrina was thirteen, she stayed out all night and a scandalized neighbor phoned to alert me. I was on a twenty-four-hour trip to the Cannes Film Festival to shoot a *Vogue* cover of the French model Laetitia Casta. Cannes has no airport, and in order to catch the first flight home I had to charter a helicopter to take me from the shoot to the closest airport in Nice. I wanted so much to fix things for Sabrina; to fix her hostile, suspicious approach to the world, and to me.

The following year we had an almighty fight when Sabrina was suspended, yet again, from her school; this time for stealing and smoking dope. Suddenly I, a magazine editor and a stylist with a frantic schedule, had to face the inconvenient reality that I'd have to home-school her through her last year of high school.

Parenting was a tough job; by far the most difficult thing I had ever attempted. Although I did my best to nurture and support her, Sabrina's childhood had been painful, and she worked that out with behavior that was much more extreme than most teenagers'. She had a therapist in Spain, but it continued to be an uphill struggle.

Things went incredibly wrong over the course of the winter of 2001, when a series of horrible teenage-nightmare escapades made me feel that I had failed her as a mother. Plus she was getting thinner and thinner; I was terrified she might develop anorexia. I was only thirty-five; perhaps I was simply too young to be parenting a seventeen-year-old who had endured years of abuse throughout her early childhood and who was stealing, lying, taking drugs, sneaking out at night, and basically breaking every rule in the book.

Her counselor thought that Sabrina needed to work on her empathy, and suggested volunteer work as a good exercise. Sabrina said she would only go if I went too, so I agreed. Our original plan had been to volunteer at an orphanage in India. Maharajahs, temples, punkah fans—my imagination, accustomed to *Vogue* photo spreads, instantly furnished a beguiling backdrop. But there had been trouble in Kashmir and a terrorist attack on a temple, so Sabrina googled alternatives for us: Ghana or Peru.

I wanted somewhere hot, since we were planning this trip in the icy damp of a European spring. In June Peru would be chilly. I asked for an opinion from my friend Hamish Bowles, who was now in New York at *Vogue* with Anna. Having known him since childhood, he was one of my oldest friends in the notoriously flickering loyalties of the fashion industry. I told him Ghana was a possibility, but that I was frightened of it already: ebola, malaria, a modern-day *Heart of Darkness*. Hamish said reassuringly, "Darling, Ghana is divine. Just think of Ozwald!"

He meant Ozwald Boateng, the dapper young Ghanaian menswear designer who was becoming such a hit. Ozwald was indeed fabulous, and he adored me, since as mentioned earlier, I had helped sneak him into a few fashion shows in Paris when he was a student. When I phoned him he told me, "Ghana is marvelous. The colors! It's such a sexy place, darling. You will love it."

It wasn't hard to get away. I was the head of my own company. I was lucky to be in demand; it meant I could routinely turn down jobs and still earn more than enough money to live quite comfortably. Also, I'd spent the previous year and a half restoring our home, and now it was finally finished. I needed a break.

We did a quick online search; white beaches, gleaming smiles. Ghana was rich in gold and diamonds and cocoa. It was also the center of the world, I learned, being the point at which the equator (0° latitude) and the prime meridian (0° longitude) intersect. A voyage to the center of the earth! Irresistible.

So Ghana it was. I signed the bank transfer—a hefty sum—to the volunteer agency that would provide us with room, board, and an orphanage where we would work. This trip to Ghana was above all supposed to create a life lesson for Sabrina. I also hoped it would mend our relationship. And of course we would be doing good for needy children, although my picture of exactly how we were going to do that was rather hazy.

The agency emailed that our orphanage would be in Gomoa, a beach town. How perfect! It was certainly not my idea of a real vacation—most summers we rented a house in Provence and splurged on restaurants—but I definitely liked the idea that a beach would be part of the package.

Ogyatanaa, wokɔ ho na woannwene wo se a, wokyea wo ti.

—Akan proverb of the Ashanti people, Ghana

If you go near a flaming fire you either show you teeth or turn your head.
(Depending on your character a dangerous situation can either push you to fight it or you turn your head from it.)

10

I had booked the trip to West Africa with the airy notion that three weeks of volunteer work would develop a sense of perspective in my wayward teenage daughter. After half a dozen vaccinations—yellow fever, hepatitis, typhoid—and stern warnings about malaria, meningitis, and worse, I had grown increasingly uneasy about this adventure. I had compiled a stock of medication that dwarfed my toiletries bag: homeopathic drops, disinfectant sprays, fungal creams. If we were going to be working with Ghana's needy children, meaning a month of wiping diapers filled with lord knows what bacteria, I wanted full protection. I had no experience with babies, as Sabrina had come to me as a toilet-trained five-year-old, so I very much hoped that Pampers weren't part of the plan.

Not much information was available to tourists, to judge by the dearth of guidebooks; I only found one after trawling through three bookstores that specialized in travel. It was in French, flimsy, and out of date. That in itself was off-putting: only *one* book on a whole country? Morocco alone got two full shelves. What, after all, did I know about Ghana?

That it was the country with the most slave forts, decimated by that bloody trade from the mid–seventeenth century until slavery was abolished in 1863. The first African country to wrestle independence from the British Empire in 1957 and now, after five coup d'états, it had a stable democracy. (Five coups in forty-five years? That did *not* sound very stable to me.) Inflation had exceeded 40 percent the previous July. AIDS and malaria were endemic. Terrible road safety statistics. *Africa for Beginners*, decreed the guidebook cheerily. Instead of a beginner, I was beginning to wish I had remained a nonstarter.

"Sabrina," I said.

"Yes, Mum?"

"Don't take any jewelry or anything; pack only what you are willing to lose. And very conservative, long clothes."

Sabrina looked at me blankly from the pile of brightly colored clothes she was packing amid the chaos of her room. She had on far too much makeup, as usual, and she was wearing a micro-mini. I tried hard not to comment.

My slowly building sense of possible disaster accelerated into outright panic when we boarded our plane in Frankfurt. I stepped into the cabin and gazed back at the rows of dark faces speaking languages I couldn't place. I don't think I had ever been the only white person in a crowd before that. Suddenly I realized what it must like to be black in a white society. I was so obviously the foreigner; the odd woman out.

The luggage pickup area reminded me of Morocco in the early days: pared down, basically an empty room with a conveyor belt and more porters than passengers. No trolleys. Everyone on the plane had mounds of luggage, TVs, microwaves; intent on bringing the full cornucopia of Western goods home to family, to show that they, too, had succeeded "in Abroad." That's what they called it, as if Germany, Dubai, and the USA were all one big place. Everyone was smiling, glad to be home, and the river of passengers squeezing through the funnel that was customs was courteous, sweaty, shedding scarves and extra carry-ons but, in general, ecstatic.

The airport meet-and-greet area similarly was in an uproar; noisy, filled with people in the gorgeous brightly colored local clothes. It seemed that it was part of Ghanaian tradition to meet people with an entourage; one little group even had trumpets and banners, brass drums and children in matching outfits. It seemed more like a fiesta than an arrivals hall. It was pitch-black too; night falls at six o'clock on the equator, something I had not factored into my travel plans. I was distracted as someone grabbed at my bag and tried to wrestle it from me, offering a taxi, money exchange, and something called "credit."

From that moment I was on my guard. For the first time I, a veteran world traveler, was arriving in a new country absolutely terrified. I wrapped my arm around Sabrina's shoulders, keeping her close. For once she did not shrug me off. I was confident that nobody would be able to put anything over on me. All those years in Morocco when we traveled together had prepared us for anything, I thought. We stood in limbo a few moments longer; just long enough for me to ask myself what the hell I was doing here.

A woman emerged from the crowd holding a signboard with my name on it. She was hugely pregnant and dressed comfortingly in a pretty pink print. Reassuringly, she did not look at all like a West African scam artist. Her name was Princess, she said in a sweetly solicitous lilt, and she asked us about our flight and welcomed us to Ghana. *Akwaaba* was the word for "welcome," she said smiling. Then she addressed me more formally.

"Madame, good evening."

"Good evening," I said.

"I hope all is well with your family back home?" she asked, for all the world as if we were in a sitting room in the London suburbs, sipping tea.

"Yes, thank you. And your family?"

I was on familiar ground here; the soothing back and forth of pleasantries essential to any Muslim society. I had not expected it in Ghana, which was largely Christian, but apparently here too politeness ranked more highly than anything else. Our new friend helped guide us safely away from the swarming crowds, a portion of whom had now burst into spontaneous song; a hymn I remembered from Bible school. For a moment it pulled at my heart.

Once out of the big shack that constituted Accra's airport and the protected circle of immigration guards, the street was full of taxis inching along at walking pace. The cacophony was overwhelming, and the pungent mix of diesel and sweat caught at my throat.

"Good evening, madame. How are you?" Again, the inherited colonial formula and another big smile; this time from a wiry young man in a singlet who put our huge suitcases in his tiny cab. My senses were on overdrive. If these people were crooks, they were the politest crooks on earth. Princess got in front, and Sabrina and I squeezed in back.

At the first traffic light, a little girl in a torn orange dress and no shoes threaded through the traffic, guiding a man with one leg and gouged-out eyes. *Standard Africa*, I thought. As they edged past the hawker girls with huge silver bowls balanced on their heads, the man tapped on the car window frame, his hand outstretched. He smiled. I could see the few teeth in his blackened gums. He wouldn't move on, face pushed at my open window.

I looked away awkwardly until the lights finally changed.

As the taxi bolted forward, Princess twisted around to face us from the front seat. "Madame, Gomoa is not coming on," she said.

"Not coming on?" I echoed dully, confused by the quaint fifties-style terminology. Gomoa was to be our destination; the beach town where the orphanage was located. Coincidentally it also held White

Sands, one of Ghana's few resorts, which I'd noted with relief when doing our research. We had an escape plan (just in case).

"We go to Teshie, then Awutiase," she explained.

I fought back a rising tide of panic. I grasped that the new plan was to spend the night in Princess's house in Teshie, wherever that was; then we'd travel the next day to an orphanage in the market town of Awutiase, three hours away.

"But why? I asked.

"The children in Awutiase need you much more," Princess said firmly. She settled down for the ride, her shoulders set. That, it seemed, was that.

As we inched through Accra in the back of the hot jolting taxi, the sudden change in itinerary really threw me. I was scared. Stuck in a sweltering nighttime traffic jam with two strangers and my trusting daughter, assailed by heat and harangued by beggars, I was already wishing I had never left the manicured avenues of home. Finally our taxi suddenly jolted free and set off at a steady pace on a clear, if narrow, road. The sea was on our right, and the air smelt briny. Sabrina looked at me with shining eyes and squeezed my hand. To her, this was an adventure. Her happiness buoyed my spirits. I took a deep breath, summoned my courage, and fixed a brave smile on my face. I wanted my daughter to see me as fearless; I could not bear to let her down.

We stepped out into the still-throbbing heat. It was pitch-black, but the high temperature remained unrelenting. The district of Teshie, in the eastern sector of the city, was a mix of violent poverty and, by Accra standards, the doggedly middle class. Battered wood shacks bleached the color of ash and roofed with asbestos sheets were crammed up against bare cement houses. A few colonial buildings had crumbling carved wooden balconies. The smell was intense: smoked fish, gasoline, and a potent stench from the storm drain, which was choked with filth and discarded plastic bags. There were no pavements; only a congested, pockmarked, staggering disorder of cars and crowds and roadside stalls.

I wasn't completely naïve; I had realized this trip to Ghana wasn't going to be a photo shoot. I hadn't filled my suitcase with Dior or Comme des Garçons; instead I wore a simple black dress. But my handbag was Chanel (because I didn't own any other kind). These bags had always been a point of pride for me, but in this harsh new environment its beautiful leather surface seemed absurdly eye-catching and out of place. My shoes as well were laughably inappropriate: stacked espadrilles. They had seemed, in Paris, so utterly simple and fit for the tropics. *What had I been thinking?*

I quickly realized that I did not blend in with this neighborhood, particularly as I was glaringly, obviously, the only white person in sight. And now, with half the street staring at me, I would have to make my way across a poorly lit muddy road, in the dark, through a terrifyingly undisciplined roar of traffic, over a drain and down an alleyway. Sabrina had already gone ahead with Princess, and the wiry young man beckoned, his arms heavy with our bags. I contemplated the choice between seeing my daughter disappear or braving the road.

The drain was squalid beyond belief; basically an open sewer. Panicked by the sudden swerve of a loaded minivan, I wobbled right at the edge of a pile of goo. One of my ankles gave way and I started to fall in what seemed to be slow motion. A strong arm shot out before the worst could occur, and I was yanked to safety by the athletic kindness of a stranger. My savior grinned widely and righted me, nodding kindly. "You be fine, lady," he said, sounding vaguely Jamaican. "But dem shoes . . . naa." He clicked his tongue, shook his head, and was gone.

Aha! My savior wasn't exactly Diana Vreeland, but this was fashion advice I knew I should listen to.

* * *

Despite having been awakened at six in the morning by a melody of cocks crowing and tinny gospel music from an unidentified source, the down-at-heel district where Princess lived didn't actually seem so bad. There were tiny sweet bananas for breakfast, white English-style bread hewn off in slices as thick as doorsteps, and tea. We actually had running water for a shower and a mosquito net to sleep under. I felt valiant and raffish and adventurous, quite recovered from my cowardice of the night before. Sabrina was radiant, chatting with Derek, Princess's ravishingly handsome younger brother.

So far, so good. The family seemed eager to retain us, and we agreed they should phone the volunteer agency and insist we stay a few more days in Teshie. It was, we solemnly agreed, important that we remain in Accra in order to understand Ghana a bit before we commenced our weeks of work. My line of thinking was this: *It seems safe enough here, but the next place may not be. Let's stretch this out for as long as possible.* We bundled out into the now slightly more predictable confusion of the street, where life was visibly treading people down— dirt, dust, flies, smells—but where everybody smiled widely and perfect strangers greeted us. The sun's fingers on my skin seemed a violation, already searing hot by nine o'clock and literally making me flinch. On our way to the roadside with Princess and Derek, we went through the greeting ritual at least five times with assorted neighbors. The children called us *obruni*, which Sabrina confidently informed me meant "stranger." She also provided a startling bit of information: there were forty-four tribes in Ghana and each spoke a different language or dialect, and that was why English was so pervasive. The journalist in me lit up. This culture was obviously so rich that I wanted to know more.

Derek showed us how to ride the *tro-tro* minibus. Everyone who crammed into the tiny bus was loaded down with bags and bundles.

Much of that luggage seemed to be alive. I counted two chickens inside and a goat on the roof. The journey took forever on the single-lane ribbon of road along the coast. The traffic hardly seemed to move, but the customers took it stoically; one man even stood up and started to read out loud, energetically, from the Bible. If you positioned yourself just right, you could catch a breeze from the open windows. I gazed longingly at the sea, but a roughly painted sign with a Jolly Roger on it said it was a military shooting range, so that rather put me off. Derek cheerfully told us that the beach was the main municipal toilet, so it quickly lost any remaining appeal.

The traffic was unbelievable, but there was so much to see that it was bearable, even absorbing. The shops in shacks bordering the road were called things like "Jesus Saves Plumbing Works" or "God's Love Auto" or "Sea Never Dry Provisions Store." The signs were naïf and roughly painted, reminding me vaguely of the paintings of Jean-Michel Basquiat.

We were headed for Makola market in downtown Accra, an immensity of gorgeous fabric and secondhand clothes jammed against stalls selling medicines and hardware, avocados and giant snails, and strange-looking giant brown tubers. As in a medieval market or a contemporary souk, it was divided into alleys that specialized in different goods; here the fabric, there the jewelry, over there the beauty products, and even farther down, the nails and hammers.

In addition women glided along like ships in full sail, selling things from boxes carried on their heads. They were wreathed in turbans and billowing with fabulous gaudy colors: indigo and viridian and scarlet and lime. Some of them had the bundle of a sleeping baby on their back, passed out from the heat. Most of them wore a very dignified, almost eighteenth-century outfit with a short tailored jacket, the *kabba* cover, and a long slit skirt; the *slit*. *A kabba and slit*, instantly I wanted one—no, several—but one at least, in one of those fantastic wax prints, preferably a pink and orange medley.

On a whim, Sabrina had her lovely long wavy hair braided into zigzag cornrows at a street stall. It took four hours, but she was happy. I had plenty to watch while I waited—the graceful passersby with their astounding, miraculous sense of color; a revelation in the almost unnaturally intense light. Apparently here it was okay for men— muscular, grizzly, unmistakably straight men—to wear floor-length pink lace. And to hold hands. Nice. And very sexy, as my designer friend Ozwald had reliably informed me. There was a lot of joking and bantering among the traders, not all of which I could understand. Many words seemed bastardized, as if they had taken the Queen's English of 1950 and made it their own, adding in a generous smattering of words in local languages with clicks and other significant nonverbal sounds. The result, Derek told me, was called *pidgin*.

There was no nature to speak of in Accra; all the buildings seemed to be either shacks, cement rectangles with ugly proportions, or occasional pompous McMansions with silver-painted burglar-proof barriers guarding their façades. After northern Africa, which was the only part of the continent I knew well, it was a big shock. In Morocco every house had at least a little flicker of beauty. But in Accra's buildings there seemed to be no easy allure or visual hint of tropical paradise; just ugly, unplanned urban sprawl, chaos, misery, stinking slums and, surging up amidst it all, the miracle of such charming people in glamorous clothes.

11

*W*hile Sabrina was getting her hair done with Derek standing by, Princess and I wandered off to explore for a bit. And of course I bought fabric. The choice of wax prints was intricate, fabulous, unending. In the shacks of Wax Alley, as I called it in my mind, the bolts were piled up to the corrugated iron sheets that served as roofs. Moreover, each print apparently had a meaning: here was food for a whole lifetime of study around the fashion traditions in this country. *Really*, I thought, *someone ought to write a book*.

There were prints featuring abstract shapes, flowers, but also mobile phones, Mercedes-Benzes, even spark plugs.

"Please, madame, what is this one?" I pointed to a white textured fabric with a print of a bird on a nest feeding a worm to her chicks.

"This one," the plump matron struggled to find the exact words, "means 'a good mother knows what her children like to eat.' You can give to a woman when she gives birth." Ah well, that made sense.

Another was a print with more birds, but with an almost Warholesque color scheme of yellow and pink against a deep fuchsia background, and with a fluorescent yellow line drawing of a cage. The woman burst out laughing as she saw me eyeing it. "This one," she managed to say through her chortling, "means 'when you go out, I will also go out.' You can give to your husband when you are married. It's a warning: if he is going to enjoy, then you too you will enjoy."

I chuckled with her. *I'll bet there's a good market for that one*, I thought.

I bought a pink graphic print called "Disc" that was very popular, the seller informed me, and hesitated over one that depicted wavy onionlike shapes with red centers. "It's called—how do you say?—'eye of my rival' because when you wear this dress you will look so beautiful, your rival's eyes will turn red."

I could have spent days in Wax Alley, learning the meanings of the endless rows of fabric.

To accompany my newfound fashion knowledge, when I returned to the street stall Sabrina told me that Derek called her boot-cut jeans "hold my thigh and leave my leg." We all fell about laughing. Ah, these Ghanaians were funny. Their humor, it seemed, as benefited an oral tradition, was all about language; double entendres and puns.

Every other woman I saw had a huge aluminum bowl on her head. They were porters, immigrants from the north. Princess called them *kayakei*. With their backs straight and heads held high, they balanced huge loads of food, fabric, and mostly anything you could think of. Princess called for one of them to carry my lengths of cloth.

On the way home I bought a boiled egg with hot black pepper sauce called, off-puttingly, *shito* (actually, it was delicious), and stopped at an eye-popping newsstand. The newspapers were pinned up with clothes pegs, creating four paper walls around the seller. They were unbelievably lurid, like the newspapers in *Men in Black*, but for real. Decorated with photos of accidents and dead bodies, they screamed random headlines in the vein of PASTOR HAD SEX WITH SNAKE, MAN

EATS WOMAN'S HEAD, AND WOMAN GIVES BIRTH TO THREE-HEADED BABY. I bought a flimsy twenty-page newspaper that was badly printed but seemed the least garish: the *Daily Graphic*. I was going to try to get under the skin of this country, I decided, and the best way was through the Ghanaians' eyes; through their rendition of their own society.

Eventually I managed to find a good secondhand guidebook; a big thick one, a Brandt's *Ghana* only a year out of date, that was to become my bible. It was sold to me most graciously out of a big round aluminum bowl of books balanced on someone's head.

After two days of enthusiastic shopping, Princess would not be put off any longer. With great earnestness, she insisted that the next day we must travel to Awutiase, where she would leave us at the orphanage. "The children are waiting for you," she insisted. I winced, ashamed to have delayed for so long. The time had come for us to sever all ties to the city and journey to central Ghana for four long weeks.

* * *

On the ribbonlike road the air smelled of wet soil. Downtown Accra, clogged with street peddlers and traffic, was now far behind us. The ugly airless cement houses started giving way to rolling hills, lush with every hue of green from celadon to khaki, the cloudy horizon broken by the occasional majestic thick tall tree. Our smoke-spewing taxi jolted past a village entirely composed of mud huts: a cluster of simple geometric shapes topped with thatch or tin. It was a thrilling sight; somehow unreal, like an illustration in a children's book. There were women washing clothes in aluminum bowls under shade trees, and shoeless children waving as we passed. I settled back to weave ideas of what their lives must be like. Here life was apparently lived outside; the tiny huts could only be meant for sleeping. They obviously had no plumbing, and plumbing, or the lack thereof, had begun to take up a disproportionate part of my thoughts.

We swept past a forest of gigantic black-stemmed bamboo and then found ourselves among coconut palms. The hills had a kind of quiet dampness to them, like photographs of the dewy gray-green mountains of Rwanda. Homes were painted fuchsia, scarlet, crimson, madder, peach. We passed women wearing lilac, tangerine, violet; supersaturated colors that seemed to vibrate into life. The paved road grew increasingly potholed and then gave way almost entirely, as we bumped agonizingly along for a further hour or so, to a track that had the surface, it seemed, of corrugated iron. The novelty of the mud villages strung out by the side of the road was now fading, although Sabrina marveled at all the children walking impassively, in a single file in the baking sun.

It seemed a good time to begin "the conversation"—the one I'd been trying unsuccessfully to have with my distant daughter for the past few months. I took a deep breath.

"Do you ever think about what your life would have been like if you hadn't been adopted?" I started.

"Not really," Sabrina shot back defensively.

We were crammed together in the car's back seat, Sabrina pushed up against the door away from me. I was uncomfortably situated between her and Princess, who snored softly through her open mouth. Even crammed so close together, Sabrina seemed miles away, her back turned to me as she stared out the window. She was pretending to be fascinated by the roadside scenery, but I saw from her hunched shoulders that she was tense and on guard. We rarely ventured into this territory.

"Well," I tried again. "Any one of those kids would probably give their eyeteeth for the kind of chances you have."

"I know," she said sharply.

"If you know, then why don't you make some changes?" I lifted one of the braids falling down her back, and she squirmed free of my touch.

"Because it's not my fault!" Her voice rose as I felt my own anger rising to match hers. Princess stirred beside me, her head lolling to the other side before she resumed snoring. I signaled to Sabrina to keep her voice down. I knew we were treading dangerously close to a shut-down; that Sabrina might just refuse to talk. One of the things that most frightened me was that she didn't know how to trust me, even if she wanted to. Her history of betrayal would always mute her.

Her voice trembled. "I don't mean to get into trouble, Mum. My friends always drag me down."

I sighed, exasperated. It was a familiar excuse. "It's about you, not about them. Have you ever thought this through? Have you ever asked yourself if bad things happen to you because you don't believe you *deserve* the good things in life? Because you came from a place where you were treated badly?"

Quietly Sabrina began to cry. I hated myself for pushing her, but somehow I had to get through. Nothing had seemed to work—not tough love, not sympathy, not rational argument. I was desperate to help her regain her course, but I didn't know how.

"Sabrina, everything that happened to you was not your fault. A lot of the kids we're going to meet will have been through what you went through, and worse. You have to break free from the memories. Don't let them hold you back."

I didn't know what the shrink would say about all this. *Am I saying all the wrong things?* I wondered when our relationship had become so cautious, so strained. I thought of the little girl in the flimsy dress I found that first morning outside my apartment; our ease sharing the strawberries in the sunlight together. *How have we come to this?*

"I'll change," she mumbled. "You'll see."

I had heard this before, but I wanted so badly to believe that this time it would be true. "Well, now you're doing something good for other people," I said brightly, although I had a knot in my stomach. The subject was closed. For now.

A police barrier halted us, and Sabrina and I began hunting among the piles of dog-eared banknotes in my handbag for the change required for a bribe. It was incredible how quickly one became used to the constant small bribes daily life required.

* * *

Awutiase was a shabby potholed place, but it was bursting with energy; a long road jammed with huts the color of the earth, and dark shops made out of empty shipping containers. There were a few new larger houses decked out with balustrade balconies; knock-off delusions of grandeur. It was noon on Saturday, and the market, smaller than the one in Accra, was in full swing; the funky, noisy clash of stalls selling smoked fish and hair products and brightly colored plastic buckets and fat plantains and cheap aluminum pans. The main road bustled with commotion. Women carried enormous loads on their heads. We passed a decayed colonial-era church, and our car got caught in a noisy procession of people in festive black and scarlet outfits: a funeral. Children darted about in mismatched Western clothes and remnants of their weekday brown and orange school uniforms, their heads shaved to ward off lice.

With a start, I thought of our purpose here. I had been so caught up in exotica that I had almost forgotten about the children we'd be working with. I braced myself for what lay ahead.

* * *

A line of one- and two-room shacks led out of town. Princess told the driver to turn down a tiny path between two houses. Immediately thick elephant grass sprang up around us: the little town lined the road, but the strip of urban life was only one house deep, and dense tropical jungle was within touching distance. This was something I had not yet seen, and it was captivating in a new and powerful way. My heart lightened, and I squeezed Sabrina's hand.

We stopped in front of a large cement bungalow with a huge palm tree in front and a hangarlike structure fifty yards farther down the hill. The place was alive with small children who immediatcly surrounded the car. They were so small; none seemed to be over the age of eight. I wondered where the older children were. *Is the orphanage only for very young children?*

All I really knew was that Awutiase was a private orphanage. Princess had informed us that it received no money whatsoever from the government and depended on charitable donations, as well as volunteers like Sabrina and me.

Princess ushered us onto a covered porch whcrc thc owncrs were expecting us. A short plump couple, they were seated on a small sofa and didn't rise when we approached. The woman held a little boy who seemed to be asleep. Princess initiated an elaborate series of handshakes and introductions. It all seemed very formal until the woman burst forward, pushing the sleeping child into my arms. "Oh!" I exclaimed in surprise, and the woman broke into laughter, grinning effusively. Reassured by the sight of her warm smile, I couldn't help but laugh myself.

At first she spoke so quickly that I couldn't understand her. "I am Maa," she said, pointing to herself. "And this is Dada," she gestured to the gray-haired man with his shirt unbuttoned beside her, who nodded enthusiastically as he gazed at us over his spectacles.

Maa made a great fuss over Sabrina, stroking her elaborately braided hair and the lovely glass beads we had bought in Makola. It seemed strange to refer to fellow adults as "Maa" and "Dada," but they insisted we call them this; everyone did, they said. In Ghana, it seemed, such titles were part of the politeness ritual. It had been Auntie Princess and Sister Sabrina back in Teshie too. Maa was a short round solid woman, probably in her late forties, in a *kabba* and *slit* and a stiff helmetlike wig of straight black hair. We sat there chit-chatting for about half an hour. There seemed to be either a baby or a cat plunked on every battered sofa or plastic chair, and the place was swarming with flies. She bustled about beaming with welcome, very keen to thrust babies into my arms.

Dada was an older man with a graying beard and a paunch; a former military man from the Ashanti region, as he informed me. The president of Ghana was an Ashanti, a proud warrior tribe. It occurred to me that I should read up on the tribes of Ghana since it was obviously going to be factor in relationships, despite the fact that "tribalism" seemed to be derided in my sources of information, the *Daily Graphic* and the Brandt guide.

I plucked up one particularly winsome and eager little child and we toured the buildings, starting with the "baby room"—an airless room with bare cinder-block walls. There were no ceiling boards; just the underside of the corrugated aluminum sheeting. In a corner lay a few broken-down beds and several rolled-up mats. There were a row of eight or so mismatched rusty cots and perhaps twenty babies and small toddlers crawling around on the floor, watched by one lethargic elderly minder. Next came a disparate collection of much smaller rooms, mostly locked. And flies; so many flies that even today when I think about Awutiase, that is what I remember most.

The bare cement floors were grimy. There were small, diaperless children everywhere. Several of the youngest were crying in a long, miserable wail that seemed to expect no answer. All of them had runny noses and crusty eyes, and three or four seemed unable to walk, dragging themselves along the floor of the bare corridors on their skinny bottoms. I was deeply shocked. "Save your tears," I reprimanded myself silently. "You can't go crying about everything, or you'll never stop." I was glad Sabrina had stayed outside to say goodbye to Derek.

"Look at this one," said Maa, pointing to a diapered child who looked bigger than a baby, perhaps the size of a one-year-old. He was lying on his back and staring vacantly like a newborn. "I don't know about him. He doesn't seem normal to me," she pronounced. "I think he must have a broken spine."

She looked up at me, her lips pursed. Maa was asking *me* for advice. I had absolutely no idea about babies, but a broken spine sounded really bad. The child didn't seem to be in pain, but indeed he did not seem able to move his limbs. His head lolled oddly to one side. He had no name—he had been found abandoned at a dump, Maa said—and he definitely needed medical attention; that was clear. I said that I could take him to the doctor. Sounding profoundly relieved, as if this had indeed been a major subject of anxiety because of lack of funds, Maa looked at me appraisingly and said I could take him to the nearest hospital. I felt invigorated and useful; so this was what we had come here to do.

By this time we were trailing ten or twenty children, and several of them had attached themselves to me. The elfin Precious, probably four years old, who had begged to be carried, was coiling my long curly hair around her hand. Since my arms were full, others were grasping my clothes. Even the smallest children spoke a few words of English and, to charm me, repeated them over and over. Sabrina was laughing as two little girls clambered onto her back and attempted to weave her braids into a megabraid. It had been months since I had seen her look so relaxed and joyful.

Maa plucked Precious from my arms and replaced her with a nightmarish figure: a tiny skeletal child with thighs I could span easily with my hands, covered with red sores. Emma was perhaps three, although she hardly seemed larger than a six-month-old baby. I had never seen malnutrition before; had never held someone so breakable, so vulnerable and fragile.

"She needs you," said Maa, her voice matter-of-fact. The poor child's eyes stared grayly at me and she made no sound. For all I knew, she was in great pain.

"I want to help however I can," I said a little shakily. Maa nodded approvingly.

Gently, holding my breath, I replaced Emma in an iron cot, carefully unbending her legs, as thin and breakable as two dried sticks. She stared up at me, unnaturally still. I felt there was an urgent story behind her huge indifferent eyes, and that it was begging for release. I didn't want to care for this terrifying baby, but already I did. From that moment on there was no more doubt in me. I knew that I could help—even partially, even temporarily—and that no matter what I could offer, it would be needed.

12

*A*t the back of the house was another veranda, where it looked as if food was prepared. Knives were in evidence, at child height, and there were various buckets of what looked like vegetables soaking in the hot shade, again with flies buzzing everywhere. In one corner was a tangle of rusting garden implements within easy reach of a small child. Outside on the red dirt were several burned-out fires laid between rows of smooth humps of mud arranged in threes, like a row of stone-age barbecues. Four young girls, perhaps twelve or thirteen, smiled at us, particularly at Sabrina, and busied themselves with cooking. They were cutting tiny shriveled onions in the palms of their hands with giant knives—the kind you would use to chop meat. I flinched. I wanted to grab the knives from them, but I had just arrived and felt I had to respect this couple's way of doing things. I reminded myself again that in this culture, politeness was probably more important than Western ideas about child safety.

It was now around three in the afternoon, and the orphanage began filling up with older children and teenagers who trailed down the rock-strewn path in silent groups, each bearing a heavy load of pineapples. They were dirty, and several of the older boys looked weak with fatigue. They said they had been working "on the farm." Maa angrily shooed them away from the kitchen area before turning to me with a smile and explaining that it wasn't time to eat yet; it was important for the children to learn to *share*.

When Maa shouted, Precious shrank into my ribcage as if she wanted to disappear. I felt for this gentle sensitive child, but clearly Maa felt that strict control was required. She oversaw the lives of 105 children on extremely limited resources. Europe would descend into chaos after a few days without running water, but this woman kept her entire operation afloat almost single-handedly in conditions I couldn't have imagined.

I felt a rush of determination. Maa was just one woman, and couldn't be expected to accomplish everything. But with two of us— three, counting Sabrina—we just might be able to get some things done around here. Marshaling the focused determination I'd seen in Anna Wintour, I marched back into the baby room with my Pied Piper procession of crusty-eyed toddlers, and took another look around.

There was the one harassed helper for over ten infants. A baby was screaming nonstop, the veins bulging on his forehead; others were passive, not even playing. The smell indicated clearly that several cloth diapers needed to be changed. The place looked as if it had needed cleaning and arranging for years. Toxic household products were on the floor, including a half-empty bottle of bleach, and dirty diapers soaking in a filthy bucket within easy reach of little fingers. A half-broken iron bed frame with a sharp metal edge needed disposal. There was nothing I could do about the holes in the roof, the cracked walls, and the lack of sheets; well, nothing I could do just yet. But I could sort out the baby room, put the baskets of medication on top of a high cupboard, find somewhere more appropriate for the cleaning products, and drag the urine-soaked bedding out in the sun for a natural dry.

At around five-thirty a flash storm erupted, slapping raindrops the size of cockroaches onto the tin roof over the veranda, where the teenage girls had begun preparing the food. The young girls flapped nervously at the fires they had built between the hard mud bumps of the stone-age barbecues outside; it was going to be difficult to cook a meal tonight. Clouds of mosquitoes rose up, and I swore to myself that I would buy mosquito nets in the market the very next day.

As evening approached birds screeched in a crazy chorus, and a crowd of hungry children began massing under the single lightbulb that held off the dark. Above them the majestic palm tree stood outlined against the still-purple sky. Maa clapped her hands and shouted for the rest of the children to gather, and they held hands in a ragged circle to sing Bible school songs in lilting English; a charming scene. All my Sunday school songs came back to me in a short sharp burst of nostalgia. It caught me off guard, again. Then Maa baptized me with what was to remain my name for the rest of my life. "Mama Lisa! Mama Lisa!" she cried, pointing at me. The children joyfully caroled it back: *"Mamalisa, Mamalisa, Mama, Mama."* My defenses were down, and I was tearing up. Everyone was else was beaming. Sabrina and I smiled back weakly; we felt welcomed, needed, loved. And exhausted.

Sabrina and I needed to unpack and settle into the house where we would be staying before the lights went out. In Awutiase, electricity was a precious and fickle resource, like tap water, and sometimes stayed off for days. A tall lean man came loping silently out of the darkness and we were formally introduced: Brother Kwame, Mama Lisa. It was difficult to tell if he was twenty-five, or thirty-five like me, as his face was strangely impassive and ageless. He was wearing a white singlet and had very dark skin and a face like an African sculpture, his muscles gleaming in the lamplight; pure visual poetry.

Kwame was a man of few words. "Please. This way," he said, his voice a rich baritone. He finally smiled, flashing brilliant white teeth, and transformed from ancestral African sculpture to a real guy, shy but welcoming. He plucked up our bags, and we followed him toward our quarters.

I glanced behind us one last time at the children, busily scooping rainwater out of a bucket with their plastic drinking cups. Children as young as three or four lined up for the older teenagers to ladle out dry, slightly burnt-smelling rice with a spoonful of tinned tomato sauce. I watched them plunk down on the beaten earth to eat their meager dinner in the deepening darkness. I glanced around for Maa and Dada, but they were nowhere to be seen.

Kwame strode ahead to a house we would be sharing with three Ghanaian families. It was large, unbelievably hot, and filthy. Kwame set five boys to work sweeping and removing cobwebs in three inter-connecting rooms. It was a traditional compound house built in cinder block, with large rooms and a long drop toilet. A shared toilet and no plumbing; precisely my worst nightmare. But strangely, at that moment it no longer seemed to matter so much anymore. There were exactly six pieces of furniture in our domain: two double beds, a large rectangular dining table, and three plastic chairs. The best was yet to come: the shared shower was outside. It was a small area about two feet square, enclosed by a chin-height cement wall with no roof. It had taps, but no water came out.

The water situation was clearly habitual; there was a water tank and a plastic bucket with a pail, with which we were supposed to douse ourselves. Then you soaped up a white froth and rinsed down with the pail. On the good side, as I realized when I took my first much-anticipated bucket shower, it meant one washed oneself under the stars. Ghanaian girls pee in the shower to avoid bogging down the loo, Sabrina informed me as we soaped up together. Okay, right; that explained the faint odor in the shower, and was why everyone wore flip-flops to bathe. The resulting draining water was rich in nutrients, so the banana trees thrived on the soapy mess and smothered the small cement structure and nearly, but not quite, provided a natural roof.

As happens so often in families, we didn't say much to each other. Instead we focused on the small things: a lost shoe, where to unpack, a quick hug in-between. This physical closeness was new to us. Like most Western mothers and daughters, we lived apart; in separate rooms with separate friends, and we often had separate meals. A woman called Sister Aisha brought us servings of very spicy fish stew with rice and fruit. Even on that first day, bemused as I was, I realized that we were getting better food than the children. This made me uncomfortable, although there did not seem to be much I could do about it in the immediate short term. There were also mosquito nets over both our beds, but Sabrina and I headed to the same one. We needed the comforting relief of each other's proximity.

Sabrina fell asleep in minutes on the sagging foam mattress, deaf to the crazy noise of the African night, which included the whirr of the fan, the unbelievably loud crickets outside, the scratching of geckos, and the night movements echoing in the pitch-black darkness: snoring, coughing, people talking loudly to someone who may or may not have been in the room, or neighbors moving back and forth to the toilet.

I lay beside her carefully, not moving, trying to give Sabrina enough room for comfort in the clammy air. I felt an enormous wave of compassion and respect for Maa. Of course I felt empathy for the children, but I was overcome by how sorry I felt for this saintly woman, who despite such terrible hardships was struggling as best she could to deal with it all.

There was no point in pretending; I would not be going to sleep that night. I was being tugged by the abandoned children of the Awutiase orphanage back into my own childhood; my own abandonment in the years of my mother's Mediterranean dream-gone-sour, when I was rescued by a family not my own.

The fostering experience with Paul and Barbara had helped lift my mum out of poverty, and through my entire childhood they provided a precious alternative family. Even though they did not support us with money, they gave a richer, more stable dimension to my life.

Now I had become a confident and competent adult, with energy and drive and the power to get things done. I had pitched up in West Africa, with children whose desperation was much greater than mine had ever been, and who faced dangers and pain on a completely different scale. And yet, quite simply, I felt that their story was my story. One kind gesture had turned my life around. Surely I could do the same for them?

I had of course fostered and then adopted Sabrina. I had of course been a huge force for good in her life already. *Or had I?* Expelled, uncertain of her direction . . . maybe I had failed her. The shrink kept telling me that her issues came from her young childhood, before we met: abandonment, betrayal, an environment thick with lies. She said that I had done my best, but still I felt guilty. Maybe if I had traveled less for work, had a stable marriage, led a more bourgeois life. Or if I had moved away from Paris earlier, denounced the abuse I had begun to suspect, cut all ties with her family. But I could not have moved Sabrina, since she was initially only in foster care with me and therefore unable to live anywhere but the Paris *département* until she was twelve. I heard the shrink's voice in my head: *You have got to stop beating yourself up about this. You did your best.*

I realized that my determination to help these children was a kind of compensation for feeling as if I'd failed Sabrina. A karmic debt, so to speak. *You have not failed Sabrina,* my mother's angry voice boomed inside my head. But as I turned to look at my daughter's beautiful sleeping profile, I realized I would never be quite sure of that. I remembered something I had once heard. It seemed so true in that moment: "It is easier to love the whole world than to love just one person." One person, with their issues and troubles; a world of disappointment and frustration. Maybe by throwing ourselves into altruism, into work, and loving the whole world, Sabrina and I would both find our way.

Very quickly Sabrina and I developed a routine that drew us close—at first almost wordlessly, and then with an outpouring of conversation. The simple acts of sharing a bedroom, a bed, and a couple of meals together every day pulled us into each other's orbits. As we became partners in our cleaning operations and major expeditions to the market, we began sharing our impressions, laughing together. We became friends again.

Each day we would wake around six. Eat breakfast of the soft sweet bread and omelets with onions, green peppers, and tomato. And walk down the lane to the orphanage where all the boys over the age of eight were heading out to the fields. I made it my business to hand them each a hunk of bread and margarine as they passed.

The other children were up and doing chores: dressing the smaller ones, washing them, changing diapers. Every morning when Maa arrived on the scene, usually long after Dada had trooped the boys off to work on the farm, she made a great fuss over Sabrina and me. Sabrina was *so* pretty, far more pretty even than the day before! And I must take Emma in my arms and look after her: "She has been crying all night for you. Only when you feed her will she eat."

Predictably, my heart melted as the tiny Emma uncurled her fragile fingers and gripped mine. As she sipped eagerly from the teaspoons of special infant formula I had purchased and made up, I held my breath, smitten. Maa knew very well what she was doing.

At seven the children ate their breakfast—a small and watery bowl of rice soup called, fittingly, "rice water"—and then the younger kids left for school at a long, low, three-room building on the fringes of the orphanage's land. In two of the cramped rooms and a corridor half filled with boxes, two of the older girls and a short elderly man named Osei gave basic reading, writing, and English classes to kids who shared not only books and textbooks, but also chairs.

Osei was not a bad man, but his English was dreadful and his teaching methods worse. The children were required to learn lists of words by rote, and when they made a mistake they were called to the front of the class and hit with a ruler. Rarely, if ever, were they allowed to come up with their own sentences. It was a miracle that so many of them managed to speak English. The younger children stayed in this "school" from nine to twelve on most days, which was at least a respite from their long days of work. After about the age of twelve, there would be no more classes. Junior secondary school cost money, and very few of the children attended.

While these classes droned on, the older girls were busy doing chores. Teenage children did all the marketing, washing, cleaning, and cooking. The washing (including diapers) was done by hand—in the same plastic buckets later used for soaking vegetables. They fetched the water for all of this from a dank brown pond about half a mile away.

I was deeply shocked by everything I was seeing. I immediately started a wish list:

1. Access to clean water
2. Proper nourishing food
3. Good education to secondary school level (note: no corporal punishment)
4. Hygiene lessons and cleaning products

For the first two days I concentrated on the baby room. This involved buying industrial quantities of bleach and scrubbing brushes, as well as sheets, mosquito nets, and new mattresses. Everything I saw was broken and needed repair. It was frustrating that the most ordinary things were so difficult to come by in the orphanage.

Scissors? No.

A mop? No.

Needle and thread? No.

A broom? Oh yes! *Of course* they had brooms. I was proudly offered a sorry bunch of twigs tied together with a strip of cloth.

I bought several bags full of square, white, ready-made mosquito bed nets in the Swedru market, and insisted that instead of ending up in a locked storeroom, they must be hung up immediately and the nets set up over every cot and mat. I sorted out the ancient debris, and put some children's beds back together. I bought extra food at the market, and medical supplies. I bought another lifetime supply of bleach. I learned to haggle. I learned to question every price, always, even on the *tro-tros* or taxis; and I learned how to ask for a discount.

The mostly silent Kwame seemed to surge up out of nowhere when I most needed help. All these marketing trips ended in chance meetings with him; he always seemed gratifyingly delighted to see me, and would carry everything back home. His English was halting, but in an environment where everyone seemed to be either under fifteen or gray haired, it was nice to have an attractive man to talk to.

13

*D*uring our third week, I asked Maa for a full tour of the hang-erlike building so I could look for spare rubber sheets to protect the new mattresses I had bought. At each locked door, everyone came to a solemn halt while Maa poked through the huge bundle of keys that jangled on a cord around her waist. Several rooms that apparently had to be kept locked contained only broken items: broken fans, broken metal bed frames, broken lamps, all thrown together and blocking access.

I smelled and then spotted a pile of rotting pineapples in a cloud of fruit flies. That made me angry; the children needed vitamins and here they were, in their purest form, rotting away. Other rooms were half filled with boxes and big woven plastic bags stuffed with old clothes. One room she didn't open, but I looked through the window; it was filled to the ceiling with old clothes, almost like a modern art installation. I felt a little faint. This was surreal.

"Donations," Maa announced importantly.

If this was a joke, it wasn't funny. I glanced around the halls, where the children's bedding was piled up *outside* these locked rooms.

While some rooms stored donations that were apparently never used, and others were solely occupied by broken rubbish, children slept on thin mats in the corridors. It was so ludicrous I didn't know what to think, except that surely there must be some kind of explanation. It had already struck me during the revamp of the baby room that it was impossibly hard to throw things away; broken plastic cots were kept, as were buckets with holes in them, and odd shoes. I could only surmise that it had to do with scarcity; some fear of being without. I knew there had been a near-famine in Ghana in the early eighties, a time of great want. I had to keep reminding myself that I wasn't in a position to question the hoarding. "Their house, their country, their kids," I whispered under my breath.

When I looked up, Maa was watching me with a shrewd expression. I didn't know how to read her look and interpreted it as embarrassment, or maybe defensiveness. It made me uneasy. I decided not to rock the boat too much right away; I didn't want to risk souring the relationship. I'd wait for the right moment to question her about the contents of the locked rooms.

We crossed the open space and headed to the large white-painted cement annex that we had seen in the distance. Again, the ritual of the keys—and lo! Toilets. Ten clean white toilets in spotless cubicles. Again, locked.

"Donations," Maa repeated. She seemed quite proud.

This was too much. The orphanage had *ten* brand new toilets that were not to be used? So the children had to squat in the dirt instead? Color flooded my cheeks.

"I don't understand," I stammered, steeling myself for the argument I'd hoped to avoid. "How can you keep them locked up? They must be put to use!"

Maa clucked quietly and hung her head, shaking it slowly. "We cannot," she said sadly.

"But why?" I demanded. "You must open them. It's dishonest not to. They are for the children!"

"They don't work," Maa said, leaning down to tap the back of one toilet where it should have been connected to a pipe. "Bio-gas. Doesn't work."

A wave of comprehension flowed over me, quickly followed by shame. They couldn't use the toilets because some well-meaning donor had installed a fancy new ecologically sound waste management system, bio-gas, and then apparently disappeared without ensuring training or maintenance. It was the first time I had stumbled upon one of the aid world's big white elephants, and it stunned me. I felt terrible for accusing Maa, for embarrassing her because of my own poor grasp of the macroeconomics of the developing world. I was furious with the installer and the shoddy job. The toilets stood there, a monument to expensive folly and lack of follow-up. I was so privileged, so naïve in my assumption that the orphanage would have the luxury of toilets. I saw in an instant that Sabrina wouldn't be the only one receiving a moral education on this trip.

Overcome with emotion, I placed my hand on Maa's shoulder. "I understand," I said feebly. "I'm sorry I questioned you." I felt guilty as hell; the donor would invariably be a white bleeding-heart liberal like me with ecological principles, probably on the other side of the world, confident that his toilets were being used. Worst of all, the bio-gas plant was connected to a (securely locked up) real kitchen with a roof, and an industrial-size gas stove that would allow the cooking to be done safely and hygienically. It was, however, dependent on the bio-gas emissions from the toilet waste to work; no waste, no gas, no kitchen.

"I can email the donor, if you give me the contact," I promised Maa, "and we can fix this." She looked at me doubtfully.

"All right," she said vaguely. Once again I was consumed with a burning ambition to right the ills here. I added "5. Toilets, sanitation,

infrastructure" to my list. And then, after some hesitation, "6. dona-
tions/financial management."

Sabrina made immediate friends with Afi, a girl her own age,
and the two of them simply fused, disappearing together all day.
From time to time I would catch sight of my daughter with her hair
in a turban, pounding cassava for *fufu*—gooey balls eaten with a
groundnut or palm nut sauce—or fanning the coals underneath the
baked-mud fires where the older girls cooked every meal. When we
met up Sabrina was cheerful, grateful, a delight to be around; a total
transformation from our months of struggles in Europe. She was the
only one with a mum, pretty much, and that must have some value
here, at least.

Despite the dismal restrictions of their environment, many of the
children were lively and bright, full of hope and possibility and the
desire to create and succeed. They learned in a second how to take
photographs with my little Canon, and one or two had a genuine
eye for composition and light, in particular a gorgeous five-year-old
boy called Salami. Vida, a particularly cute long-haired girl of about
nine, caught on right away when I taught the kids to play charades.
She was a hilarious mimic, and what she wanted to become, she said
seriously, was a journalist.

My heart broke when she said it, for it should have been easy
for me to help her achieve that, and yet I knew it would be nearly
impossible. The children didn't even have colored pencils or paper
for drawing. Poster paints and books were an inconceivable luxury,
and yet Raymond, a tall skinny teenage boy, had an obvious flair
with drawing. Benjamin said that what he really wanted was to be a
doctor and, horribly, all the other children around said so too, although
it was clear that for them to manage such a thing was about as doable
as flying to the moon.

As their confidence blossomed, several of the teenagers confided
that they reused their old exercise books as personal journals, and

they showed me bits of writing. What impressed me was not so much the skill, but how much they cared about this work and how touched they were when I asked them questions. I added number seven to my list, "Counseling and therapy (and other creative stimuli: books, games, paints, paper)."

They were all ambitious, despite having so few role models who had made it out of Awutiase. A common dream among the children was to be adopted; what they wanted was out. I could understand that.

Number eight on my list was self-evident: "Health education and access to proper health care." The rainy season was now in full force and at any time, it seemed, three or four children were bedridden with malaria. They developed high fevers and shivered quietly. It was terrifying to see, and made the breath catch in my throat. I knew that malaria kills more people each year than any other infectious disease, and yet these kids caught it as often—more often, even—than European kids catch the common cold. The reaction was just as casual too. Maa said there was no need for a doctor; all we needed was malaria medicine from the market. But to me it seemed important to confirm the diagnosis first. In my world you didn't just go to the market and buy some (possibly bootleg) pills, and then push them down your sick child's throat.

When I shared my concern, Maa shrugged. If I wanted to waste my time taking children to the clinic, she implied, that was up to me. The clinic was more than an hour's ride down the bumpy road in the port of Winneba, past a crossroads called the Fetish Priest Junction because of the dark sour-smelling voodoo shop that sold talismans and dried animal skins. The clinic itself was a series of verandas with ceiling fans, packed with people waiting for their name to be called. You paid upfront and then waited, sometimes for two or three hours.

I would be called to fill in registration details for children who had never previously attended the clinic, which was every single child whom I accompanied there, and then wait again for the name to be called so a nurse could take the child's vitals. Then of course we waited for the actual consultation itself—five minutes—and finally we emerged with a prescription.

In 2002 it was always the same prescription: chloroquine. Throughout Ghana during the rainy season, malaria is so overwhelmingly common that blood tests are rare. The diagnosis is simply assumed. The pharmacy was right outside the clinic, and now all the people who had waited for hours to see the doctor were waiting at the pharmacy for their medicine. The whole thing was an all-day experience, as the food and water sellers outside the clinic testified.

By the twenty-first day of my arrival in Ghana, I woke up with fever and chills. Dada came and stood by my bedside, stroking his beard. Maa doled out chloroquine; against my better judgment I took it. I had no test, went to no clinic, saw no doctor but, unmistakably, I was experiencing my first bout of malaria.

I was very scared, but I wore the dreaded malaria attack like a badge of honor, figuring that somehow it made me African. (Hey, if only it were so easy!) I tried to be as nonchalant as they were.

"I'm not surprised Maa and Dada were so worried," Sabrina said gaily on the fourth day, when I was feeling much better. "The last volunteer died of malaria."

"What?" I sprang up off my sweat-soaked pillow. "Who? When?" My words tumbled over themselves.

"Yes, Mum, didn't you ever wonder why we were the only volunteers?"

I had actually been asking myself that, as a perfunctory investigation had revealed that volunteers had been steady source of income for the orphanage in the past.

"The agency won't send them any more since it happened. They only sent us because the place we were meant to go was closed."

I gulped. "How did it happen?"

"Mum, I don't know the details, but all the kids were talking about it when they heard you had gotten sick."

Sabrina had proved invaluable in terms of getting information on the inner workings of the orphanage by chatting to the children. Her darker skin color, her youth, and her sociability quickly made her one of them.

"Ye . . . es, they were wondering how Kwame was going to deal with it. If you died, I mean," she continued.

"Kwame?" I blushed, and looked down.

"Yup. Everyone knows he's sweet on you. They say you should marry him."

"Marry him?" I was feeling a bit dazed. "I just met him."

"Yes, but you know the way people keep asking us to marry them in the *tro-tro* and at the market. It's just something people say a lot here . . ." Sabrina's voice trailed off. "But, Mum, you like him, don't you?" She shot me a sharp glance and continued before I could respond. "Because I don't. He's fake." She twirled the end of one long braid. "He actually knows what the children go through, but he's always on the side of Maa and Dada."

Finally she paused, but I didn't quite know what to say. I didn't think there were sides here; just a kind couple doing their best for the children.

"But I can see their point," sighed Sabrina. "You and Kwame would make a much better job of running Awutiase than Maa and Dada do."

There was a lot to think about, and my malaria-addled brain wasn't up to it. I fell in and out of a wet sweaty sleep in the noisy bird-dominated twilight, always the prettiest time of day in Ghana.

When I woke up, Kwame was standing over me with a bowl of soup. It smelled delicious.

"What's in it?"

"*Aponchie enam.*" Goat meat.

I sniffed it suspiciously. The man next door, an emancipated northerner, was a great one for rat and even bat soup. Ever since the day he was seen skinning a snake as long as my arm, I had grown suspicious of the unidentified pieces of meat floating in the thin red broth that we were served on a daily basis. Some tribes in Ghana ate dogs and cats; dogs in particular were prized, and sold under the euphemistic name "better meat." I could just see myself requesting "better meat" and ending up eating a relative of Brioche's by mistake. However, having witnessed true hunger here, I understood the need to eat everything that moved. For most of these children a whole rat was an unimaginable luxury. I wasn't in a position to judge. I sipped my soup, feeling a little ashamed.

Kwame was silent, as always. Pre-malaria, he had been my faithful partner in cleaning, shopping, and hospital expeditions. Although I had worked out that he was ten years younger than me, I trusted him. In this strange new environment, he was the closest I had to a friend.

"Kwame, what will you do next?" I asked him. I knew he had finished school but had not been able to go to university.

He answered unequivocally, "If I find a sponsor, I will study agriculture in Kumasi and then come back and run the farm, so that the orphanage is not dependent on donations. The donations are not regular; that is what is causing all the problems. The land is very good here. We could grow pineapples as a cash crop."

That was definitely the longest I had heard him speak so far. *Hmm*, I thought to myself, *I've got to see this farm.*

The farm, and a better volunteer program, could be income earners, for sure. I added number nine to my list: "Sustainability." That was it, then; I had a nine-point action plan to improve Awutiase and turn it into a place the children could actually thrive in. Kwame watched me silently as I chomped the gristly goat. I had no appetite since I was convalescing from malaria, but I was so frustrated with

the aches in my bones and the killer headache that I was determined
to eat myself well. I was beginning to feel the pressure of time; our
days in Ghana were running by very fast.

The next day when Maa and Dada came to visit me on what I
had thought could be my future deathbed, we talked business. First,
I quizzed them on how much money they had received from the
agency for our stay. The response was a mere $200, which was just
about 10 percent of what I had paid the volunteer agency. I was
furious. Sweet Sister Princess, in the pink dress, had been a scam
agent after all. I had been well and truly deceived. So had the orphanage, I realized, when Maa and Dada's eyes popped out when I told
them what I had paid. A total of $1,800 went to the agency for five
nights in a shared room in a slum and a ride to Awutiase, and only
$200 to the orphanage (and its 105 hungry children) for nearly five
weeks' room and board. I was determined to put this right.

"We will organize our own volunteer program," I proclaimed,
unknowingly sealing my fate.

"I'll set it up on the Internet. We'll ask volunteers to pay the
whole amount to you."

Maa and Dada looked positively bowled over. "But we have to
have a sick room, with medicines and a nurse, for the children and
the volunteers," I said sternly. "I know what happened to that last
volunteer."

14

*I*t was a few days more before I could walk to the farm, but I used the time to compile an accurate list of the children; a document that, unbelievably, Awutiase did not appear to possess. This turned out to be a herculean task of byzantine complexity, because in Ghana most families do not have a surname. The newborn is given his own first and second name, irrespective of the surname of the father. The first name is determined by the day of the week the child was born. For example, a boy born on Monday is called *Kojo*, derived from the word Monday in Twi, the language of the Akans who constitute nearly half of the population. A girl born on Monday is called *Adwoa*. A child born on Tuesday is *Kwabena* for boys, and *Abena* for girls, and so on; different names for each day of the week.

The second name is often given based on the birth order within the family; for example, the third-born girl is *Mansa* in the Twi language. Simple, right? Day name and birth position name. Well, that's the way it should work, in theory.

Occasionally all such formalities are blithely dispensed with, and the child is simply given the name of the deceased family member they are thought to resemble. Or a name that tells you something about the day the child was born; if it was sunny, for example, or if it was in the middle of a drought. If you think that's complicated, add this in to the mix: the Ewe tribe names their children after the virtues they want them to have. Among the Ewes your accountant could be called Prosper, your bank manager could be called Rich Love, and your CEO could be called Famous. You could visit Beauty, your hairdresser, and Innocent, your tax attorney. The possibilities are endless.

Another level of complexity was brought in by the fact the Ghana is presently undergoing an evangelical fixation, and many people in the south have an additional "Christian name," such as Mary or Emmanuel or Moses. In the north they have an additional Islamic name, such as Mussa or Aisha. But rest assured if all this seems a little complicated; the truth is that nobody in Ghana, except officials, use any of these names. In day-to-day life people use only nicknames; usually a teasing play on a physical characteristic. The fashion for these nicknames pervades the whole country: Keeper, for example, for a footballer. Oxygen, if you have big nostrils. Taller—well, you get my drift.

Thus, when compiling the list of children at Awutiase, I would have on a scrap of paper from Maa: Abraham (church name), Kofi (Friday), and Mensah (third-born male). I would then wander around asking to meet the little chap with the big name, Abraham Kofi Mensah, so I could measure and weigh him, only to discover that nobody knew who he was. I returned to Maa and announced that there must be some mistake; maybe the child was no longer in the orphanage.

"But of course he is," she remonstrated, "he's over there." She pointed toward a lively eight-year-old in impossibly dirty shorts and a thick, torn sweater, kicking a rag football in the sweltering heat.

Ahh, the kid everyone called Striker because of his prowess at football. Got it! Silly me.

I grabbed Maa, who was heading off purposely toward the kitchen area, and asked her a question that had been weighing on my mind for a few days. I already feared the answer.

"Do you have um . . . any files on these children?"

"Files . . ." Maa looked thoughtful, as if the idea had just occurred to her. "There are files at Social Welfare."

I heaved a sigh of relief; the files would definitely be safer anywhere else than here.

Still, I added a tenth point to my plan that was by now inscribed in a flimsy green Ghana school exercise book, with multiplication tables on the back: "10. records, social welfare paperwork." Now, that felt complete; a nice round number.

"Sabrina," I said that night as I pored over my list in the light of a smelly kerosene lamp, "do you have a nickname?"

"Yup." She was correcting someone's homework.

"What is it?"

"*O didi papa*." She flashed me a smile. I laughed out loud; *O didi papa* means "eats a lot" in Twi. My fears that Sabrina would develop anorexia seemed very far away.

When I felt stronger, I asked a group of teenage boys to take me to the farm. They were reluctant, but I insisted. It was about a quarter mile down a jungle path. The rain forest was strikingly beautiful; huge towering trees surging out of the soil, immune to storms, their canopies stretching far above our heads as we progressed in single file. In that powerful hothouse atmosphere, the farm was a well-organized place with the dark-green indigenous pineapples called "sugar cake" growing vigorously on their long stalks. There were also oil palms and a few dark mango trees, the fruit drooping down heavily from broad shady branches.

The children became almost mute as we approached. They stopped skipping and chattering, and became fearful and sullen. I asked Brenya, one of Sabrina's friends who was walking with me, if they liked working here. He shook his head scornfully.

I was stunned by the order and cleanliness of this place. The contrast between the unkempt dirty orphanage and the organized clean farm buildings was striking. Hundreds of chickens were kept in the poultry equivalent of luxurious hygiene; not something that could be said for the humans. I was also shocked that whereas I'd been trying to buy cut-price eggs in the market, the farm was selling eggs for a sizeable profit. Not one of those eggs went to the children. This was obviously another hard conversation I would have to have with Maa and Dada.

Walking home in oppressive silence, I was bitten by a grass-cutter—a guinea pig–like creature, frequently hunted for food, which is known as the marsh cane rat. I had to go all the way to Winneba Hospital for a tetanus injection. I resented the interruption since there were only ten days left of our volunteer experience, and there was so much still to do.

I was particularly horrified by the children's diet. Although they did hard physical work, they were given virtually no animal protein. Occasionally a smoked fish would flavor the sauce on their rice. Curiously, despite their constant farm work, they were almost never given fruit. In short, it felt as if almost everything was lacking in their diet.

Slowly it was becoming evident to me that the children's biggest problem was malnutrition. That was why they were getting so sick. This meant negotiating the best possible price for large quantities of eggs, cheap protein, so that even after I left Ghana the children would get an egg every day. I sat down with Maa and Dada to negotiate giving eggs from the farm to their kids, but what seemed a no-brainer to me took forever. The eggs, they protested, were the only source of ready cash. If they gave the eggs to the kids, how were they to pay for medicine or secondary-school fees? Again, I could see their point, and felt embarrassed. It seemed that I kept putting my foot in my mouth. Last week when I had asked about the use of the children as workers on the farm, Dada had been very clear: "This is not child labor; this is part of our culture. In Ghana, children work alongside their parents. It is just the way it's done. The stars do not ask the sea if the sun is coming out."

What?

Kwame explained the proverb to me. The stars were in the sky and therefore closer to the sun, so they would not ask the sea about the sun's movements, would they? I must have looked confused. It means the man on the ground knows the situation better than the stranger, he finished by explaining. I finally realized the implication; I was a foreigner and had no right to question them. Embarrassed, I tried to backpedal furiously by mentioning my ten-point plan for improvement and the fact that I could buy them more land for the farm—on the sole condition that they employ professional workers, not the children.

That afternoon Maa and Dada called me to their office (the greasy couch they lounged on) to introduce me to an architect called Kwabena. He was interested in supporting the orphanage. His sister, Afua, who was the head pediatric surgeon at the main hospital at Korle-Bu, also wanted to help. Kwabena was a soft-spoken highly educated man; I had not yet met anyone like him here. He was surely a representative of Ghana's cultured middle class that was not often seen in the villages. That day and in our following meetings, we decided together to open a charity in Ghana, with an office in Spain. My ten-point plan would be its manifesto, and the mission would be to create happier and healthier places for children to grow up.

A few days later Maa decreed a day of fasting. Evangelical Christianity was a big part of their lives, so the children attended church services on Sundays and had prayers every day. Annoyingly, out-of-tune gospel music played super loud and very distorted on every tinny radio in the place. If children arrived with Muslim or traditional names, Maa gave them a Christian one, and (I winced at this) made no effort to hide her attempts to convert them. So far that had been the worst of it. But a fasting day for children this skinny and vulnerable to disease?

There was no food, she explained to me with dismay and regret. The expected donations from the English and American charities that supported the orphanage had not come through. The day of fasting would motivate the children to pray to God and encourage him to provide.

Maa and Dada made the solution seem so simple: all it would take was a little money, and everything could be sorted out for the best. I started thinking about how many times in the stormy muggy heat I had taken the two-hour minibus ride to the little Internet café near the market square of Winneba, the nearest place with a painfully slow dial-up connection, so that I could email my patient accountant in Spain to send me another money transfer.

The money went fast. A nurse who could visit twice a week had been found, and I set up a full sick room. I also paid to have the orphanage professionally painted; the filth was making me sick. I bought a mobile phone and chip for myself and Kwame, and a wheelbarrow of tools for fixing things.

Like Sabrina, I was transformed. I never looked at myself in the mirror (actually, there was no mirror). At dawn I washed in a scoop of water, wrapped my hair in a bright Ghanaian cloth, pulled on a kaftan, and got on with my day. I also didn't spend much time thinking, as there seemed to be far too much to do.

Perhaps that last part was a mistake.

The children taught me so much. I was caught up in the desire to lose myself in their culture; to be with them and share their lives.

I learned the niceties of how to interact with elderly Ghanaians. I observed with concern the culture of absolute deference to one's elders; the children's bowed heads, the downcast eyes, the curtseying, the feigned shyness, how to nod and make low clucking noises to show you are paying attention, the elaborate greetings that are absolutely nonnegotiable. I learned that one click of the tongue means "yes" and two means "no." I saw children prostrate themselves to adults to atone for some minor wrongdoing. That level of submission freaked me out; surely it made the children more vulnerable to bullying and ill-treatment?

I learned useful things too. That it is vital to use only the right hand to greet people, because the left is for unclean things like scrubbing, which I did a lot of. I learned that 1950s-style long tight underwear isn't just a weird retrograde fashion in West Africa, but a first step in rape prevention. (In Ghana, an estimated 60 percent of women have experienced sexual abuse of some sort or another.) I learned never to cross my legs in public and—most useful of all for a woman, and a special skill I used daily in a country that has few toilets and a lot of long *tro-tro* rides—how to pee in the bush standing up, under a long skirt.

I saw the older children, boys included, stepping in and acting like parents to the younger kids, which was inspiring. I felt that I was becoming part of a family. This feeling was intensified by the fact that Sabrina had, for all intents and purposes, merged with a bunch of the older kids and become part of their group. After dinner she used to bring a group of them around to our house to do their homework at our dining table. There were no tables at the orphanage, as people ate sitting on stools and crouched over their food, Ghana style.

With these teenagers, I felt a helpless outrage at the narrowness of their destinies. None of them could attend school after about class six level (and even "class six" was a euphemism, given the poor quality of the primary education the orphanage dispensed). When I learned that the cost of attending secondary school was only about $30 per child a year, it became obvious to me that I could, and should, pay for them. For the price of a pair of Ferragamo shoes, I could buy a year of high school education for six kids. How could I refuse that?

Brenya was my favorite among the teenage boys. About seventeen, he was very quiet, not boisterous like the others. Still, there was always a smile dancing around his lips, and humor in his eyes. He was obviously intelligent and prime college material, but he was stuck at the home like most of them. "No worries," I said to him, determined that all that was going to change in September.

As I busied myself trying to arrange the paperwork, money transfers, and school uniforms, I sometimes thought about the scholarship that had enabled me to attend an English-language school outside Barcelona in the 1970s, even after my father took off. That school had literally transformed the trajectory of my life.

* * *

One night there was a new face around my dining table-cum-youth club.

"Who is that?" I whispered to Brenya. I was starting to feel that our makeshift home was becoming a bit too much of a free-for-all in the evenings.

"That's Kwesi. They brought him back today."

Something in the way he said it made me take a second look at the boy. He was stocky, strongly built but not tall, typical Ghanaian build. Just now he looked very depressed, sitting in the corner, not joining in the banter centered on Sabrina.

"He's Vida's brother," Brenya explained. "He was adopted, but the man married a woman, and now the wife says she does not want him in the house. He has been returned."

I felt an icy chill in the pit of my stomach. *Returned.* He had been brought back like unwanted baggage. I walked over to him and said, "Hi, I'm Mama Lisa."

He looked up. "He-he-llo," he said with a stutter. "Let's talk," I said, and took him out onto the veranda where we could hear the dry rattle of the plantain leaves in the wind, the piercing sound of the frogs and insects; the generally noisy riot of the African night. It was about to rain, as it did often in the afternoons and evenings, and I could feel the heaviness in the air.

Kwesi did not open up that night, but I got the rest of the story from Brenya. His foster father had just dumped the child and his baggage in front the of the orphanage door and sped away. He hadn't even bothered to get out of the car.

Over the next few days, I managed to find time to go with Kwesi to his old school to pick up his transcripts and so that he could explain the situation to this teachers and friends, maybe finding some closure. I found him a new senior secondary school near Awutiase. During our excursions we had a lot of talks, although he was painfully shy and crushed by the sudden change in his circumstances. It was so sad to witness.

Kwesi, Brenya, and Afi became Sabrina's squad. It made me so sad to think that they would not have the opportunities she would.

With the teenagers, I projected my own experience, or that of Sabrina. But with many of the toddlers and older babies—like paralyzed Prosper, as we named him, with his putative "broken spine"—I could feel the anxiety that was knotted up inside them. They lay crying (or worse, not crying) wherever they happened to have been plunked down by this or that harried caregiver.

I had no time; no space left in my brain. I felt an incredibly important clock ticking, reminding me that it was my task to try to fix every detail of the children's lives in my allotted time. My mind raced with what needed to be done.

Sanitation. Open the toilet block. Buy toilet paper. Buy sheets. Stop them from sleeping directly on disease-infested mattresses. Scrub every surface with bleach. On medical care, which seemed insanely difficult to access, get proper medical records for every child; set up a financial medical fund for emergencies.

I realized that none of the children had birth certificates, and Maa did not even keep a basic record of their arrivals, birth dates, or medical treatment. Most kids had never been vaccinated. . . . But I digress. Improve their nutrition. Send them to school. Get their beds fixed. Patch the roof that lets the pounding tropical rain in.

On and on, the items hammered at me, and I made no attempt to analyze, to prioritize based on urgency, to take a broader view. As the days swept by, I felt choked by a growing sense of urgency. How could I leave these children, whom I now knew so well, in this state when I had managed to achieve so little?

Before we left I was determined to take little Prosper to see a specialist. There was something odd about him, and it wasn't only that he couldn't move his torso. He had uncontrollable spasms and seemed to have trouble eating properly; there was something wrong with the way he swallowed and held his head. He needed to go to Korle-Bu, the big teaching hospital in Accra, to see the pediatric specialist.

This was a complex trip involving several changes of *tro-tro,* and I didn't think my minibus skills were up to it. Thankfully Kwame offered to accompany me. The hospital was pandemonium. There was a special room at Korle-Bu for people who hadn't paid their bills; mothers, for example, who had gone in to have a baby, but— perhaps because the mother was a teenager, the child was disabled or stillborn, or for no reason at all—nobody had paid. I had never seen anything like this hospital; people waiting in the corridors, two or three children to a bed, mothers sleeping on the cold cement floor, a prevalent smell of urine, and cloaking it all the sense of vast human indifference, or at least desensitization to suffering.

The doctor was harassed but very competent. She said that Prosper had massive cerebral palsy (CP) with perhaps some autism, as well as seizures and probable mental challenges. Not only was it unlikely that he would ever walk, but his difficulty in swallowing might well prove fatal if he didn't receive proper care. There was no attempt at niceties.

No treatment was being proposed, apart from pills to control his epilepsy. What he really needed was the entire spectrum of care: physiotherapy, special education, rehabilitation, massage therapy, walking aids. Quite simply, what a child with CP would have gotten in the West. The diagnosis was like a death sentence, since a child like Prosper had no possible future in Awutiase orphanage. It was not an environment where he could count on help with swallowing. I knew that several of the children and helpers actively disliked Prosper; something about him came off as cold and demanding. All the babies were neglected at times, but Prosper worst of all.

When I got on the plane to go back home, that would be it. Not being able to swallow, Prosper would slowly starve to death. I had already heard almost casual mention of children dying at the orphanage, notably from malaria and meningitis. Life seemed expendable there. It was obvious the pediatrician was saying that Prosper was going to die.

I wasn't crying when we walked out of Korle-Bu Hospital, but Kwame must have sensed the pain that was welling up inside me. He took Prosper out of my arms—he was unbelievably heavy for a baby—and announced it was time I went to a chop bar. He said it was unthinkable that I'd never visited one of these local restaurants, an institution as fundamental to life in Ghana as a French café is to Paris. It was a dark shack heavily shielded from the street; in Ghana there are all kinds of elaborate rules about not watching people eat, particularly tribal chiefs. Chiefs are considered part divine, and gods of course do not eat. There was a plastic menu: hamburger, pancakes, and, oddly, Chinese food. My mouth watered, but Kwame pointed out that the menu was purely aspirational; none of that kind of food had ever been prepared there, and probably never would be. There was rice and chicken or *fufu*. Period. Kwame ordered *fufu* with grass-cutter soup. It was served with ginger scraped on top, and we ate it hungrily with our hands, out of the same big terracotta bowl called an *asanka*.

Very gently, over that bowl of sticky spicy *fufu*, Kwame talked me back from the brink of utter misery. He was a good man; I could feel that. It seemed to me that he had dedicated his life to the orphanage, which meant a great deal to me. There was something attractive about how he could appear almost brutish when he worked, hard and focused, and then so tender when he carried a baby, or helped me. Obviously he was no intellectual, but then he had never had the opportunities to become well read. I could not judge him on that. I was drawn to his generosity and dependability. He told me that after I left he would make it his business to look after little Prosper. On the long final bumpy *tro-tro* ride back to Awutiase, Kwame held the baby, and I fell asleep on his shoulder.

When Sabrina and I finally packed up and prepared to return to Europe, with tearful goodbyes all around, I felt I had found a path to every aspiration I'd always yearned for. I no longer wanted lovely free clothes and front-row seats at fashion shows, or to be paid $20,000 a month for finding delightful locations for photo shoots. I was thirty-five years old. I had thirty-six pieces of Yohji Yamamoto and a museum-worthy collection of solid silver sculptural jewelry, and I had just suddenly realized that despite everything I had amassed, something was now more important to me. In fashion all I had been doing was selling dresses; at Awutiase orphanage I could be saving lives.

Sabrina and I rode the *tro-tro* back to Accra, the friendly sweaty pressure of our fellow passengers jolting us at every bump. As the groves of bamboo and mangos gave way to the ugly cement blocks and ramshackle shanties of the city's blighted outskirts, I found myself smiling at the familiar dark little shops selling loops of electrical cable and toothpaste and one-use envelopes of everything from shampoos to sugar. I would sell my house in Barcelona. I would work a little less, organize my life better, and return to Awutiase every two or three months. I could use my credit with the bank, network some of my fashion friends into the loop, and set up a structure that could support the orphanage; something durable, with real impact, that followed my ten-point plan.

I felt energized; driven. I felt that finally my money had meaning.

At the Accra airport there was a rush of air conditioning and a crowd that seemed unbelievably well dressed. I looked at Sabrina as we strode onto the airplane and felt a surge of joy. Burned almost black, she was regal in her African robes. She was smiling, relaxed, and happy. She spoke only of the children. I was confident that she would agree with my new plans for our future.

Then I looked down at myself—drained, malarial, and in tears at leaving the kids. My eyes drifted to my personalized silver Chanel handbag that had been made just for me by Karl Lagerfeld; it was absolutely ruined. I couldn't have cared less.

15

When we reached home, the backlash from the reencounter with a material culture and Western civilization was savage. I had not expected this. I hated—literally hated—my old life. Electric light, water coming out of the taps, endless clothes; who needed this?

Sabrina felt the same. She had stared fixedly at the row of toilet stalls with their generously flushing loos at Frankfurt airport and turned to me wordlessly, tears in her eyes. The boundless choices at the supermarket revolted us. I had never felt closer to her than I did in that moment. It was so odd, to be repulsed by comfort and plenty, but we both felt the same. Conversations with old friends seemed frivolous and trivial. We felt that none of this was real; that the real world was what we had left behind. The first working day after my return I called Raquel, my trusty travel agent, and booked another ticket to Ghana for October, two months later.

"Did you bring back any children?" she teased.

"Yup," I answered, "a hundred and five of them. They all live in my heart."

I had lost a lot of weight, which suited me. I looked brown and happy, but I could not enjoy the sleepy August vacation time. I was calling all my friends for donations, trying to express everything that had happened to me in a few simple sentences; to express all that endless need in a way that people from my world could understand. From the beginning it was clear that some of them would have nothing to do with my African infatuation, which would have distracted them from the real work of becoming more fabulous by the hour. Others were more receptive. Carla Bruni called me several times asking for more details; Rossy and Victoria and Patricia were all interested, openly pledging future support. Charles-Henri had been involved with philanthropy since his childhood and had lots of advice on setting up the charity.

It was only about a week after our return that the unthinkable happened. I got an email from Awutiase announcing Brenya's death from complications of malaria. I screamed out loud when I read it; wailed and banged doors and wept. I was first red-hot angry, then sad. Sabrina came home to find me wracked with sobs, and she cried her eyes out with me. He was such a gentle, calm boy. The fact that death from malaria was so preventable made it even worse.

I was sad and furious, angry and guilty all at once. But if Brenya's death did one thing, it sealed my fate; there was no longer any walking away from Ghana. My resolve was like steel. I was determined to change things; determined to make a difference. I put a photo of Brenya in my wallet. I would never let this happen again, I promised myself. I promised *him.*

Sabrina's school results had arrived in the post. All she had left now was one A-level exam to do in June, and she would be qualified for college. I sat her down and we discussed our options, both of us red-eyed and exhausted in the aftermath of digesting the death of our friend. I would start the charity officially in Spain, ask for donations, and travel back and forth. If I was to be gone for longer than two weeks, she would stay with friends. When she was done with her exams, she would join me there. We had never been so united; we shared the same goal. The issue was very clear: Awutiase could not wait.

I was naïve, dazzled—overwhelmed by an immense feeling that I was needed. I felt that Maa was a kind of saint, but the children had awoken a warrior instinct in me; an enormous, fiery, almost angry kind of love that was unlike any emotion I had ever known. I understood that it is possible to truly listen to someone who can't speak, and that such appeals must be answered. I felt that I could, and *must*, make a difference for them.

My fiery resolve yielded spectacular results. As usual, when you really want something and feel passionate about it, doors open and everything becomes possible. The charity was registered on the fourteenth of October 2002, within two months of my return. Its mission was basically my ten-point plan from the school exercise book. We had a board, under the good offices of my former tax attorney Ramon Maciá. They were legally in charge of the charity in Spain, and of fundraising and releasing money to Ghana. We had a bank account, a logo, an office space, and even a mailing campaign and flyer that featured a photo of Kwame and me surrounded by children. We registered the website and the name: OAfrica. Photographer Christian Rodés agreed to accompany me to Ghana with her teenage niece so we would have some decent photos of the children. I asked Patricia to buy my car and thus, armed with a little more cash, I hurried back to Ghana.

As we approached Awutiase, my heart was beating wildly. I knew that Brenya's death would weigh heavily on the adolescents, but I was excited to see Vida, Kwesi, Salami, Prosper, and of course Kwame, with whom I had been exchanging constant emails. It seemed as if our relationship was definitely more than just a friendship now. Especially when you factored in the fact that he had to ride all the way to Winneba to send them.

Kwesi was the first to grab a moment alone with me. "I want to change my name."

"You do?" I wondered where this was leading.

"Yes. I'm going to change it to Courage, because I'm bold. I'm not afraid of anything anymore."

I nodded delightedly. Names were a big deal in Ghana, and we split a soda in celebration.

It was immediately apparent that Maa and Dada now considered me and Kwame a team, or rather, a couple. Slowly it began to seem clear to me too that he was my knight in shining armor. It is hard to emphasize the loneliness I felt, trying almost single-handedly to change an entire system. Kwame's presence by my side gave me a certain legitimacy. He was a Ghanaian; he understood the impossibly complex rules of the culture and the language. He gave me a justifiable role. Those delicate liberal sensitivities about not presuming, or not trampling on other people's cultural values were making me hesitant to ask for urgent changes, such as no child labor, no corporal punishment, no fasting. On the one side it was a human right, but on the other it seemed to be the accepted thing. With Kwame agreeing with me, my middle-class fears of insensitively trampling on others' cultural traditions faded.

After a week I came down with malaria again. This time Kwame stayed by my side the whole time, but I only spent three days in bed and was up and working as soon as I could stand. Again, I felt that time was running out.

As I was recovering, one day he timidly held my hand. The next day we kissed, although I quickly discovered that kissing was not one of his "cultural norms." Kwame was not an affectionate man. Hardened by his own experience of abandonment as a child, what drew us together was mainly a shared goal. Our aim was to stop the children from losing their lives through such apparent carelessness. From the beginning, it was more of a working partnership, although after all that hard work a little romance, however perfunctory, was agreeable.

Kwame brought round a little one-year-old chubby-cheeked chap with rosebud lips called Johnny, together with his friend George who was about two. These boys were Kwame's personal responsibility. George was due to be adopted by an American and would soon be leaving, but Johnny had no one. Kwame suggested we adopt him when we got married. *Wait, married?* And that was it: the proposal. It was not extended in the context of our feelings for each other, but in the context of giving a beautiful baby a family. My thwarted womb literally ached as I took Johnny into my arms.

Of course I wanted to say yes. In total I had suffered two ectopic pregnancies, and I knew I could not have children; here was my chance at an instant family. But for once my good sense persevered. I called Sabrina, who was not surprised. There was an I-told-you-so tone in her voice. But after her own cathartic experience in Awutiase, and Brenya's death, she was almost as determined as I was to invest ourselves in the situation.

Then arose the problem of how to tell Maa and Dada that we were a couple. There was no question of an illicit romance in the highly evangelical atmosphere of Awutiase, where gossip flowed like water (which of course didn't, actually). I was not ready to marry a man I hardly knew, but I knew that the traditional tribal engagement rites were not binding, and so I bought myself some time and acquiesced to a "traditional engagement" when they asked me to. It was a ceremony that meant nothing legally; just an old-fashioned ritual. The entire orphanage erupted in joy at the idea of the ceremony. My friends from Europe, caught up in the general atmosphere of exoticism, also seemed to agree. Christina and her niece loved Awutiase, and that helped me to make my decision. I was comforted in my need to dedicate myself to these children; this would seal my commitment.

I learned a few words of Twi, the main language of the Akan people. I learned to have some gumption; with Kwame behind me, I felt I was entitled to an opinion. Now I was no longer the sea but part of the stars, surely. I was feeling more Ghanaian by the second, understanding that the way to get what you want is to cajole, make a joke of it—never make a direct demand, never play the power card. Never come across as rude or domineering. Humor and proverbs would get you a lot further. This of course was in complete contradiction to everything I ever been taught.

Dada muttered under his breath that no matter how long a log lies in the water, it will never become a crocodile; another proverb, less than flattering to me, which means foreigners never fully assimilate. I knew by then that speaking in proverbs was considered the mark of an erudite and sophisticate. I knew too that many Ghanaians were suspicious, and who could blame them, considering the country's four-hundred-year history with white slavers. As I had observed the orphanage children threaten each other—"*Obruno*, I will beat you"—I made the connection with the ubiquitous Twi word for white person: *obruni*. In horror I realized that it probably meant "he who beats," not "stranger." Ancestral shame prevented me from imposing any more demands.

Dada was only pretending to be grumpy, anyway. Kwame said he was mollified by the $3,000 we had invested in land and the car we bought to get the kids to hospital faster. Kwame himself was busy learning to drive. Much to my embarrassment, he seemed to think that the concept included constant pressing of the horn in a kind of rhythmic accompaniment to his (very) slow progress. Still, I sat in the front and smiled stoically, happy that at least the car was my new charity's signature color: bright orange. It wasn't a snazzy convertible, but it was a definite step up from a *tro-tro*.

During that trip I was immediately concerned by a skinny little girl called Akua, who was always bullied by the other children. Her behavior was extremely odd. I knew nothing about mental illness, but I could see that her situation was unsustainable. Awutiase was a rough-and-tumble place. A kid who was a fighter did well, such as little Salami with his street smarts, or outgoing Vida. But the sensitive ones like Brenya, Courage, Prosper, and Akua were going to have a hard time surviving. I added her to my mental list of special protégées.

A few of the children were physically handicapped, and several seemed to behave oddly, although it was hard to pick up in the general brouhaha. Many of the kids were troubled. There was no way I could ignore the dark and even violent screaming matches; the storms of shouting that descended on the orphanage children from the staff; or the brutal way the kids sometimes spoke to each other, indicative of how many disputes they had witnessed and the pain they bore. About a third of the younger kids were incredibly passive; they smiled, but there seemed no light or energy inside them. And I didn't realize it then, but a very large percentage of the toddlers were also self-harming. They rocked themselves violently back and forth, repeatedly knocking their heads against furniture or walls.

* * *

Just before Christmas I returned to Ghana with Sabrina, both of us maxing out the extra baggage allowance with gifts for the children. She was thrilled to be back among her friends, although the change in the weather took us both by surprise. Dry and dusty, it seemed like a completely different world. The entire red dust content of the

Sahara Desert appeared to have been dropped on Awutiase; we lived in a permanent gritty haze, and there was no moisture in the air. It was most unpleasant. During our previous trips it had seemed to rain punctually at four in the afternoon on alternate days. This time there was no humidity at all. The sun's relentless rays were dulled as if it was wrapped in cotton wool, and the sky was a uniform light-ash color. The wind shredded the leaves of the plantain trees into long brown ribbons. What had been green was now yellow: the grass, the flowers, the undergrowth. At this time of year even the slightest burst of rain, which happened maybe twice in a month, with clouds menacing for days beforehand, was landscape changing. The green would push up temporarily for a day or so after the rain and then fade back into brown. It was a different country from the Ghana I had known.

By the end of the year I had raised over €23,000, including funds donated through a charity concert in Barcelona. I donated almost as much myself. We had about ten volunteers, including (*yes!*) a fully qualified nurse, all of whom had paid the orphanage $600 directly to participate in the program. Armed with little bottles of hand sanitizer and malaria-prevention tablets, they were at work implementing our ten-point plan. They worked their hearts out on the train wreck that was the health and hygiene system.

Sabrina, the volunteers, and I lived a life of great sameness. Get up, work all day in the usual filthy conditions, sweat, fall into a hot, uneasy sleep, and sweat some more under the horrid corrugated roofs that stored all the heat. Most of us had a permanent low-grade fever—typhoid, malaria, amoebas, worms; the gruesome possibilities were endless—and an exhaustion hangover.

Therefore the preparations for the engagement ceremony provided a welcome diversion. All the volunteers were to play the role of my family during the ceremony. We hired a *tro-tro* and went on a preengagement day out to the sea. We lazed under the coconut palms, and the children were nonplussed by the gray rough Atlantic. I realized that most of the kids had never seen the ocean. We visited White Sands, the resort close to where I had been intended to volunteer, before a twist of fate sent me to Awutiase and changed my life. White Sands reminded me of Ibiza, with a tropical twist, and was heaven. I wished longingly then that Awutiase was by the sea.

Maa had informed me in no uncertain terms that in Ghana a lady had little to do with the ceremony. Traditionally she was kept in a room until the families negotiated her "bride price" to their satisfaction: a white chicken, a traditional stool, and several lengths of cloth being the extent of mine. Of course the whole thing was a farce, since my "family" of volunteers had no idea what they were negotiating for. I was resentful and excited in turn; resentful because I was starting to feel pressured into something I wasn't sure about, and excited because the whole orphanage believed this was one big fiesta. Kwame seemed strangely detached for the whole thing, which seemed to prove to me that it was a simple formality, a way of becoming official "boyfriend-girlfriend." At least the kids would get a couple a square meals out of it, I thought. I consoled myself with the thought that it was an ancient ritual that was meaningless to Europeans (I hadn't even told my mother). It was just to reassure Maa and Dada that I wasn't a flash in the pan; I was here to stay. And that bit, at least, I was sure about.

My mother pregnant
with me on the crossing from
Italy, when
my parents moved
to Spain in early 1967.
Personal collection of Lisa Lovatt-Smith

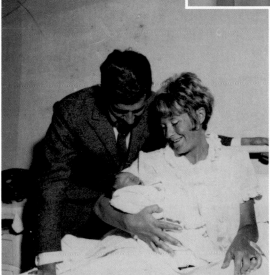

The one picture I have of myself
with both my mother and father,
at my birth, April 15, 1967,
in Barcelona.
Personal collection of Lisa Lovatt-Smith

My father and me, about a
year before he disappeared
from our lives.
Personal collection of Lisa Lovatt-Smith

Jonathan and I (aged about four) during the year I was fostered by his parents.
Personal collection of Lisa Lovatt-Smith

Paul, my foster father, watching Jonathan and me (age four) play. It ended in tears as we got stuck in the basket!
Personal collection of Lisa Lovatt-Smith

A photo of me at seventeen, modeling for Helene Curtis hair products.
Photo courtesy of Helene Curtis

A photograph published in American *Vanity Fair*, February 1989, of me with Pedro Almodóvar star Rossy de Palma (center), later to become one of our premier OAfrica ambassadors. The transgender artist Bibiana is on the left.
Photo courtesy of the estate of Eric Adjani

Eric Adjani and I, post-breakup, with Sabrina in Paris in the early nineties. His mother is on the left.
Personal collection of Lisa Lovatt-Smith

In Paris with my father the day I met him for the first time as an adult, in 1993.
Personal collection of Lisa Lovatt-Smith

Karl Lagerfeld's Polaroid of me in his garden with Tony Ward, Madonna's then-boyfriend. Karl loved my long neck, but hated the cheap, grungy clothes I was wearing that day.
Photo courtesy of Karl Lagerfeld

Sabrina and I in our rented house in Tangiers, circa 1994, during the period when I was working on my Moroccan book.
Personal collection of Lisa Lovatt-Smith

Sabrina, Charles-Henri, and I at his home, the Château de Botz, Besson, France, in 1994.
Personal collection of Lisa Lovatt-Smith

Happy 1995! With love Lisa Sabrina + Brie

Our Christmas 1994 greeting card while we were living in Paris, six months before I was to become engaged to Olivier.
Photo courtesy of Marc Plantec

Photographer Mario Testino and me at a signing event for my first book, in 1994.
Photo courtesy of Graham Kuhn

Olivier and I with Sabrina and the mayor of the 7ème arrondisement at our wedding in Paris, September 16, 1995.
Photo courtesy of Gerlinde Hobel

At a fashion show in Spain in 1998, looking very "fashion editor."
Personal collection of Lisa Lovatt-Smith

A very skinny me, with Mathias and Beth in 2004, during the stressful first few years of OAfrica.
Personal collection of Lisa Lovatt-Smith

The type of storage room, full of mess, waste, and dirt, that we would often encounter at the orphanages.
Personal collection of Lisa Lovatt-Smith

Fashion designer and "It" girl Margherita Maccapani Missoni, on her first volunteer visit to Ghana in 2003. She was later to become the president of OAfrica, Italy.
Personal collection of Lisa Lovatt-Smith

With baby Prosper who had just learned to sit up straight— a huge victory. Taken December 2003, at the celebration of one year of marriage to Kwame.
Personal collection of Lisa Lovatt-Smith

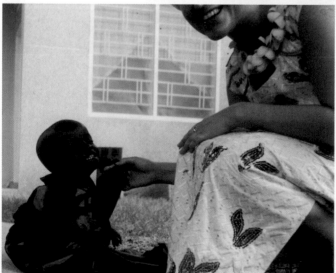

Sabrina, just arrived
in Ghana and in one
of her first batik dresses,
with two neighbors.
Personal collection of Lisa Lovatt-Smith

The mud building built
by OAfrica in Ayenyah
and then turned over
to the village
as a school.
Photo courtesy of Marti Ros

One of my favorite
pictures with the
children.
*Photo courtesy of
Alberto Heras*

Sabrina with her first son, Marcos, only a few days old.
Photo courtesy of Mari Carmen Cordero

My traditional engagement to Kweku in July 2006.
Photo courtesy of Agbeko Lucien Massame

Me with (left to right) Ernest, Fatima, Beliratu, and Mensah, the four children I either adopted or fostered in Ghana; my precious family. November 2013.
Photo courtesy of Cori Deterding

16

*T*wenty-four hours before the now dreaded event, Maa suddenly informed me that I was supposed to fast. *Seriously?* I was already wiped out by hard work, the emotion of all the preparations, and two successive malaria attacks. Fasting would probably knock me out completely. But still I complied, desperate to integrate; desperate for the "log to become a crocodile." By the next morning I was woozy, so I was allowed milky tea. A gaggle of giggling older girls and Sabrina woke me at six o'clock (why, oh, why did important events in Ghana necessitate getting up before dawn?) and bundled me into Maa and Dada's private sanctum. This room was where I had first seen Prosper. It was, as then, filled with the woven plastic carry-alls they called "Ghana-must-go." The name came from the forced migrations from Nigeria in 1983 when these light and capacious bags first became commonplace. The bags seemed to be stuffed with donated clothes, and I paused to ask myself what they were doing in Maa's room. Ditto for the mountain of stuffed animals on her king-size bed. The kids were woefully short of toys.

But there was no time to think. I was plonked down in front of a dressing table covered in bottles and powder, perfumes, stray earrings, and greasy little tubs of shea butter.

"First, you will wear *kente*," Maa announced proudly.

My heart sank. "First?" Was this going to be like those Moroccan ceremonies where the girl changed five times?

"Only twice," Maa reassured me.

The *kente* was the most prestigious cloth in Ghana, hand-woven in strips in the Ashanti region and then sewn together. In Ghana clothes speak, and each *kente* also had a story. The colors chosen by the weaver could mean riches, envy, fruitfulness, and so on, and branches of the Ashanti (Dada's tribe) had their own tribal *kente*. What concerned me was that it was not a cotton dress, but almost wooly; hot and prickly, heavily lined and tight fitting. The weather that day seemed even more sultry than the day before, and although Maa turned the fan directly on me and Sabrina sat next to me fanning me industriously, I was already sweating.

"Is this really happening?" I mouthed at Sabrina.

"It'll be fine, Mum." She was applying my makeup, which she had a natural ability for.

The woven *kente,* which had a lot of dark blue in it (for love and harmony) and yellow (for riches), actually looked really good on my newly slimmed-down post-malarial body. When I was dressed, I was ushered out to sit next to Kwame.

My "family," the cluster of volunteers and Sabrina's teenage squad, had been presented with the white chicken, the stool, and several lengths of cloth. Pride of place was given to three bottles of the local spirits, *akpeteshie*, and also imported schnapps in a square bottle. This was the legacy of the slave trade. The Dutch slavers, the first to begin the bloody commerce in Ghana, had sealed their deals with a gift of their local booze. No chief worth his salt would give a judgment on anything without his schnapps or, in a pinch, imported gin.

My role was saying a wobbly "yes" when Dada, seated across from my "family" with several older people unknown to me, officially informed me that this young man had come to engage me. Did I accept?

We posed for pictures as I held hands tightly with Kwame, who looked suitably proud. Then I was rushed off to Maa's room again.

"This is for the church," proclaimed Maa, shaking out a concoction in cotton cream. It had been one of line items on the "budget" I had been presented with a few weeks back, but I had not actually seen it yet. I looked it over with a professional eye. On a base of vanilla lace were embroidered gold, pale-pink, and pale-blue teardrop clusters of sequins and a short length of beads. It was a *kabba* and *slit*, with a tall matching headdress in the same material. In fashion terms, it was Christian-Lacroix-meets-bridezilla. I sighed. Did I really have a choice?

"Why are we going to church?" I asked.

"Oh come on, Mum, did you really think you'd get away without Sky Daddy having a look-in? You know how crazy religious they are," whispered Sabrina.

"For the blessing," said Maa sternly.

By this time I had been granted a Coca-Cola, but the rising heat had my makeup melting and my head spinning. I got into the orange car for the short ride to their local church, a colonial building squarely situated on Awutiase's main road. Dada escorted me inside.

When the door opened I nearly fainted. The church was packed, and not with children from the orphanage, whom I had fondly imagined as our joyful witnesses. None of them seemed to be there at all except a few of the teenagers. Instead it was crammed with row upon row of town people in their Sunday best. Like a lamb to the slaughter, I trudged down the aisle with Sabrina. Kwame was sitting to the side at the front. Even from a few feet away, I could see that he was terrified. One of the elder boys was dabbing the sweat off his face with a handkerchief. After plunking myself down next to him, Sabrina followed suit and compulsively patted my sweaty face with a grimy scrap of cotton.

I sat there in a daze as a full three-hour church service, a typical Ghanaian ceremony, was rolled out: dancing, preaching, testimonies, loud prayers and all. Just as I was about to doze off in the furnacelike heat, we were called to the front. The pastor said a few words in Twi and then prayed for us, shouting at the top of his voice. "The devil is a liar!" he yelled at me as I flinched. The congregation replied with a roar. "The devil should not come into this marriage and spoil this union!" Another roar.

Wait a minute—marriage? Wasn't this supposed to be an *engagement* ceremony?

The back and forth went on for ten minutes, then the pastor finally subsided. Maa strode over and led me and Kwame to the lectern. "Sign here," she said.

I stared blankly at the document, which was effectively a marriage certificate. If I refused to sign, I felt the entire congregation would label me as an uncouth stranger who had deceived them. Miss Manners triumphed. I signed dully, as did Kwame. This was looking undeniably like a marriage, but I no longer cared. I was so woozy I felt as if the ground was coming up to hit me.

The rest of the day went by in a haze of heat. Complete strangers lined up to shake our hands and have their pictures taken with us. Kwame and I were not left alone until evening, where close questioning revealed that he had not been expecting the church ceremony and signing, either. We looked at each other disconsolately, not at all the picture of two thrilled newlyweds. Maa had won this round; that was for sure. We fell into an exhausted sleep, side by side, for the first time. Maybe, I thought, things would seem better in the morning.

With our marriage, which was of course what it turned out to be, Kwame's attitude toward Maa and Dada underwent a sea change. He became more critical and drew away from them but also, I felt, from me. He was on the farm from dawn until dusk, although I knew that during the dry season there was less work, not more. He categorically refused to go on a honeymoon, saying that he was too busy. I sensed that he had little experience with women. Since we had started dating the physical relationship had been perfunctory, but I could not work out if that was because he was inexperienced or because he was just not naturally sensual. In any case, it was clear that he had not chosen me because he was drawn to me physically; instead he seemed to be with me because we were good work mates. That was all right, I thought, because I was completely focused on my work too.

I could not give the situation much thought; after all, I had not come to Ghana for romance. I had faith in him and in our relationship as co-workers, and I believed that time would heal the situation. Sabrina and I had Christmas to get through, which included our firm pledge to get every child a gift. We had a nativity play to produce, with Vida playing Mary and Salami as a talkative angel. We had to compile the children's medical files for the new local nurse, who was now coming two days a week. The other volunteers had begun to speak up and voice their concerns too. I had made a lot of excuses for the poorly run orphanage, but now they were starting to seem flimsy.

I knew that there were no proper records at the Awutiase orphanage; no receipts of any kind, and no screening of volunteers or staff, apart from those sent by OAfrica. This meant that anyone who wanted it had unlimited access to young children for hours on end every day, therefore creating a potential magnet for child abusers. These things were not the result of poverty but of mismanagement. None of the children had any privacy or personal belongings. They were not vaccinated. They didn't go to a proper school. They were frequently ignored and/or hit, and were kept in rooms that were both squalid and dangerous. They almost never had three square meals a day. Very few learned any skills other than farm work, housework, and child care. Perhaps one of the worst things was that the orphanage was operated on the basis of extensive and exhausting labor by the children themselves. As I thought about it, I could see that most of these abusive conditions were avoidable.

But I wanted to believe that people who look after orphans are good and kind. And I assumed that Maa and Dada truly had no financing. I also believed Maa. I excused the neglect, the indifference and exploitation, the exposure to danger. My brain made a comfortable liberal shortcut and jumped to the assumption that Maa's system was the inevitable outcome of being poor. It was an assumption that was both lazy and foolish. Mosquito nets cost very little yet the children had none, resulting, of course, in malaria. Shoes do not cost much but almost none of them had shoes, so they had open sores and cuts on their feet, even a toe or two torn off, and snake bites. I had witnessed the "fasting days" that deprived them of nutrition whenever Maa declared there was no money left; and her proposals of prayer at signs of even serious illness. Decent medical care would cost a little money, true, and it also took forever to get to Winneba on the rough roads.

Luckily, because it was the dry season, fewer kids were ill, and there seemed to be fewer crises. Or perhaps the money I was pouring into providing them with fruit and meat and eggs was finally paying off.

On Boxing Day three separate church groups descended on Awutiase from Accra. Each one brought bags of rice and pasta, boxes upon boxes of tuna fish and sardines, cookies and juice, and even rolls of toilet paper. The first two were Ghanaian Baptists who submitted the children to two consecutive two-hour impromptu services in Twi. The kids obviously enjoyed the frenetic dancing, and they knew all the hymns. There were, however, no breaks for food or drink. My heart went out to them.

I also noticed that there seemed to be more children around on holidays. When I mentioned it to Sabrina, she said that Maa's extended family and the neighborhood kids were commandeered to make up the numbers for the donors. The more kids they saw, apparently the more money they gave. I blanched at that thought, but realized it was as close as these kids were ever going to get to a party.

After the second church group left, the children were ordered out of their finery and into their usual ragged clothes and given a cursory lunch (not making use of any of the donations, I noted). About an hour later, when the heat was at its very worst, a bus drew up and the children were called back to the assembly ground (having changed into their best clothes again) for a third donation ritual; this time from a group of American missionaries. The ladies cooed and ahhed over the little kids, and had their pictures taken. Then they delivered a long sermon, all in English with strong American accents. It was about "obey thy father and thy mother," which seemed singularly insensitive, but I figured that none of the kids understood it anyway.

At one point the main lady minister, who was standing next to a carton of cookies, asked the children with a flourish, "And how many of you know where you will be going when you die?"

Now, I knew these children and their English were not up to that kind of abstract thinking. No one under ten spoke more than a few monosyllables, but a few kids put their hands up hesitantly. The other kids (those who weren't asleep in the heavy torpor of the afternoon) looked at each other worriedly.

"Will you go to hell?" asked the lady minister.

The children who already had their hands up waved them frenetically. A few more joined them, wanting a piece of the action. The minister was delighted, since here were obviously a lot of lost souls.

"Who would like to give their life to Jesus?" she roared.

The children were silent, straining for some kind of cue. Again the same hands went up.

The pastor was flummoxed. She tried again. "Come forward, little children! Come and give your life to Jesus!"

The waving arms and come-hither hand gestures were unmistakable. I could see the kids thinking that *maybe now, finally,* the cookie distribution was about to take place. What the pastor did not know was that life at Awutiase was all about the survival of the fittest. The whole ragged assembly surged forward as one and basically knocked the good pastor flying. I turned away, no longer able to contain my giggles.

The kids got their cookies after they said "the prayer."

"How many of you have prayed this prayer before?" All hands flew up enthusiastically. This time the pastor must have realized that the children did not understand the question, so she rephrased. "How many of you have never prayed this prayer before?" Again, all hands flew up.

As the missionaries slowly got onto the bus, I heard them talking amongst themselves. "Did you see how many lives we brought to the Father today, Edna?" an earnest young lady asked. "Such an amazing day for the Lord."

Lord, did I need a drink.

The contradictions between my values and the way Awutiase was being run could no longer be ignored. I decided to take a few

days off over New Year's to think things over, and took a taxi down
to the seaside with one of the Spanish volunteers. Kwame was to
meet us the next day. Tight as ever with her group of friends,
Sabrina did not want to come. Since she was nearly eighteen, I felt
I couldn't tell her what to do, especially because she had behaved
impeccably since our first trip to Awutiase. I trusted her now; we
were in this together. Plus she had her finger on the pulse of the
place and had become an insider. As my suspicions around Maa
and Dada's motivation grew, Sabrina provided the children's point
of view.

The day at the seaside was a fiasco. To make a long story short, as
dusk was falling the volunteer and I were attacked and nearly raped
by two men. I had no time, as usual, to think about myself. The worse
had been avoided, but the volunteer was still hysterical. Kwame and I
booked the volunteer on an emergency flight for January 2. Her
nerves were shot. It had been traumatic for both of us. The night
before her flight we slept over at the comfortable estate home of
Kwabena, the architect who was helping me with the charity. It was in
Teshie, but this was quite a different side to the Teshie where I had
landed almost six month ago: running water, reliable power, comfortable spring bed mattresses and, the holy grail, hot water.

As promised, Kwabena had registered the charity in Ghana. Our
certificate to commence business was about to be issued, and I was
acknowledged as co-founder. I held the paperwork in my hand,
thrilled. I spoke to him about the doubts I was beginning to have
about Awutiase; about how difficult it was to impose change, about
the volunteer complaints, even about the crate of rotten eggs I had
come across in a storeroom a few days ago. I wanted to drive home
the point that the children were suffering from malnutrition. He listened and nodded. It was not easy, he agreed. "Have heart," he
advised. "After the holidays we'll go to Social Welfare and ask their

advice." The crude reality of Awutiase seemed very far away from his tastefully decorated front room.

After the volunteer's departure, Kwame and I headed for the police station to report the attack. As we walked into the cool low colonial building toward the chest-high wide wooden counter, I held his hand. The last few weeks had been brutal. I was caring for Sabrina and the volunteers, many of whom had legitimate issues with the way the orphanage was run. Kwame had been completely thrown off by the whole wedding fiasco and had retreated far into himself, to a place I could not reach. My marriage seemed to be floundering before it had even begun. Johnny was still in the hell of the Awutiase baby room; with my and Sabrina's imminent departure for Europe, I had not given myself permission to love him just yet. The attempted rape and the volunteer's subsequent breakdown had been hard to deal with. On top of this, every morning the sun seemed to grow angrier, hotter, and larger until it pervaded all our waking hours, flattening us with its intensity.

As Kwame filled out the paperwork, my eyes were inevitably drawn to the left, through the door made of iron bars to the cells inside. It was a long, dark room and the men were all naked apart from shorts or underpants, because of the heat I supposed. There were a lot of them for such a small cell, and several hung their arms and legs out of the door, for the breeze I assumed. The chiaroscuro of the cell had the effect of making their arms and legs look separated from their bodies; a muddle of spare limbs, as in a tableau of a Dantesque small dark hell. They were less than three yards away, and the stench of sweat and fear was terrible. We had been told that my attacker was in there too, but I could not recognize him since it had been dark on the beach. However, I was sure that he could recognize me—the foolish *obruni* who had walked across the sand in the gloaming. The hair on the back of my neck rose. I knew all the suspects in the cell were watching and appraising me, a privileged white woman coming to complain. I felt sorry for them and fearful of them, all at once.

Suddenly I panicked. "Please, let's go. I don't want to press charges."

I tugged at Kwame's sleeve. Once we were in the orange car riding to the orphanage, I finally cried.

17

*W*hen I got back from the police station, completely drained, Sabrina was waiting up for me. She said there was something I needed to know. Her friend Afi had a boyfriend, she said. He lived across the street, and the two of them would go over to his place in the afternoons. Sucking in my breath, I wondered what news of disaster was coming next. A pregnancy? A drug bust?

But Sabrina seemed calm and clear-eyed. She looked at me and said, "If Maa finds out, she will beat Afi with a long cane and lock her in a room with no food for four days."

"Oh darling, don't exaggerate. Of course she won't," I said, to my eternal shame. "Maa is just concerned about her, as any mother would be."

"But the children say that Maa always goes by the Bible," Sabrina insisted.

"I'm sure she does, but what do you mean 'by the Bible'?"

"Well, if you commit adultery, you should be punished."

The very words sounded medieval and had a Ghanaian inflex-
ion to them. For the first time I wondered if I had done the right
thing in bringing Sabrina here.

"And if you get pregnant, she will beat you, too, and harder."

Beat a pregnant girl?

"Yes, and if you do stay pregnant anyway, after you give birth
she will take your baby away and give it to someone. It happened
last year. The girl ran away to find her baby, but they said it had
been sent abroad."

At this point I should have questioned Sabrina far more deeply.
It should have occurred to me that Maa was doing something completely unacceptable with these newborns. But for some reason I
brushed it aside; gossip, I thought, or Maa's blunt but rather efficient
way of making the underage girls stay away from boys.

"That's just Maa's way of frightening the girls so they stay out
of trouble," I said. "But she would be better off giving sex education
and contraception. I'll talk to her about it."

"But Mum, the door to the teenage girls' dorm and the boys'
dorm is always open at night, and there's never a watchman. Honestly, it's no wonder they get pregnant. It almost seems like she *wants*
them to have babies."

Sabrina had put her finger on the crux of the whole matter.

At that moment, though, I chose to focus on something different.
That bloody watchman. I had long suspected he slept on the job.

It was time to fly away to Barcelona with Sabrina and Kwame,
albeit unwillingly, leaving the volunteers in charge of the children.
My trust in Maa and Dada had pretty much been eroded, but
Sabrina had her exams to do, and I was still a full-time mum until
the following summer. Sabrina was ready for me to make Ghana my
home after her eighteenth birthday and graduation. I hoped that she
would be going away to college, so it made perfect sense. I aimed to

return to Awutiase more or less full time by the summer of 2003. I was sure that was what I wanted more than anything else.

Kwame studied his permaculture course, which we had identified as an ecologically responsible practice that could be appropriate for Ghana. The course was given on a freezing wintry mountain in eastern Spain. Kwame's utopian vision of Europe as a rich land where everything would be easy, an illusion common to many untraveled Ghanaians, fell away rapidly. The land was less fertile than in Ghana, and the cooler climate made life a lot less comfortable. He was not enjoying it one bit. Meanwhile I was on the receiving end of emails from the volunteers at the orphanage who were increasingly disgruntled. I hadn't yet seen Maa's punishment system—depriving children of food and care for one or two days at a time, beating them until the blood flowed, locking them alone in a dark room filled with broken furniture and walking away—but the volunteers had. They also testified to the continued use of child labor to run the farm, and that the farm was not supplying food for the home, despite my insistence that it should.

I decided I needed a second opinion. I sat down with Josh, my business partner, to get a businessman's rational perspective. Here, after all, was a man I had known since I was twenty. Despite having the most to lose from my passionate involvement with Ghana (since his livelihood stemmed from my continuing to produce shoots for glossy magazines), he had staunchly supported my charity since my first trip, serving on the board in Spain and giving advice.

We stood sipping coffee in my brightly colored kitchen in late February.

"Why don't you have OAfrica staff at Awutiase, with proper job descriptions and mandates, who respond to you and not to Maa and Dada?"

I mulled it over. "Would the staff have their own budget?"

"Yes. Just don't send the money to the orphanage anymore; send it to the OAfrica account and give it to your staff."

"We have a part-time nurse, so the next person I would employ is someone for the baby room. They're the most vulnerable." I did not add that Johnny was in there, but I thought it.

"And, Lisa, do us both a favor. Get an assistant here in Barcelona who is solely responsible for your OAfrica work, so you can delegate some of it."

I knew Josh was hoping I would be able to juggle my fashion work with my Ghana commitments. I think we both knew that was not going to happen, but an assistant, just for my Ghana work, was a great idea.

"I have the ideal person," Josh volunteered. "She's from Chicago."

And that was how I met Beth.

There was a "before Beth" and an "after Beth" in my life.

It quickly became apparent that this petite strawberry blonde, who had spent her adolescence as a rebel punk in a Catholic family, was the perfect fit. Funny, fast, and gratifyingly appreciative of my fashion career, very soon she had a handle on the charity work, and I did not feel so alone any more. She became an assistant, a precious new friend, and very soon the second in command at OAfrica.

I also made my first paid hire in Ghana: Lena from Ontario, a psychology graduate with extensive hands-on experience in child development, including stints in orphanages in the developing world. She was my dream come true. I had spent the last nine months as a jumped-up nurse-cum-counselor, a role I was hardly prepared for; here was a woman actually qualified to do the job. I wrote enthusiastically to Maa and Dada about her arrival.

At the end of the email—I knew they had their emails printed out and read to them on a weekly basis—I added: "I have assured her that she will have the independence and space and budget necessary to implant her concepts. Please welcome her."

Maybe the last bit was a bit of wishful thinking, but it was my last-ditch attempt at working within their structure. Lena started on the fifteenth of April, my thirty-sixth birthday; surely a good omen.

As May rolled around Lena was still hanging in there in Ghana, Beth was on top of things in Barcelona, Sabrina had dived into her exams, and I was still doing a balancing act between journalism and charity work. Soon I discovered common ground between the two worlds. The need to be resourceful and imaginative at finding quick solutions was a finely honed skill from my *Vogue* days (as when Snowdon had wanted a white stallion at the Paris couture, or Patrick had needed to photograph a nearly extinct toad, or when a model was stuck in Tokyo and we needed her in Miami in twenty-four hours). Also, with nearly twenty years of journalism under my belt, grant writing was a natural progression. Since we were involved in agricultural projects, our tagline became "The most sustainable way to help."

The children, I argued in my pages and pages of painstakingly researched prose, did not need a handout. Instead they needed a "partner" to lift them out of poverty, an idea that proved far ahead of its time. It was based on the concept of "sustainability" in development, long before it became mainstream for small charities to look for "trade, not aid" solutions. I wrote to everyone who I thought could help. Of great importance to me since the deaths of so many of my friends, HIV quickly became my passion. I really wanted to focus on getting kids diagnosed and on to the best regime of care as soon as possible. This was of course before the arrival of antiretroviral (ART) medication in Africa. The life expectancy in Ghana had fallen to age fifty-eight, yet no child at Awutiase had been tested for HIV. As far as I knew, no child was even vaccinated. When I thought about it, I wanted to cry.

At the end of March Sabrina celebrated her eighteenth birthday. Suddenly, completely unexpectedly, it was as if all hell let loose. I

had put a lot of thought into her birthday gift, and decided to give
her a magnificent album with photos from her earliest days. We had
a few photos of her biological family, and masses from our adventures and holidays together. It was to be a chronicle of her wonderful
life to date, and I left lots of blank pages at the end to fill up with
more memories. Preparing that big album took a lot of secrecy, and
I had photos and photocopies tucked away all over the house. On
the day of her birthday I made her breakfast in bed. Josh had sweetly
agreed to come over and prepare a lunch of sushi (her favorite food)
for her, her boyfriend, and all of her teenage friends. There seemed
to be a lot of arguing during the meal, and soon I realized that someone had stolen some of my money and, more important, my phone,
which contained all of my precious Ghana numbers.

When I confronted Sabrina there was a lot of yelling and tears.
She stormed out in the heat of the argument and did not come back
until the middle of the night. She screamed at me, slammed doors,
and said what I most dreaded hearing in the whole world: "*You are
not my mother!*" Afterward in that awful dawn I looked at myself fixedly
in the bathroom mirror, wondering what I had done wrong. My
world crumbled around me, again.

The next day I wandered around in a daze. My naturally analyt-
ical mind pushed me to ponder why this had all happened on her
eighteenth birthday. I recalled all the times I had told her that from
eighteen on I had been completely independent, and that when she
was eighteen she would be an adult and responsible for her own
destiny. I had given her these pep talks in the hope of making her
more responsible. However well intentioned, my words had perhaps
backfired and made her afraid to be an adult; afraid of who she was
expected to become.

I called the therapist. She reminded me that Sabrina's biological
half-siblings had always told her that the stay with me was just temporary, and that as soon as she was eighteen she would inherit from

her parents. (Her father had since passed away, although nobody had told us at the time.) On that day they would come and get her and, naturally, they would all live happily ever after. This of course was a fantasy, as both her father and mother died paupers and she was a ward of the French state when I adopted her. The shrink surmised that having to face up to the fact that all those stories were lies may have triggered a psychotic episode, and she suggested I call a psychiatrist. I made an appointment for Sabrina. A few days later, and against my better judgment, the reassuring doctor put her on antidepressants. He tested her for other drugs and later called to assure me that no hard drugs had shown up in her system.

We sank into an uneasy truce. I felt guilty for my new passion for charity work, thinking that maybe Sabrina was feeling put aside. No, she assured me, it had just been a bad day. She was okay now; she would take the medication, she would complete her exams, and she would be fine.

Still uneasy, I flew down to check on Lena. Twenty babies, including Prosper and Johnny, were in her care. While there I was to be filmed by a Spanish TV crew. The resulting projection on national TV brought us €5,000 in donations in about ten minutes, and a number of monthly donors—the life blood, as Charlie had dependably informed me, of any charity. During the filming Dada stayed away, planting ten thousand yams on the new land donated by OAfrica. Maa was clearly annoyed at Lena's arrival, despite the fact that the babies all had proper (and unbelievably expensive) baby milk and baby food for the first time.

My heart rose; the atmosphere in the baby room was completely different now. It was brightly painted and properly staffed, with clean sheets and repaired furniture; even the flies had bowed out. Every weaned infant received at least three eggs per week. Every child was in school, and the school had three new teachers. There was a new brightly painted kindergarten; in all, Awutiase was a much nicer place. The money donated by me and my friends was really making a huge difference. I hoped we could keep Maa happy, and that the transformation would continue.

To appease Maa and Dada, we agreed to build them a new bungalow.

A fully qualified Spanish nutritionist visited Awutiase while I was there and, horrified by the lack of fruit and vegetables in the diet and the lack of vaccination, wrote a report that resulted in us demanding three simple commonsense changes:

1. Basic hygiene (washing hands, airing bedrooms, providing more water to babies)
2. More proteins and vitamins in diet
3. Vaccinations

I took up these three points with Maa, but since we had taken the cash out of her control, the staff was finding it impossible to work with her. She would stay inside her room, ignore them, refuse to respond to their questions. The atmosphere was poisonous.

Very confused, I flew back to Barcelona and confronted Kwame on the weekend. Why was it so difficult to improve the children's lives?

He looked very uncomfortable but finally opened up. For the first time in his adult life he must have been feeling out of reach of Maa and Dada. They had dominated his life since he was twelve, as he came from a broken home. He confirmed that the farm made a profit and, as I had suspected, none of the money was being reinvested into the orphanage; Maa and Dada were keeping it. Worse than that, he confirmed that several charities, such as the Seeway Trust, donated on a per capita basis, so the pressure was on to "recruit" as many children as possible. And many weren't orphans at all; just kids "loaned" by their families in exchange for a promise to educate them.

Educate them? At that school? If I hadn't been so devastated at his admission, I would have laughed. Some of the kids' families, he added, even paid to place them in the orphanage as a kind of boarding school. Now *that* I could not believe. *Pay* to live in that hell?

I was in conflict, but I trusted Kwame. His revelations proved his allegiance to our marriage. He explained that the marriage had been Maa's way of assuring my continued involvement with Awutiase. That he had known nothing about it. That he had been forced into it.

It was a surprisingly cool morning in early June. I looked away from the gray skies outside the window and back to Kwame. He looked so miserable. He hated the rough life on the permaculture farm; his fantasy of European roads paved with gold had fallen flat. What all this meant for our relationship was unclear, and neither of us wanted to explore it yet. At that moment it seemed as if all we had was each other.

I was in a very delicate position. I loved the children at Awutiase; I had changed my life because of them. I could not just leave them at the mercy of Maa and Dada. It seemed there was no way that we could pull out. Kwame gently insisted that we must. If they ever found out that he had told me, he would be . . . he hesitated . . . *persecuted*.

18

*O*n June 11 the Spanish OAfrica board met. They decided to issue an ultimatum to Awutiase orphanage: either cooperate with our staff or we would pull out. Josh requested a vote. I knew that Maa would never accept any more controls. With a heavy heart, torn between the children we would be leaving behind versus the proper use of funds, I voted yes. It was finally clear to me that the completely unlicensed Awutiase orphanage was a shockingly lucrative little business. The owners skimmed off the vast majority of goods and cash donated by well-meaning evangelical charities, and pumped starry-eyed tourists such as ourselves for all we were worth, while also exploiting child labor on their huge plantations for profit.

In other words this orphanage, which on the day I arrived was housing 105 vulnerable children, most of whom were not orphans but instead children whose families paid for their keep, was a criminal enterprise. Back then I had been far too artless to see it, but not anymore. I flew back to Ghana alone, with a knot in my stomach. I presented the board requests to Maa and Dada.

By June 18 it was all over.

That momentous morning Maa, Dada, and I were sitting on the veranda where we had first met almost exactly a year ago. There were a few marked differences: there were no more flies; there were no babies lying diaperless on the floor; and the place was brightly painted. I could see that work had begun on the new bungalow for Maa and Dada; how ironic.

I explained that we could provide the orphanage kids with secondary-school scholarships, quality schooling and housing, hygiene, toilets, kitchen and farm infrastructure; but that in return, Maa and Dada had to support the children's rights. I explained that some of their activities were questionable, and that child labor, corporal punishment, depriving the children of food, water, medical care, or sleep were all things we could not be party to.

"Very well then," said Maa, "if you don't like the way we run the place, just go and take your people with you."

I blinked at her harsh words.

"That is the way we do things here. What do you know, you *white woman*, about our customs?"

I nodded my head sadly; it was inevitable that it would end like this. Heavily I arose from my seat, feeling my whole body ache. I stumbled out in a daze.

I called my Ghanaian partner Kwabena and explained the situation: I and my staff had to leave, pronto. He was very concerned, and agreed to meet me in the next day at Osu Children's Home, the biggest state orphanage in Ghana, in the capital Accra, only fifty miles but about three hours away.

That night over the usual pineapple, Lena, a few of the volunteers, and I dispiritedly discussed our options. Each of us was individually attached to at least one or two specific children. Pulling out was very hard, but we seemed to have no alternative. There was bound to be a need for our program somewhere else. I felt that we should prioritize services to HIV-positive children: early testing, better nutrition, treatment of opportunistic infections, ART drugs if we could get our hands on them. I promised that I would look for a new orphanage; a place where the children were looked after properly, where the owners' hearts were in the right place but they simply needed financial assistance and a great staff. We would all move there and get on with the job.

As I lay in the bed I had shared with Sabrina on that first night a year ago, I thought about the children: Vida and her wish to be a journalist; Courage and his football ambitions; Akua who would fall victim to the bullies as she roamed around in her private and puzzling world; Prosper who was doing so much better under Lena's constant care; and especially baby Johnny. I could not imagine leaving any of them behind.

At dawn I went to see Maa and asked permission to take Prosper, Akua, and Johnny with me when we left. Of course I would have wanted to take them all, but I knew that these were the three who would suffer the most if I left them there. To the first two she quickly agreed; after all, they were more a burden to her than anything else. As for Johnny, she said, Kwame would have to come for him. It sounded a lot like a threat.

My new husband was in fact very much on my mind that morning, as I prepared to tackle the mysterious world of Ghanaian public transport on my own. He was usually by my side on the longer *tro-tro* journeys.

The first bus took me into Accra without mishap, although we were squished like sardines five to a row (despite the customers' muttered complaints of "four, four"). It was hot, but what else was new? And the traffic was terrible as it was a market day in Kasoa, the junction town where the Awutiase road met the main Accra thoroughfare.

This market was massive, with traders selling anything from sheep to cows to bicycles to secondhand clothes, spread out on either side of the road. Their customers blocked traffic; the hawkers selling

ice water and donuts blocked traffic; and the policemen directing the
traffic blocked traffic. It took nearly three hours to reach the Kane-
shie station in Accra. What looked like hundreds of *tro-tros* were
parked bumper-to-bumper in the midday heat in a dustbowl of a
bare-earth parking lot. Each one boasted a bumper sticker with the
IF IT'S NOT ON, IT'S NOT IN HIV-prevention campaign, designed to
promote condom use. AIDS KILLS proclaimed a dusty billboard that
hung over the depot. Long-distance drivers were considered a vector
for infection, as they were said to have a girlfriend in every town.

I hopped into the first taxi. "Madame, one minute." Wearing a
dirty singlet and jeans, the driver hopped out to tie his boot with a
bit of old string.

"Madame, where to?"

"Osu Children's Home please, sir," I said nonchalantly.

"Ten thousand," he demanded, flashing a mouth full of broken
teeth. I was used to dealing in tens of thousands, hundreds of thousands, and even millions and tens of millions by now. I knew that he
was giving me the *obruni,* or white person's price.

"Five thousand," I responded.

"Oh, madame . . . why? Six thousand? Fine!" he smiled tooth-
lessly at me again, surprised, but appreciative at having been bargained with. His eyes took in my elaborate *kabba* and *slit* and head
wrap. I was in full regalia, as I would be visiting orphanages.

"Ahhh, madame, your dress, it dey fit you paaa . . . are you
married?"

"Yes, I am," I replied wearily. Kwame was so unhappy in Spain
that it really was not my favorite subject.

"Ahh . . . a black man, heh?"

I nodded perfunctorily, and he nodded delightedly.

He gunned the motor loudly, and we set off at the only speed that
exists for taxis: very fast. Shaggy was playing on the radio, crackly

and dissonant. I was lucky that it wasn't an impassioned sermon at full volume from one of the millionaire evangelical pastors.

Finally I arrived at Osu Children's Home. Staffed by social workers, it housed 160 children within a huge compound in a pretty residential area right in the heart of the city.

Kwabena met me in the entrance and shooed me inside to the reception area. A formal introduction (or five) and a very formal chat later revealed that at this orphanage, none of the children were admitted unless they were truly orphans or abandoned children, usually left in one of the city's marketplaces, public toilets, or hospitals. Apparently many women who could not pay their bills for the assistance received during birth would just walk away and leave their newborns in the wards. The alternative was to be forced to stay at the hospital, sometimes for months with their newborns until they could pay the bill. These mothers were unable to care for their other kids until their extended family somehow found some money and paid up. I gasped; obviously, even after all the hardship I had seen at Awutiase, I had only experienced the tip of an enormous iceberg of need.

I explained what we did. "We make orphanages happier, healthier places, and bring in expert staff."

The lady in charge looked stern. They were open to help, but as a government institution, that would be a complicated process since she could not accommodate foreign staff. My heart dropped. Lena was in the country already, but also a doctor, a nurse, and a women's health specialist were coming. Their credentials would have to be approved by the Ghanaian medical association, the lady told me sternly, and probably sit another exam.

"Why do you have so many medical staff coming?" she asked.

"We want to specialize in HIV," I said.

"Well, we can certainly refer children to you in that case," she said brightly. "We have several children here with HIV, and we never know what to do with them. The staff refuses to handle them."

My heart sank. The poor kids . . . I had recruited an ace team that was arriving in Ghana in a week. We could help them, but I needed somewhere for the new staff to live and work *now*. I began to realize that we were in an impossible situation. The ramifications of leaving Awutiase were becoming more complicated by the second.

Walking around the Osu Children's Home was instructive. I realized that the children were being cared for by qualified social workers who had well-kept files, and that the kids could receive help in finding their relatives, if they had any. The school situation seemed much better, probably because they were in the center of Accra and had several scholarships to local institutions. They had what seemed to be a good kindergarten, with toys and games.

In addition the level of hygiene and nutrition seemed better than at Awutiase, although there were definitely too many children. The staff seemed cold and unresponsive; they were government employees who worked in shifts. In fact the whole place had an institutional feel. The children with special needs, of which there were many, looked to be as neglected as in Awutiase. I realized that this place was no party either. I swore that we would help Osu as soon as we were settled.

Kwabena offered to take me to his home, and on the way we stopped off at Teshie orphanage. Here there was the opposite situation: the tiny house sheltered only a few children (about twelve), but a robust baking business made sure they had enough to eat. There was not enough work there for my growing team, so we thanked them and said goodbye. Just as we were leaving, the owner stepped up to the car and asked us if we knew anything about HIV.

"Why, yes," I replied. "It's one of our main areas of interest."

In that case, she said that we should come back soon because they knew several children in the community who were very sick.

As Kwabena started the car, the owner rushed toward us again. "Oh, and by the way, we do not have a toilet. Could you please provide that?" My heart sank. No toilet in the relatively sophisticated city of Accra? Was there no end to this bottomless well of want?

The next morning Kwabena had to go to work, but he had arranged for me to meet a board member of another children's home. The situation, it seemed, was a little unusual. Missionaries had set up the orphanage, and when they eventually pulled out they had appointed a board of local people to keep the place going. It was quite a distance away, but when we got there it was worth it. Famenya, with its fifty-five children and five staff members, was run down, and it definitely had absentee-landlord syndrome. It needed renovations for sure, but otherwise it had a lot going for it. The man who ran it turned out to be educated, affable, and open to all my suggestions. There was a large government school across a football field that dispensed education from ages six to sixteen. And, wonder of wonders, it had a well-stocked library! This was kept permanently locked, they explained, for lack of staff. My blood boiled; another generous foreigners' project gone wrong! The volunteers would soon sort that out, I told myself.

There was a building with three rooms chock-full of secondhand European and American clothes, to the extent that you could not open the door; the same situation I had seen Awutiase. Well, we could empty them. There was an abandoned vegetable garden, but Kwame would make short work of that, I said to myself.

The children seemed sad, undernourished, and understimulated. This too I was familiar with. In a burst of enthusiasm, I thought to myself, *Here there is nothing we can't improve! We have fixed worse than this!*

In my newfound excitement, I inquired about housing. As luck would have it, there was a housing estate across the road with individual homes (some even furnished) for rent. I visited one, and it took my breath away: large, airy, three bedrooms with terrazzo floors and two bathrooms. This was a level of luxury that I had not yet seen in Ghana. And it was cheap. "I'll take it," I whispered.

The next day the three new medical staff members arrived. I settled them, Prosper, and Akua into the new digs, and we spent a week organizing our work schedule with Famenya orphanage. As June slid into warm July and the tropical rainy season came to an end, they were busy laying down the essentials: enough beds for all the children, clean mattresses, sheets, and apparatus for hygiene, as well as blackboards, pencils, and paper for the school. Although Famenya had a better basic structure than Awutiase in terms of things like dustbins and hand-washing basins, and the meals contained at least two elements of protein a day, there was still a lot to do. Much of the infrastructure was very run down, there was a huge rubbish dump in the middle of the land, and the children were very short on essentials such as pens and schoolbooks.

Our first donation at Famenya was a bunch of drums (an African orphanage without music is unthinkable), and the children were thrilled. You should have seen them dance! We started with a piece-of-fruit-a-day project, and three of the volunteers taught in the nursery school and organized afternoon activities like dancing, painting, reading, badminton, and football.

Lena started a baby unit in one of the rented houses. We decided to specialize in taking care of the babies with particular problems: malnutrition, cerebral palsy, post-traumatic shock syndrome, and babies born prematurely.

By the end of the month I was back in Europe. As it was the summer holidays, Kwame was preparing to return to Ghana permanently, having completed his six-month practicals. He would now take over at Famenya. I needed to help Sabrina pack for her internship in the south of Spain, where she was going to work in a friend's hotel over the summer. She was keen to cook for a living, but I wanted her to experience the outlandish hours for herself as an intern, before she made a commitment to a career in catering.

But first I returned to my beloved Paris with another of my Chanel bags in tow, where plans were afoot to set up OAfrica France. My important date was with the Spanish actress Victoria Abril. From the moment I had first set foot in Ghana, she had supported the project. A friend of Josh's, David Del Bourgo, was to investigate the options for setting up the new fundraising office. I dressed to the nines and visited my fashion buddies, as well as Charles-Henri of course. It was wonderful to be back in my old world for a week. Ines de la Fressange proposed hosting our inaugural event at the Inter-Continental Hôtel. It was a blast from the past: the same majestic hotel where, at twenty-one, I had watched my first haute couture show, front-row center.

It was difficult to go from being a behind-the-scenes organizer to being a fundraiser. Asking was a new game, and I wasn't sure how to do it. I managed to snag an hour at UNESCO with Luc Montagnier, the doctor who had co-discovered the AIDS virus. We talked about his AIDS research and treatment in Ghana's neighboring country of Côte d'Ivoire, and about access to antiretrovirals. I told him that I wanted to specialize in children with HIV, as it stood to reason that they would constitute a large percentage of children in orphanages, and no other nongovernmental organization (NGO) seemed to be doing that. We talked about how the kids could possibly access his center. In addition Montagnier put me on a course of a new papaya enzyme food supplement, telling me dryly that my immune system was shot. In fact I had lost so much weight that a story in a Spanish gossip rag confidently reported that I had AIDS. Perhaps they thought that was the only plausible reason for me to leave the glory of the fashion world for Africa.

On my last night in Paris I attended a lavish Bulgari party in a cordoned-off section of the gorgeous Place Vendôme. Two important things happened at that party. It is odd how you can go to so many galas, dinners, and cocktail parties in your life, but only a few leave a lasting mark. This was one of them.

First, someone tried to introduce me to my ex-husband. "Have you met Olivier Gagnère?"

I got to drawl the classic line, "Yes, darling. We used to be married to each other." Very Joan Crawford.

The friend blushed and awkwardly bowed out.

Appraisingly, like gladiators in the ring, Olivier and I eyed each other. He looked much the same, although it had been almost eight years since our impulsive wedding and subsequent divorce.

"How are you? How is Sabrina?" he asked. I told him about Sabrina's internship, about the bust-up at her birthday, about the medication. I told him about Ghana.

He said something like, "Darling, you don't really think you can solve Africa's problems with your little charity, do you? Don't throw away your incredible career! You know everybody; you have so much credibility in this world, your books . . . Seriously, just write a check every few months. You'll do more good that way."

I saw clearly that we were not on the same page, as usual.

"Actually, the high-society thing wasn't really me. There was something beyond the mirror, and this is it," I said stiffly.

The sexy, dapper Parisian looked me up and down. With red African dust under my fingernails and circles under my eyes, I probably didn't meet his standards anymore.

"Do you really think you can save the world, *cherie*?" he asked. I thought he was laughing at me.

"I'm not trying to change the world; I'm just helping one damaged child at a time. And then two, and three, and four. If I don't, I can't sleep at night."

I turned on my Ferragamo heel and dived into the crowd. I needed more champagne, pronto.

On my way to the bar I ran into Margherita Missoni, who looked fantastic. She was all grown up, living in New York, and fascinated by my story. "I'll come and help," she said spontaneously. "If I knew anything about the Missonis, she really would.

These two opposing responses were indicative of the reactions I would receive from the fashion world regarding my decision. About half of my "friends" didn't want to have anything to do with me, now that my interests had broadened beyond hem length and the hot new photographer in town. The other half—people like the Missonis, Victoria Abril, Ines de la Fressange, and the talented Franca Sozzani from Italian *Vogue*—were to be the lifeblood of OAfrica; demonstrating that fashion was not always fickle.

When I flew back to Barcelona, I was exhausted. The stress of the last few months was beginning to tell on me. I fell into a deep dreamless sleep, only to be awakened by the phone ringing at four in the morning.

It was about Sabrina, the caller said. She had attempted suicide.

19

*N*ervously I dialed a cab, fumbling, confused, and went straight to the airport to catch a flight to Madrid that left in less than forty minutes. The connection to Badajoz, where Sabrina had been staying with friends, was five hours after that. It was afternoon by the time I arrived at the provincial hospital, shaking like a leaf.

The friends with whom she had been staying told me they were convinced Sabrina was doing drugs, but I blamed the antidepressants. Research said that in younger patients these particular drugs could produce a severe reaction, and there was data on teenage suicides in which antidepressants had been a factor. Quickly I found the doctor, who told me to calm down.

"I see attempts like this all the time in teenagers; overdoses of pills mixed with alcohol," he told me. "The only unusual thing about this one is that it happened on a Monday night. Usually we see them only on Fridays and Saturdays."

His matter-of-fact words comforted me somewhat. I went into the ward to see her.

"I'm so sorry, Mummy. I'm so sorry." Sabrina was sobbing, I was sobbing, and we were both apologizing to each other. How had we reached this point, both of us afraid of the other person's reaction, both of us feeling guilty? After Sabrina was discharged we took the long trip home, with the weight of everything unsaid between us.

In Barcelona we went straight to the psychiatrist. I showed him research on the side effects of the antidepressants. However, he was not having anything to do with my theories. He made me sit down while Sabrina went for some blood tests.

"Just look at this girl's history," he said. "Both parents dead; double abandonment. First disrupted attachment. Her half sister was delusional, told her all kinds of fairy tales about reuniting as a family, and flaked out on her when she was five. Second rupture. Then she was passed on to you. Interrupted attachment, for the second time. There is a history of drugs, alcohol, and abuse within the family. A trail of broken promises, leading to her inability to trust. It is no wonder she dabbles in soft drugs and takes all kinds of risks. The world has never proved itself to be a safe place to her.

"Every day this girl is alive is a kind of miracle. And it's a miracle you have made. You should not beat yourself up about it. You have done your best, and you have gotten her this far. Now you need to disconnect a bit. This may be the lowest she can go, and hopefully she will start to climb out again. In any case, she's an adult, and she needs to make her own decision to live. It is a decision you can't make for her."

When Sabrina came back into the room he asked her if she had heard of cognitive dissonance. This is when you hold on to a set of beliefs, and then when faced with evidence that contradicts these beliefs, you become uncomfortable. Yet you continue to hold on to your beliefs in spite of events that disprove them. He said that the events around her eighteenth birthday had been a good example of that; it was clear that he blamed the untrustworthy people in her past. I left his office deep in thought. I could see the truth in what he had said, but that did not stop me from feeling like a failure.

From there we went to visit my own mother, who was none too happy about all the gallivanting in Ghana, but was quite excited to be planning her first visit over Christmas. When we were there something amazing happened. Sitting on my mum's couch, Sabrina opened up for the first time about how bad things had really been in her childhood. She confirmed everything I ever suspected. For the first time I heard the truth, straight from her, without having to conduct an investigation. When she started talking it was as if she couldn't stop. Listening to her, I became furious all over again at what unscrupulous adults had done to my little girl.

From that moment on I never spoke to any of them again. The experience at Awutiase had taught me a lot about abuse; what I did not observe, I had now read up on. I knew we had no hope of prosecuting, since Sabrina's abusers were in three different countries. But I also knew that a cathartic experience was occurring; a first step into the healing process. I had the distinct impression that by opening up and telling me everything she had hidden, by relinquishing that shame, recovery had started. I hoped that the simple ebb and flow of sharing would start her on the road to healing.

I was booked to go to Ghana on the fifteenth of the month, but obviously I could not leave Sabrina behind. I cheered her up by telling her that Margherita Missoni, who was her age, would be in Ghana too, but she did not need the encouragement. "Mum, Ghana is where I feel best. Maybe I'll do a course on child development during the holidays while I wait for my results," she said. "You know they're always advertising courses in the *Daily Graphic*."

It was true. The entire literate population was on some huge campaign to better itself, if you believed the *Graphic*. In its flimsy pages there was a course for everything from rabbit rearing to water harvesting to faith healing.

"I'm interested in understanding what happened to me, and also preventing its happening to others. I want to work with babies, Mum. They are so vulnerable. Every time I see an abandoned baby, it's like—" she hesitated. "I see me."

I knew what she meant. Every time we were able to save another life, I felt redeemed in part for the failure I felt in parenting her. We certainly would be in the right place for working off our combined trauma, I reflected bitterly.

This time I felt that Kwame was truly glad to have me back, as this time he had embraced me passionately and whispered "I missed you" into my ear when I got home from the airport. He had driven over to Awutiase and come back with Johnny. I had no idea how he managed the negotiation with Maa and Dada, but my life suddenly got a whole lot more complicated. I was pleased, as I sensed that my husband had a loving impulse to create a family unit. It made me feel warm and fuzzy inside. Kwame was such a distant man, so restrained, and that was difficult to live with. We had been married off before we knew each other, as virtual strangers. The only time he seemed really happy was when he was playing with Johnny, carrying Johnny, feeding Johnny. The image of the huge no-nonsense dark-skinned farmer I had married cradling the tiny walnut-colored baby was both tender and erotic to me.

Johnny seemed to be the glue that would hold us together, so I dedicated myself to being a mum. I wanted to give it a go on my own, without a nanny, despite my crazy work schedule. This was my first personal experience with an infant, and I painfully realized that it required late nights and early mornings. We were not set up for babies; I had to bathe Johnny in the kitchen sink, and I used industrial quantities of nappies. Yet his dimpled little face and tiny smile were all the reward I needed. I took him everywhere, tied to my back, *à la Ghanaian*. The inexorable routine of babyhood—bath, feed, nap, change, play, feed, nap—worked like meditation. I was so focused on Johnny that the fact that I had thrown up my career, my life in Europe, and was fast burning through my savings disappeared into the background. I dissolved into love.

* * *

Sabrina's presence in Famenya produced another wave of arrivals: a week or so after we landed, a group of her friends from Awutiase appeared on the doorstep. Among them was Courage.

"What are you doing here?" I gasped in surprise, hugging them madly.

"Maa told us to curse you. We defended you, so they asked us to leave."

The short response threw me. I knew the teenagers were a burden to Maa and Dada because they were less passive than the younger kids. They realized they were being exploited for their labor, and made their feelings clear. No matter how stunted they were, how many hours they worked or how little they were fed (rebellious kids were simply deprived of any food at all, it turned out), they still talked back. They had burned their bridges by coming to me.

Kwame was furious with them. I thought perhaps he felt threatened by the boys' allegiance to me. At night in bed I tried to understand his feelings, but as usual he was hermetic and closed. I felt waves of pity. Whatever he had been through as a little boy must have been terrible if he was this uncommunicative. I imagined growing up in a place like Awutiase, and shuddered, holding Johnny tight. At least our son would have a normal childhood with two loving parents, I reflected.

So now I had twelve teenagers to cater to, and senior secondary schools to find. My project seemed to be growing by the minute. Sabrina, however, was thrilled to have her posse back.

The next wave of refugees from Awutiase included Vida as well as her mother, Mama Georgina, and her two sisters, Akos and Benedicta. Mama Georgina had a job in minutes, since recruiting mothers for the new baby unit was turning out to be very complicated. We had one mother, Mama Rose; one of the many Ghanaians who had been evicted from Nigeria in 2003. She came with two stepsons, Mensah and Jewel, big lanky boys of twelve and fourteen who were bright and better educated than the others. Mama Rose continued to prove herself to me by really helping Prosper; he could sit up and drink on his own now, which constituted unbelievable progress in the face of his disabilities.

Now no longer physically present at Awutiase orphanage, we were paying local staff to work there. I wanted to continue doing that, as the support was vital to the children's well-being. I realized that for a long time now, people had been building and buying and fixing material things in Awutiase, confusing material enhancements and improvements with respect for children's rights and improvements in their lives. In particular, foreign donors were likely to not look beneath the surface at the whole rotten edifice, but just try and improve or add to it. And Maa and Dada knew how to exploit the legacy of the continent's dark history of slavery that many of us foreigners dragged along: the white man's burden; the respect for anything disguised as a cultural value that in this case served as an excuse to starve, beat, and humiliate children.

So I decided to make those salaries we were paying conditional. My lofty vision of an improved Awutiase orphanage was basically reduced to the addition of a piece of fruit a day. There were problems getting even that done, although an uneasy truce was established. We did not want to pull out completely because of our attachment to the children, but it was getting increasingly difficult to work with Maa and Dada.

At Famenya, Margherita Missoni proved to be a disciplined and extremely hard worker. She did fun things with the kids like drawing and playing, but she was also given the wretched (and extremely dirty) task of organizing and cleaning the rooms that were clogged with donated clothes. Just imagine three good-size rooms, filled floor to ceiling with secondhand clothing that stank of mothballs and was covered with dust. I expected it all to be lovely wax cloth, but in reality they were secondhand European clothes. The markets of Ghana were flooded with the misguided dumping of excess and preborn clothing on Africa, slowly killing the local fashion and fabric industry. This was the downside of the garment trade that we two fashionistas had never seen before.

I was very grateful to Famenya orphanage for making this cleanup possible; those rooms were then turned into an infirmary and volunteer quarters, ensuring health and also bringing in money with the fees they paid (as I had). It was a no-brainer, but I now knew that there was nothing obvious about orphanages relinquishing their excess, even if they were sacrificing perfectly good floor space to their hoarding habit.

I knew all about need at this point but also, sadly, much more than I wanted to know about waste. Margherita turned the key to a previously unopened storeroom in Famenya one day and found it full of rice (and fat mice). Rice! While children in other orphanages were going hungry! My anger and frustration had to be felt to be believed. Margherita and I just stood there and looked at each other in amazement. Bucking the hoarding trend, the Famenya board then unbelievably agreed to donate 250 kilograms of that rice to another orphanage. The volunteers banded together and hired a massive truck, and we drove up to the Ashanti region.

The Awutiase experience had made me more perceptive, less innocent. By August we had reached out to a total of six institutions.

During my visits I had seen the most atrocious things. In every orphanage I visited I saw proselytism: the forced conversion of Muslims to Christian beliefs, or vice versa. The children would, it seemed, always need to fit in with the belief system of the majority. None of these orphanage owners seemed to have heard of the right to religious freedom, or even the right to keep your own name.

The orphanage we transported most of the clothes to (which were riotously received) was run by an Australian pastor. All the Issas became Issacs, and all the Ibrahims became Abrahams here. This orphanage was in Obuasi, where the largest gold mine in the world (and the world's most profitable, for the owners, that is) created horrific problems. Prostitution and AIDS abounded among the migrant workers, despite the gold beneath everyone's feet. We stayed in a ramshackle hotel in which the beds sagged and the rooms were lit with pink and purple lightbulbs. I considered sleeping on the floor, but that was as dirty as the sheets. During that long and horrid night I realized that I had reached an all-time lifestyle low, but also that there was no turning back.

Unsurprisingly, judging by the activity at the "hotel" that night, a lot of babies ended up abandoned. The orphanage was huge; nearly as big as Osu. Sabrina was drawn to it immediately, and asked if she could come back and work there. Shamed by the desperate need I saw, I hesitatingly agreed. Famenya had no babies. In our own house we had the twelve teenagers who were runaways from Awutiase, as well as Prosper and Akua. The Obuasi orphanage represented a better fit for Sabrina, so I promised her that she could come back.

Margherita left, but the trip had made a strong impression on her. She was to remain one of OAfrica's most powerful advocates in the world outside of Ghana. As a result of her stay Margherita became president of OAfrica in Italy, and has supported us inexhaustibly ever since as "her charity"; the one she always thinks of whenever she is asked to do a charity fashion project. This faithful attachment, rare in the celebrity world, has been a key ingredient to our success.

With September came school issues. Of the kids living with me, there were nine at senior high school level, three at junior high, and one at primary level. They all needed placement. Manuel and Marlowe Garay were two new staff members who had joined us from their last post in China. Marlowe was African American, and as wry as they come. I liked her at once. She was methodical too, and through her and her husband's work, one thing became immediately apparent: without improving their education, the opportunities for these children were strictly limited. I always tell donors looking for projects that improving education is a sure-fire way of helping. But how much to help without increasing dependency was to remain a quandary for many years.

Ghana had gone from having an educational system that was admired throughout Africa, immediately post-independence, to having something that seemed like a travesty of the British system. There was nursery and kindergarten, which were optional, followed by six years of primary and three years of junior high, which constituted the nine years of basic education. After that they had three final years of senior high school, up to grade twelve, and then at eighteen they sat for a final exam.

The hiccup lay in the fact that only primary school was free (although uniforms and books were not). Given the prevalent belief that children should do much of the house and farm work, attendance was irregular. By the time they finished their studies, the students were often well over twenty, since lags of three to four years were common, and even seven-year gaps were not exceptional. This led to the perception that schooling was an almost impossible luxury. Every single poor child that I met in Ghana had one overriding dream: to be allowed to go to school.

At OAfrica, we burned with the determination to help make that dream come true. The scholarship program we founded in September 2003 continues strong until this day. By the following school year the program had more than 170 beneficiaries, and I truly believe that it is one of the best ways to help children in the developing world. This being said, as soon as you have a handful of children attending school, you have to engage with the educational system of the whole country.

There were so many problems: the fact that teacher absenteeism was so high (it remains one of the highest in the world; around 40 percent according to the World Bank); that many of the teachers were so ill equipped to instruct; that some of the class sizes were monstrous (fifty to sixty kids were not uncommon); that many of the schools were under trees or had leaking roofs, and therefore could not be used in the torrential rainy season. In a surreal twist, impoverished children were not allowed to attend these battered schools without wearing the official uniform and shoes. No shoes meant no school—in a country where most adults wore flip-flops, and where shoes were an unimaginable luxury? The illogic left me speechless.

Even worse was the reality that corporal punishment—caning, or "hitting hard on the buttocks with a pliable switch" (which the children were tasked to provide for the teacher at the beginning of each term)—was used in every classroom. If you forgot your homework, you got caned. If your hair was too long (beyond a quarter of an inch), you got caned. If the goat ate your homework (a perfectly possible scenario), you got caned. This really had me seeing red. If we said anything to the teachers about the caning, we were glared at scornfully and dismissed with the old biblical lesson "Spare the rod and spoil the child."

Marlowe called an education meeting, which involved me and Beth (who was visiting). We sat down and looked at each other in dismay, not really knowing where to start. The situation was much more complex than we had thought. Marlowe presented her shopping list. One of the first things we should do was have a home school at OAfrica that would coach kids intensively until they had reached their grade level in the three Rs and prep them for entry into the mainline schools. Marlowe had cleverly started the discussion with a proposal that was small, practical, and eminently doable. A great idea.

Her second proposal was more hefty. "We have to improve the kindergarten, toys, teachers, reading books, etcetera, because what the children learn there will set them up for primary."

Okay, I thought, *kindergarten is only two classes full of cute four- and five-year-olds, so that seems possible. It would be easy to find a donor for that.*

"We need to get the kids free textbooks, pencils, paper—oh, and desks, uniforms, and shoes." Marlowe rolled her eyes as she spoke. "Most have nothing to read and write with, and are sitting three or four to a double desk."

I nodded. I had seen the children squashed into tiny wooden desks. She continued, "We have to train the teachers. They can take courses in the summer holidays. And top up their salaries."

"Okay," I said, thinking she was finished.

"And," Marlowe took a deep breath, "we need at least fifteen more teachers to make the class size at all reasonable and the learning effective."

I gulped. Fifteen more salaries would triple the size of the OAfrica staff. "And it's the only way it is even worth getting involved." Marlowe was unrelenting. "It's either that, or we don't go into it at all."

It looked like I was going to have to find some funding, and fast. My lawsuit against Taschen for back royalty payments promised to bring in substantial money, but that had been dragging on for eight years by this point, despite my lawyer Narboni's best efforts. Beth was already helping me to rent my lovely house in Spain, but only selling it would give us the injection of cash we needed.

Johnny was fidgeting on my back. He was hungry; I had to go. I told Marlow to go ahead and hire the teachers. Selling the house it would have to be.

20

I trawled the orphanages of Accra and beyond. They were mind-blowingly awful.

There was the ironically named God's Grace, owned by a bombastic Ghanaian TV-star-cum-politician. The place was incredibly mismanaged, dark, and overcrowded. We were to renovate their collapsing kitchen, open an infirmary, employ a manager and nurse, and build them a magnificent school in the hope of transforming the palace. There was Osu, of course, where we renovated a whole building and then used it for the care of special children, a nutrition facility, and an infirmary. We had installed a nurse there, as well as a physiotherapist, a masseuse, and several carers for children with special needs. At Teshie we built the toilet they so badly needed, and repaired their leaking roof. There was overcrowded Obusai with its room full of wooden cots in rows.

But the place that most affected me was the Reformatory. All over the developing world, juvenile justice is one of the most problematic areas for children's rights. Even knowing this, I was not prepared for what I saw. In the long low colonial-era government

building, boys and girls as young as nine were kept in cells behind
bars. Some of these girls even had babies. As we were given a tour
from hell, small grubby hands reached out from behind bars and
gestured wildly at us. The children were often stuck there for years
for "crimes" such as stealing food to eat, simply because there was
no one to pay bail; no one to take them to court to plead their case.

Then and there, I pledged a salary for a social worker and for
two teachers for this institution. The complexity of the situation was
immense, but I knew one thing: I *would* make a difference here, no
matter what. For a start, I encouraged them to refer their freed mothers and babies to us. Sometimes they stayed on the compound because
they had literally nowhere to go. At least we could keep infants out of
that hellhole. Then we started a sports program to get the children out
of their cells for at least a few hours a day. We fed them nutritious
snacks, and struck up an agreement with some generous young Ghanaian lawyers to represent the children in court. This was to ensure
that the easy cases could be moved out of the Reformatory quickly; a
significant transformation, as innocent children were often abused by
older ones in the confined cells. My priority was to get their cases
heard and if possible dismissed entirely, and then move them out as
fast as possible. As a consequence, the decreased numbers meant a
better life for everyone in the Reformatory.

By October our own baby center had moved into a bigger OAfrica house that combined the baby center and the teen home, both
maintained by Child Priority, Italian *Vogue*'s charity. We now had the
capacity for twelve teens, twelve four- to thirteen-year-olds, and
twenty babies in much larger premises with a big garden. We were
then able to bring in eight children from Obuasi for specialists' care
in the capital. Afua, the head pediatrician at Korle-Bu Teaching Hospital, operated on six of them. The kids from Obuasi were in a terrible state. There was twelve-year-old Christopher, a Liberian whose
hands and tongue had been cut off in the civil war. Throughout the

war it was accepted practice to sacrifice, eat, murder, or maim individuals in order to attain prowess in battle. Christopher had been one of the victims, but we were to see many more. He now ate and wrote with his feet. Despite the unbelievable atrocities he had witnessed, he had a wonderful smile, and was a joy to be around.

From Obuasi too came a tiny baby nicknamed Butterfly, because although she was already one and a half years old, she was not much bigger than a doll, and malnutrition had kept her fragile. After a few weeks with Lena, she was eating every two hours and growing fast. She became Sabrina's special love. When the children from Obuasi went back to the orphanage, Sabrina went with them, convinced that there was where she was most needed, and that she had found her vocation: childcare provider. I let her go, remembering that she was nearly nineteen and needed me to trust her.

In the months that followed, Lena also moved there after having been shocked into action by the terrible scene of a room full of high cots with two or three babies to a bed. The conditions at OAfrica were paradise compared to Obuasi.

Near Famenya Foster Home we had recreated an orchard and vegetable garden, volunteers' quarters, a new kindergarten and infirmary. Marlowe, our education director, was spearheading the formation of the kindergarten, and had her hands full.

Around that time my family life took a terrible hit. It happened like this. Kwame and I had been trying hard to make a nest with Johnny, although Sabrina and a dozen teenagers lived with us. Kwame was the only person from OAfrica who still managed to keep the channels of communication open with Awutiase. Unexpectedly, Dada sacked the last staff member we still had on salary there, the Ghanaian nurse, and that proved to be the final straw for the board in Spain. They decreed that we should pull out completely. It just seemed wrong to continue to fund an organization that had proved time and time again that it did not care about the children.

I was frantic about what would happen to all the children I knew and loved, and for whom I had come to Ghana. The lady from Osu had gotten me an appointment with the Department of Social Welfare (DSW), the body responsible for monitoring orphanages. In tears, I told them about what I had observed: about the lack of monitoring, about the children with special needs who did not get proper treatment; the child labor, the deaths, the inadequate staff, the violence by staff, and the inadequate food and health.

The director was a large lady behind a large desk, poured into a fabulous blue print *kabba* and *slit*. "I know, I know," she said wearily. "We know about that woman. Very soon now we will be closing the place down." My heart leapt.

Relieved, I focused on creating a facility where the children of Awutiase could find proper care, when and if DSW did close them down. One of the first to arrive was a pregnant teenager, Emma. Courage showed her into my room. I remembered her well from the first few stays there. She had always been very close to Maa, preparing rich and generous bowls of food for the couple (in stark contrast to what the kids ate) and warming bathwater for her by laboriously heating it over an open fire. Now she was in tears. Maa had starved her and locked her in a dark room ever since she started showing. She had not seen a doctor or received any prenatal care. She had no idea when she was due, but thought maybe it was around December. She had fled Awutiase, fearful that when she gave birth the baby would be taken from her and sold for international adoption.

Illegal adoption, she added, was how they made most of their money.

I sat down. The shock of this revelation was physical. I had been naïve, dazzled, overwhelmed by an immense feeling that I was needed when I arrived at Awutiase. But then I had seen the efficient money-making machine that duped unsuspecting evangelical charities in the United States and Europe. Even still, I did not want to believe the worst: that Awutiase was a business. Sabrina's gut instinct had been absolutely right; the sale of babies was its most lucrative sideline.

Emma told me that most of the clients were American, arriving with a cushion under their dress and leaving with a baby.

The next morning I rushed to the American embassy on a *tro-tro*, Johnny on my back as usual. The man behind the desk listened uncomfortably. After I was done with my breathless revelations, to which he made sympathetic noises, he walked me out of the premises and down the road, as if to see me off. It struck me as odd, but I immediately realized he had something to say that he did not want to talk about in the office.

"Look," he said glancing away from me. "The situation is this: I'm the person who has to go and verify adoptions, and I often interview birth mothers. Sometimes they know their child is never coming back, sometimes they don't. But in all cases, middlemen have paid them off. The middlemen are making the money, and they usually have ties to the private orphanages."

I stared at him, speechless. The authorities *knew* all this?

"But how can this happen?" I asked.

"Well, if the kids fit the USA definition of an orphan, we can't really say no to our American families." He sighed. "The USA definition of an orphan includes 'abandonment of or desertion,' so if the baby comes from any kind of orphanage, that's it. It automatically qualifies as an orphan, once the kid was in the orphanage, even for a day, it can be classified as abandoned or deserted. Even if we trace the mother."

He mopped his brow, noticeably unused to the street conditions beyond the cocoon of antimicrobial air conditioning provided by Uncle Sam.

"But there is nothing we can do. We know it's an industry, but we have Americans in front of us and, in most cases, they have already bonded with the child, spent three months in a hotel, taken time off from their jobs. They are weeping. They want the kid. They are tax-payers; we work for them. It's all legal. What can we do?"

Obviously this was a good man with a conscience, and he was being consumed by the injustice of what he was doing.

"We make our reservations clear to them; that this child may have been stolen or trafficked. But after they reach a certain point in their adoption journey where they have bonded with the child, they just don't care. They believe they can give the child a better life. They are beyond reason; they just want that kid. We tell them, *this kid has a mom,* but they don't want to hear."

He wiped his brow again. Finally he looked at me.

"It's terrible. I hope you can get the Ghana government to do something about the way the orphanages go around recruiting kids that aren't orphans."

He turned on his heel and left. I could tell that he thought he might have gotten too emotional.

I got into a cab and drove to the Department of Social Welfare for the second time that week, where I recounted the conversation word for word. Again, vague promises were made. I was angry. It seemed to me everyone knew what was going on, but no one was doing anything about it.

Obviously Maa had impeccable sources at DSW and probably, I was beginning to fear, inside OAfrica. Her retaliation to my activism was instant and brutal. Shortly after these meetings occurred, she drove up to me in the street in Accra. Like in a scene from a movie, she literally ripped Johnny out of my arms, got back in the car, and drove away. I stood in the street and bawled my eyes out.

My heart was broken, again. I had spent months with that baby, wrapped in cloth on my back in the markets, cuddled in my arms at every meeting. Every moment he was with me. After holding back while we were in Awutiase, I had finally allowed myself to love him. How could I endure life without him?

The situation brought on an almighty row with Kwame. Of course I expected him to go and bring Johnny back. When he showed no signs of doing so, I lost it. Why, I asked him, could he not stand up for Johnny, for our family? I stamped my feet, slammed doors, and asked him to leave the house. I was overcome with grief. I even wrote him a letter of goodbye: *I am horrified you cannot stand up for Johnny. It is a deep shock to me, and I cannot be married to a man with no moral backbone. What Maa and Dada are doing is very, very wrong. You need to stand up to them. You are surrounded by hypocrisy.*

Within a week I had received three threatening emails from Dada and a number of anonymous death threats by text message. The vitriolic content was intensely personal. How could they have gotten this private information? Things about my past, about my marriage, about Sabrina. Did they have an informant among the teenagers? Who were these people? I was thrown off-balance; I had never seen real evil before. I was so horrified by the greed and cruelty that my view of human nature was irrevocably damaged.

I was sure that Maa had no paperwork on Johnny, and therefore had no more right to him than I did, but the Ghana OAfrica board cautioned me. I could not be seen to do anything remotely illegal if we were officially reporting Awutiase for child trafficking. "Yes, I know," I told them wearily. "We have a proverb for that too."

Foolishly, I reacted as a European. First, I reported the threats to a police station. The police drove me over to Awutiase (in a taxi I paid for) and called Dada to the police station. I did not stand a chance from the moment we walked through the door. The orphanage was a financial motor in that town, and Dada was a "big man." I had dreamed of seeing him behind bars, but it was I who was nearly locked up for slander. Nobody believed what I was accusing him of. Dada protested that he did not know how to use a computer, so how could the emails have come from him? I escaped the cursed police station before I ended up behind bars.

This was my darkest hour. Sabrina was in Obuasi; Johnny and Kwame were gone. I was so alone. I felt adrift and lost without Kwame, so when he came back with apologies, I took him back. In return, I made him promise not to go near Maa and Dada. Taking Johnny away from us was an act of pure vindictiveness. They knew he would have been happy with us; they knew how Kwame loved him, and how I treasured him.

I spoke to the teenagers about the death threats. All of them denied any involvement, but I could see that they felt uncomfortable. The contents of the emails were such that Maa and Dada had to have a spy in my own home. I obsessed and worried, and then slowly began to see the ridiculousness of the situation. Emma had told me that nowadays in Awutiase, almost the entire prayer session was taken up with cursing me, and that Dada encouraged the children to pray for my damnation. Then I remembered the evangelicals, and I remembered the children. I knew very well that half of them would be praying they could run away *to* me, as opposed to my being consumed by hellfire. Anyway, words couldn't kill me, could they? I began to see the more comical side of the situation when I received a piece of hate mail that opened with the usual "You will rot in hell" but that ended in a conversational tone with a question (in capital letters): "HAVE YOU SEEN HOW YOU HAVE BECOME LEAN?"

I was now so thin that even my worst enemies had noticed! In this country, wealthy Ghanaians were expected to be fat as a mark of prestige; an advertisement of their life of indolence. My newly slim body was a big Ghana no-no, but I was very happy with it. Looking good would help me in my fundraising forays.

That month *Vogue* came back into my life with force. Child Priority was the foundation run by the renowned editor of Italian *Vogue*, the endlessly creative Franca Sozzani whom I had known since I was eighteen. That organization made a substantial donation, and has remained our partner until this day. This partnership, along with Victoria Abril's indefatigable efforts on French TV and the steady support from the Missoni family, have been the cornerstones of our success, and they were laid that autumn as I battled with Dada's threats.

In mid-December we had our introductory event in Paris: a star-studded kids' tea party with an African storyteller and magician. Our international godmother, Victoria, attended the tea, and followed up with two great TV shows. The event was the brainchild of Ines de la Fressange, who understood exactly the kind of support we needed. Politician Frédéric Mitterrand made an impromptu speech and, yes, I cried. David Del Bourgo, our OAfrica man in Paris, organized the event in a lovely salon. Nobel Prize winner Luc Montangier brought gravitas; the party made money and reestablished my faith in what we could do. Help seemed to be flowing from all sides.

However, the fundraising success and the golden glow that went with it was easy to snap out of once I got back to Ghana. Now that Johnny and Sabrina were gone, Kwame and I had decided to move into a wing of the larger OAfrica center in the housing estate near Famenya orphanage. This we figured would cut down on rent. We wanted every penny to go to the children. We had two rooms and a bathroom, down a corridor from the child care facility. This also meant that the dividing line between our personal living space and the children was not clear, either physically or in our minds. Our relationship was definitely on the rocks; the issue over Johnny's abduction was proving hard for me to forget.

The children's stories were traumatic. Paajoe was nine years old, but weighed less than the average five-year-old. He had full-blown AIDS. A gentle sweet kid, he now came to live with us at OAfrica. Two new babies that were brought to us were also HIV positive.

Just before Christmas I went to visit Sabrina in Obusai, to bring her up to date on all the news. Sabrina was in her element. She was mightily attached to Butterfly, who didn't deserve her name any more because she was quite plump now after my daughter's careful ministrations. Sabrina had also started a diploma course in child care.

In the meantime we had received her exam results. It seemed that after the nightmare of homeschooling, she had actually done okay. She would have access to any number of further education options, anywhere in the world. What would she like to do now? I was about to sell the house in Barcelona, so we could invest some of the money in her education.

But Sabrina replied, "I'm happy here. I love the work. Let me do this for a year, and then we'll see."

Like me, Sabrina was fighting off wave after wave of malaria, and she was skinny. In addition—and this came as a surprise to me—she was not living in the orphanage, but in her own apartment with a girlfriend. The place looked rundown, and the neighborhood was obviously a slum. In particular, the tiny scruffy house and the lack of protection worried me.

"Mum, when you live in a neighborhood like this, everyone knows you; they *are* your protection." She made fun of my bourgeoisie hopes for her. She certainly looked happy, and laughed a lot.

We parted with a promise that she would review her plans in June. A year off working in a charity would not look bad on her CV after all, she said. She was right, but still I left with an uneasy feeling. Sabrina had become a born-again Christian under the influence of the pastor who owned Obuasi orphanage, and seemed to be behaving impeccably. But I also knew my daughter, and I was very worried that this new outlook would not stick. I confided as much to the pastor, who disagreed strongly. Sabrina is doing really well here, and is safe, was the gist of the conversation (*unlike when she was with you,* was implied). And Jesus, the pastor reminded me with a smile, was in control. We had a nice lunch and that unimaginable luxury, dessert, and then they all prayed for me after coffee.

I left with a heavy heart. Both the pastor and Sabrina had made it abundantly clear that my meddling in her new independent life would not be tolerated.

21

*A*t Christmas, stocked with antibacterials, antimalarials, and anti–
everything else, my mum visited Ghana for the first time. I rented
her one of the air-conditioned and furnished estate houses, and
directed her to the nearest pool (over two hours' *tro-tro* ride away),
where she spent her days teaching the teens to swim. In the garden
of her rented house, Kwame and I celebrated our first anniversary,
dressed up, once again, in our wedding clothes (which had to be
taken in massively, in my case).

It had been a very hard year. Sabrina had moved away, I was
juggling a new marriage with someone from a very different culture.
I'd had an instant family with an eighteen-month-old baby who had
then literally been snatched from my arms. I had moved to Ghana,
effectively transformed my career from writing and styling for magazines to charity work, and opened three companies: OAfrica in
Ghana, Spain, and France. I had given away almost all my money. I
had learned so much, and made a difference in so many lives. I had
also seen pain and suffering beyond anything that I had experienced

before, and was forced to deal with evil, staring me in the face, kicking me in the butt. It was a lot to take in.

But sitting around in the garden with all the children, for a very short moment it seemed as if things were finally settling down. I looked at Prosper who, unbelievably, could now sit up straight and feed himself. I wondered what had been the decisive moment that had moved me from an ordinary sweaty wide-eyed volunteer to an organized, well-staffed, and internationally financed activist. Was it Brenya's death? The guilt I felt about not magically erasing all of Sabrina's problems? The refusal to let Prosper and Akua suffer anymore?

We took a celebratory trip to the beach with twenty kids and my mum. She stayed in a hotel, whereas I was in a rundown rental with the kids. There was a merry (and loud) dance-and-children-filled Christmas, when I wrapped up loads of presents: towels and soap and clothes.

A day after Christmas, when Emma had danced and eaten her fill, she went into labor. At dawn we rushed her to the pitifully under-resourced local clinic, and we waited. It was the first birth I had witnessed. She was sweating and panting and screaming in the tiny room while I held her hand. The teens had warned me that midwives often caned the women as they were delivering the baby, believing that it sped up the process. I was there to make sure that did not happen. It was an agonizingly difficult delivery. There was no equipment to monitor the baby's heartbeat, let alone an ultrasound. Eventually, after about seven hours of difficult and intense labor, the baby was delivered. He was a strangely pale little boy, perfectly formed in every way, but curiously immobile. Stillborn.

The shock of this birth and preventable death had me down for days. At home, everyone tiptoed around Emma's room with long faces.

The day my mum left, not much impressed with Ghana and still hoping it was only a phase in my life, I was recovering from a bad attack of malaria when Courage asked to see me. I got up from my sweat-soaked bed and shuffled into the next room. Kwame had been gone all day on some errand, and I was hoping he would soon be home and bring me some soup. I had been calling his mobile phone, but it seemed to be out of coverage. In any case, the phone lines here were notoriously unpredictable.

"I know who has been informing Maa and Dada."

"What?" Who?" I sat up straight. *Yes!* I thought to myself, and mentally punched the air. I had been convinced that the gossip machine would eventually bring us the information. I was a hundred percent sure they had planted an informant in OAfrica; the threatening emails and text messages were so well informed about my daily life. Who could it be?

I looked around the room. All the teenagers were standing around, looking worried. No one seemed to be missing except Emma, who was still in bed, recovering.

"It's someone close to you, Mama Lisa."

The kids looked apprehensive. I could see that breaking the news had been a controversial decision for the group. Some of them fidgeted uncomfortably and looked as if they would rather be anywhere on earth than in that hot, dark room with me.

"It's Kwame."

My head reeled with confusion about who this was. It was, after all, a common name in Ghana.

"Which Kwame?"

But I knew the answer when I searched the kids' faces. *My husband was the informant.*

As the story came tumbling out, it got worse. Kwame had another "wife." He had already been engaged when he was forced to marry me. Maa and Dada had wanted to have a hold on me, and thought my marriage to him was the best way to secure my never-ending support to their orphanage. Initially he had not wanted to marry me, because he was already involved with a woman, but they had bullied him into submission. They had connived with him to seduce me, and believed they would have access to my money through him.

It was a real conspiracy. Things had started to go badly wrong with their plan when it became clear that, unlike most orphan tourists, I was actually going to come and live in Ghana and supervise the use of the money. They had imagined that I would live in Europe and visit on occasional holidays; that Kwame could stay cozily married to his local wife while they all spent my money as they wished, with impunity. They had not foreseen that I would actually open an NGO with a local board, put in financial controls, and insist on the measurement of results.

These new details about the couple's capacity for evil were simply additions to the long list of unthinkable things Maa and Dada had already done to me. Kwame's betrayal, however, was much more upsetting. My throat went dry and my stomach contracted. Kwame's lies affected me as a woman, not as a philanthropist, reaching much more deeply into my heart than anything Maa or Dada could ever do.

"Who is she?" I whispered.

"Sister Angela."

Her face floated in front of my eyes. She was a plump young junior staffer whom I remembered from my first visit to Awutiase.

"Johnny is with her now," Courage told me.

So many things suddenly made sense. The unexplained long absences that I had put down to the terrible logistics of living in Ghana, and traffic. The fact that he had not seemed as distraught at Johnny's departure as I had thought he would be. The coldness in and out of bed. Despite myself, I understood. How could the tenuous hold of his new wife, whom he had been coerced into marrying, match that of the woman he did love?

The only advantage to him of our marriage was his perceived access to unlimited cash. However, they quickly realized that I had a tight hold on my budget and monitored every penny. Their Machiavellian double-cross had been a flop.

"But wait," I asked the older kids. "What about when we were in Spain, and Kwame told me all that stuff about Maa and Dada? He seemed sincere."

Yes, the kids knew about that. They believed that for a moment he had actually tried to break away from the hold Awutiase had on him and align with me, simply (they were quick to clarify) because he thought it might be more beneficial for him. In the end, however, Maa and Dada had used Johnny as a negotiating tool, and he had come back to their side.

I felt dizzy. The level of double- and triple-crossing was confusing. For the first time in my life, I was forced to look greed, the bastard offspring of poverty and ignorance, straight in the face. All this had been done with the sole purpose of getting access to my supposed wealth. The irony was that after almost a year and a half involved with the children in Ghana, my personal money was fast running out.

In Ghana, sadly, marriages for money seemed to be par for the course; after all, whenever one of the foreigners so much as left the house, they were proposed to. By now I was familiar with the sex tourism industry in Ghana, the so-called rent-a-dread trade, whereby handsome young guys (usually with dreadlocks) pimped themselves out to older foreigners, both men and women. I knew it existed, but I hadn't thought that it was part of *my* marriage bed. I felt ashamed.

When Kwame arrived a little later, all the pent-up anger I held inside exploded. In the best tradition of Bette Davis, I slapped him across the face. I thrust a suitcase into his hands and sent him packing back whence he had come. There were going to be no second chances; I was done with him.

The anger carried me through the sadness, the regret, the shame of feeling like an idiot. It carried me through the court proceedings and the divorce, and even the summons to the Women and Juvenile Unit, the police department that usually dealt with domestic violence. Kwame had reported that I had slapped him.

I sat on a wooden bench outside the police commander's room with a couple of the teenagers who had escorted me. The irony of the situation was not lost on me. I had been taken for a fool, fleeced like a lamb, and mentally tortured by these people, and *they* were reporting *me?* The whole thing was more slapstick than tragedy.

I was aware of the racism in the civil service and the administration; my work at OAfrica meant that I encountered anti-white prejudice constantly. Many middle-class Ghanaians were thrilled to have an *obruni* "at their mercy" so to speak, and delighted in making things as difficult as possible. Again, the memory of colonialism haunted me. Who could blame them? If I were a Ghanaian, I would be a whole lot more pissed off than they were. Even today foreigners control the bauxite, gold, and aluminum in the country. Foreigners made the profits on the biggest and deepest gold mine in the world. The World Bank's economic adjustments had created famine and scarcity. By now I knew the backstory well.

I was therefore prepared for the female police officer's sneer. I asked why we were there, since Kwame was nearly thirty, so not a juvenile and not a woman either. This made her eyes twinkle despite herself. Someone in the back snickered.

She asked Kwame to present his case. Without Maa to egg him on, he was lost for words and practically inarticulate. Despite myself, I felt sorry for him.

"So you beat him?" the police officer asked as she turned to me. She was obviously enjoying this.

"I slapped him once, across the face, like this." I demonstrated on myself, a bit of slapstick that the audience loved. There was an audible wave of merriment through the room. "Because he had another wife and was hiding her from me." The audience gasped.

I knew they would like that. My married life was like a *telenovela*, and Ghanaians loved those dramatic over-the-top shows imported from Mexico and shown ceaselessly on daytime national TV. Ghana is a polygamous society, so it was not the fact that he had another wife that they were reacting to, as I well knew. The law allowed him up to four wives. It was the fact that I had not been informed; an unforgivable breech of etiquette. Manners were so important here.

By this point, I weighed 125 pounds for my five feet six inches. I was skinny and must have looked drained. The continued death threats and threatening emails had upset me. My long blond hair was covered, making my blue eyes look enormous in my emaciated face, set off by a demure white *kabba* and *slit*. White, by the way, symbolized victory and joy in Ghana. The children had given me strict instructions: a head wrap, no cleavage, nothing short, no arms showing, but a tightly cinched waist. The result was chaste nun gone va-va-voom. Kwame was a broad-shouldered farmer well over six feet, lean but strong and muscular. I slipped off my high heels and walked over to my soon to be ex-husband. I barely reached his armpit.

"Madame," I said, "do you really think *I* could beat *him*?"

By now the rest of the room was in convulsions of laughter. The case was dismissed.

I was proud of myself. I was beginning to understand what made this country tick, however crazy that was.

With Kwame gone for good, I settled myself in to a small room in the orphanage. I painted it pink, and dedicated myself full-heartedly to the children.

* * *

Within a few weeks I had a new darling to attend to. Her name was Beliratu, and the first thing she did was to bite me. She was carried through the door with her leg in a cast from thigh to toes, followed by her adult sister. I sat down next to her and tried to hug and welcome her. She bit and punched me; a first. The Mama Lisa magic was clearly not working on this young lady. I would have to think of something else. She wore an old ragged blue dress, which hung slightly off one of her shoulders. It was striped and had a print of what looked like white birds taking flight, although they had turned a musky gray color due to the dust. Her left leg bent awkwardly inward, as if she were trying to sit cross-legged. Her right leg was straight out in front of her, wrapped from thigh to foot in a cast. Her hair was shaved very short, like all young girls in Ghana, and she had two thick dark tribal scars cut horizontally into her cheeks, just below her eyes. The empty look she gave was as bare as her feet, though just as strong and resistant. She was tough, and I was unsure who was more intimidated, this injured little girl or me.

We made them comfortable in a corner of the main hall. The sister spoke some Twi like the other children, but Beliratu only spoke Mampruli, her tribal language. They had never seen a house with indoor plumbing, windows, doors, light switches, and beds. It was a huge learning curve for both of them, but the little girl in particular was like a frightened animal striking out at anyone who came near her. The social worker called me outside and told me what had occurred. Beliratu, who they thought was around nine years old, was hit by a car while selling water in the busy street out in front of the Tema bus station, where she was taking refuge with many other women and children. Like numerous other girls her age, she had been sent to the capital from her rural village in the north of Ghana to work the streets for money to bring back home.

I later saw the conditions of the open-air bus station where she was living, and even later had an encounter with the man "in charge" of all those women and girls. I can honestly say that being hit by a car was probably the best thing that had ever happened to Beliratu. It was her ticket out of that place, where rape and violence was a daily occurrence. The driver who hit her immediately took her to the hospital and offered to pay for treatment for her broken knee. A social worker was called onto the case, and she concluded that Beliratu's family had neglected her and put her in danger, so she could not return to them. Knowing OAfrica's good reputation, the social worker called us to take her to our children's home, where she would receive proper care and an education.

After the first few days, one of our staff took the older sister back to the north of Ghana to report to her tribal elders what had happened to Beliratu. We intended to set her up with an income-generating activity in her village, so that she would not have to face the rigors of the annual ritual of economic migration to Accra. As the village culture in the north of Ghana has evolved from one of farming and barter to a money culture, in which modern things such as plastic buckets and aluminum pans have become the must-have status symbols for women of marriageable age, the migration of teenage northern girls to Accra and Kumasi has become a rite of passage.

In some villages it is an annual event during the dry season, when there is not much to do on the farms. This exposes the girls to rape, AIDS, pollution, violence, and dangers such as the car that knocked down Beliratu. It also affects the village, with fewer women present to ensure family life, child care, and the maintenance of the houses, traditionally a woman's job. And they are leaving home at younger and younger ages; when Beliratu was taken to live in the bus station and become a porter, or *kayayo*, who sold water, she was only seven. At the age I was in school plays, she was cowering at night in the shadow of her sister, sleeping rough and working full time.

There are no words to describe the eerie feeling that crept through my veins when I heard Beliratu moan the first night after her sister left. It was not quite a lament, nor was she crying, but everyone in the house understood the melodious utterance as one of pain and fear.

Obviously my presence terrified the poor girl. A strange *obruni* who didn't speak her language had come to take her away. She began hysterically singing that same mourning song whenever I walked into the room. If not for her cast, she would have hightailed it out of the house.

I finally found a way to distract her when I handed her my first digital camera that someone had given me as a gift. She sat there in silence, curious, and then took multiple self-portraits: of her foot, her eyes, her mouth. She would then look at the photos on the screen and smile. I realized from then on that to keep her smiling, all I needed to do was bring out my camera. Just because she had lived through more adult experiences than children her age ever should, she was still a little girl amused and distracted by toys.

Beliratu was the most beautiful little girl I had ever seen. She emitted a light that is hard to explain, and when she smiled, your heart just melted. Those big powerful eyes stared at you, full of curiosity, courage, and experiences that we could never imagine. In only a couple of days, I noticed a huge difference in her. She smiled a lot, showed interest in the other children, and was making an effort to learn. Her first words in English were "I am fine." She particularly loved watching the other little girls dance to the African drums, her eyes big, taking in every move, determined to participate eventually. The first time she said my name, I almost had a heart attack. I felt like a mother hearing her baby speak for the first time. But big plates of food and the camera notwithstanding, Beliratu was not yet tamed. Three days later she was reported missing from the house, and by the time we tracked her down, she was almost at the roadside. She had somehow managed to wriggle down the mile-long red dirt track by walking on her elbows, dragging her leg in its cast behind her.

22

Since Brenya's death, health care in the orphanages had become an obsession for me. Babies died easily and far too soon. Parasites such as intestinal worms killed. Anemia killed, particularly girls. Mammals and reptiles and microbes killed. Above all, AIDS killed.

Nobody in my new world seemed to simply catch a cold; every single disease that came to our attention seemed to be life threatening. Except the blasted scabies outbreak that was just annoying, and which meant we had to burn all the clothes and sheets and paint every child head to toe with a white ointment (which they thought was a fun new game). Matthias, a doctor from Mexico, and Winnie, a Dutch nurse, traveled to our infirmaries at Osu, Famenya, God's Grace, and then to our own stand-alone infirmary that was open to the public as well. By this time, with the increase in the number of HIV-positive kids in our care, the focus at OAfrica was on antiretroviral therapy (ART) access. A month's course on the black market in Ghana was $400, and we had identified least twenty kids who needed the medication. Needless to say, we didn't have that kind of money.

I took a short course in Spain on pediatric AIDS, and we attempted to sort out the different currents of thought: starting the drugs early, waiting as long as possible, or not starting them at all. The medical community was divided, and we were confused. We knew that you tested the CD4 cell count in the blood to decide when to start medication, and then you tested for the amount of the virus in the blood, known as the "viral load." This enabled you to make an informed decision about the real state of health of the patient. This was important because the ARTs themselves are very strong, and if the patient was too weak, the drugs could kill instead of save. Yet the viral load test was not available in Ghana. We had no way of testing for this indicator unless we sent the blood overseas; even then we didn't have the ARTs. On the worst days I felt as if we had opened a charity for children who were going to die.

We reached out to Luc Montagnier in Paris and HIV units at various hospitals in Europe for help with drug supplies. In the meantime we offered palliative care including good food, nutritional supplements, lots of rest, and medication for opportunistic infections like pneumonia and TB. In just a few months I got used to being around stricken babies, although I had always thought of myself as a terrible nurse. Then Mathias, who was always researching our options, came up with a small miracle: a cheap generic antibiotic called co-trimoxazole that supported the child's immune system if taken daily. Almost immediately we saw a change for the better in the patients he treated. It was our first glimmer of hope.

The biggest health challenges were at OAfrica, since the only reason most of the orphanages referred children to us was if they feared they had no possible future. Osu actually had enough to fill a van. A green minivan had replaced our orange car, which Awutiase had taken back. The day I went to pick them up, I settled back into my seat and looked around the van as we pulled out of the forecourt. I had never seen so many desperately ill children. No worries,

I thought to cheer myself up; OAfrica could do wonders. At Ghana's Department of Social Welfare headquarters, I had learnt that we had a nickname. With typical Ghanaian deadpan humor, they didn't call us OAfrica. Instead they called us Last Stop. OAfrica was these kids' chance at life, and I was determined that we should stay true to our nickname. If they thought we were professional miracle workers, I was unwavering in my resolution that we should be.

Our successes were earning us huge respect in the areas of child protection and care. Even today social workers in the head office in Accra will evoke the names of some of those children as examples of what can be done with proper food and medical care. These were cases in which everyone had lost hope.

There was the baby who had been abandoned in the forest and who arrived with rotting maggots under her skin.

There was Paa Kwesi, abandoned by the roadside and then diagnosed with tuberculosis. Since money wasn't available for medication in the orphanage he lived in, he was confined to quarantine at the age of three, with no human contact; he was fed from a bowl pushed through a hole cut in the door. After living in these inhumane conditions for two years, Paa Kwesi was of course deeply disturbed, nonverbal, autistic and self-harming. We did not know how old he was, due to the extreme malnutrition, but we took a guess that he was five. Paa Kwesi was a classic case of extreme attachment disorder. Attachment theory provides an understanding of how our early relationships with caregivers influence the ways in which we interact with others, and it was the most common, and crucial, psychological trouble we came across, as so many of these small children had been neglected or abandoned babies.

Then there was Naa, a little rascal who also had attachment issues, and who followed me around like a shadow. At night she rocked herself wildly and compulsively in her cot, keening to herself. It was terribly sad to watch.

There was Richard, an absolute skeleton, saved within inches of death. When I brought him through the door, the carer told me flatly that he was going to die. The doctor at the hospital, who could not find a vein large enough to insert the drip, obviously thought the same, but worked (tight-lipped) to save him.

There was a merry little HIV-positive orphan whom I called Ernest, after the man who had plucked him off his dying mother's body; he was strapped to her back in the busy streets of Accra. The man had taken them to Korle-Bu hospital and had effectively saved his life. The only word Ernest would say was *abinci*, which meant "food" in the Hausa language, so that became his nickname. Can you imagine a child so hungry that his name was Food? His only thought was for nourishment, and no doubt that is what pulled him through, despite multi-drug-resistant TB that had us all frantic with worry. I spent day after day with him traveling to the hospital for X-rays of his lungs, hoping for good news—that his TB was in remission.

Eventually all of these children lived and thrived.

There were terrible stories with happy endings, such as HIV-positive Joshua. He was born to a mother who died from AIDS, but we managed to feed him up to a respectable weight. We then sent him back to God's Grace whence he came, as we thought they could maintain him. At three o'clock one morning shortly thereafter, a frantic pounding on the door woke us all up. There was Joshua, dying again before our very eyes. He did pull through, and eventually tested HIV negative. This happens in a resource-poor situation like Ghana's, where babies are tested with simple first-line tests that can give false positives based on the mother's immune status. A tiny baby has its mother's immune system, but as the child grows, its own immune system takes over. If the child is strong and healthy, when you test again the test will read negative. That is the dry factual explanation, but when someone who tested positive suddenly tests negative, there was always something miraculous about it, and a celebration in the house. This of course was before the practice of administering ARTs during birth, a cheap and effective way of ensuring that babies are born HIV free. Nowadays that is the norm, but in 2003 that therapy had not yet been fully rolled out in our corner of sub-Saharan Africa.

And then of course there were the battles we did lose; the sad stories with sad endings. There were other deaths; kids who were referred to us too late. AIDS was a major cause, but also meningitis, malnutrition, anemia, and of course malaria.

Bianca, an Australian volunteer, was absolutely brilliant at caring for the babies. Bianca, whose efficiency and staying power belied the fact she was so pretty and petite, dealt with some remarkable cases. She often slept in the pediatric AIDS ward at Korle-Bu until her patients pulled through. The ward, it seemed to me, was merely a place where the fragile came to die. It was filled with sick children, three or four to a rusty bed, and the space between the beds was encumbered with mothers (usually AIDS patients themselves) or carers sleeping on mats next to the buckets and provisions that they used to feed their children. The understaffed nurses expected family members to do all the actual caring, and no food was provided in the state hospital.

It was a pandemic. The fact that all babies with HIV were born to mothers with HIV further complicated the situation. The health system had never had to deal with so many orphans, or so much sadness; so many sick parents, most of whom had already lost partners or other children. Those days, before ART drugs arrived in Ghana, were unbelievably tragic. Entire crowded wards were wiped out within a few weeks. It was a massacre, and we were on the front line.

I had never seen death, but now my life was soaked in it. Especially after the deception by Kwame and the hate mail from Awutiase, my close friends in Europe asked me, "Why don't you leave?" The answer was simple: there was this huge need, this huge well of despair sucking me in, making it impossible to walk away. In retrospect, actually, I think that my chief virtue was not to give up. Helping people is tough. Humanitarians are doing a very difficult job, and local situations often don't work out as planned. The chief thing is to stick at it and be flexible, because it is incredibly important work.

* * *

Those early days of the epidemic in Africa were terrifying, since the facts around transmission were not understood. At that time the stigma surrounding HIV/AIDS was huge; all the nurses wore gloves and refused to touch or cuddle the patients. People panicked so much that AIDS patients were neglected and literally left to die in the streets. I had no such issues; I had been around people with AIDS continuously since the mid-eighties, and knew normal day-to-day contact could not result in contagion. Everywhere I went, I defiantly doled out hugs and kisses and touched and held dying people, attempting on a tiny scale to lead by example.

Bianca took special care of a tiny baby called Benedicta, who had full-blown AIDS, pneumonia, and possibly TB, which, we had learned from experience went hand in hand with AIDS. Bianca took her to the Trust Hospital one evening as the baby worsened. The nurses could see that Benedicta was a lost cause as she was pale and emaciated, her thin skin stretched over matchstick limbs. But they did not want another death on their books, especially from AIDS. They gave Bianca a prescription for some palliative medication and sent her home. They did not, however, tell her there was no hope. No sooner had Bianca's taxi pulled into the orphanage than Benedicta stopped breathing. Her little life was gone; another statistic of that dreadful disease.

Devastated, Bianca got back into a taxi to take Benedicta's tiny body to the morgue. The Trust Hospital refused her, saying the morgue was full. Although the taxi did not want to carry a dead baby, Bianca finally made it to the 37 Military Hospital, but the morgue there too was full. Bianca dearly wanted to avoid Korle-Bu mortuary, as there were constant scandals in the newspaper about the sale of body parts for voodoo, even recently the sale of human livers to the kebab sellers, but there seemed to be no other option. In the dark night and on the third lap of her horrific journey with the body, Bianca finally laid Benedicta's fragile corpse down in the Korle-Bu morgue. The drunk mortuary attendants walked Bianca, clutching the poor dead baby past row after row of corpses, as they refused to carry the body of an AIDS victim themselves. They joked, alcohol thick on their breath, at the crying *obruni* and the dead child, who was nothing more than a statistic in their ghoulish world.

I could not have done what Bianca did. I knew my limits, which were somewhere between sleeping over for weeks at a local hospital and going to the morgues. I even refused to attend the funerals. There was only so much sadness I could take.

Gradually Bianca and I became friends. After her four months in Ghana were up, before her departure, we had a talk. She wanted to adopt Nana, a little girl whom she'd nursed back from death's door, despite the child's health issues. She wanted to go back to Australia, change her master's degree to development, and come back fully qualified.

"What you are doing here is amazing," she said. "All of those kids would have died without OAfrica. This is transformative."

We looked at each other in silence, and then slowly I got up and hugged her. I knew that we would make a great team. In Beth I had a strong director for the European operation, but I had very few great workers at OAfrica in Ghana. Bianca was my blazing hope. I thought long and hard about my "succession plan." Constant death threats will do that to you.

I realized that the volunteers would have to be phased out, as the constant turnover affected work badly, and that the operations should be completely taken over by Ghanaian teams who knew their country and their traditions. I had to find fully qualified and dedicated people to ensure that OAfrica became Ghanaian in more than its mission statement.

However, the experience at Awutiase had frightened me. It was now understandably difficult for me to trust people, but I knew I had to delegate. We had no other foreign staff by now, as it had become clear that we needed qualified Ghanaian social workers for our work. Foreigners just passing through were looked down upon by those committed irrevocably to their country. The culture was so unique that the learning curve for foreigners was just too long. Like me, foreigners continually got sick with malaria, typhoid, and other tropical diseases; and the cost of flying foreign staff to Ghana simply was not sustainable. But Bianca, as she had so clearly demonstrated, was different. If the free ARTs kicked in, as they were supposed to, these children would have a future and would need schooling, care, career planning, and so on. OAfrica had to expand beyond me and my money. My head spun. I scribbled an organization chart in my diary. Bianca was at the head.

For a while it had seemed that the majority of the babies in our care had HIV and would not survive. Yet we kept hearing that the new Global Fund was due to hand out a dependable free supply of ARTs in all the state hospitals, administered by trained doctors. We waited. Sometime in 2004 it began to seem true. ARTs were available in the state hospital, and for practically nothing. We were almost too depleted of hope to believe it, but gradually instead of a charity for children who were going to die, it seemed as if we might have a charity for children who were going to live. It was an intoxicating feeling; it meant that we could start to plan for the future.

I decided that although this ugly peri-urban area was convenient for Accra, it was not what our kids needed. I wanted more space to construct an ecological community in the countryside, where we could have our own farm to provide us with fruit and vegetables, and to get away from the squatters' community we now lived in. The unstoppable flood of rural migrants from the villages to Accra resulted in ancestral ties being broken, tribal systems breaking down, families scattering, and money replacing ancient barter and exchange systems. The area we lived in near Famenya was home to many of these migrants living in uncompleted buildings. Ghanaians in the diaspora, who were usually those able to afford to build, erected many of the buildings on an incremental basis; bit by bit, when they had the money to do so via remittances. Everywhere you go in the world you will find Ghanaians sending money home and that is what keeps the country afloat.

These unfinished constructions, though, left the surrounding areas dotted with craggy, dilapidated, and roofless cement-block structures whose corners served as refuge for whole families of the rootless poor. Malnutrition was rampant. Clean drinking water was a distant aspiration. That was how most of our neighbors lived, which was not, I decided, a congenial environment for kids whose lives up to that point were already a wreck. But the absolute deal breaker was when I learned there had been a rape on our street. I wanted to move, again.

The Missonis (how I adored that fabulous Italian fashion dynasty) said they would pay for it. The hunt was on for a large piece of land. My criteria were simple: it must be suitable for farming, it must be close to a major hospital with an HIV unit, and it must be close to a deprived village that we could benefit and bring our services to. In early April the intense rainy season finally started, which in the south of the country typically stretched from April until July. Donning my Wellington boots, I started the exciting search for land for the new OAfrica orphanage. I visited ten sites, dreaming of the perfect permaculture design: water and waste recycling, in addition to the incorporation of garden and farm areas with adobe huts.

When the rains started that year, I received the call from Obuasi orphanage that deep inside I had been dreading. I walked away from the garden where I had been playing a game with the children, and listened as the pastor apologetically explained that Sabrina had run away. With a boy. They had no idea where she was. Even worse, it had happened a few days before, but they had waited to see if she would come back before alerting me.

My first thought was that Sabrina was pregnant. My second thought was of the danger she could be in. I sat down on the steps and wept. All I could do was hope that she would turn up on my doorstep, and that she was running *to* me and not *from* me. But somehow I doubted that. I beat myself up about her disappearance. If I had not brought her to Ghana in the first place, she wouldn't have run away. Above all, my determination to dedicate myself to the children was beginning to look like the costliest decision of my life. I just hoped that it was not going to prove life and death kind of costly. My very existence was still threatened daily with anonymous emails, and there were some days I felt like giving up. At that moment Africa seemed very harsh. Here I was with no Sabrina, no Kwame, no Johnny, no children of Awutiase; the very people I moved here for were, as if in a sick joke, all gone out of my life. All my vital relationships lost, stolen, or broken.

Over the next few days, the teenagers brought me snippets of news about Sabrina, all of which sounded made up. She was in Accra dating a Lebanese guy; she was working at the French embassy; she had gone to France. (This I doubted, as I had her passport; she had left it with me for safekeeping.) I called the shrink in Spain, and she underlined that Sabrina was nineteen and an adult. I had to trust her and give her space. I nodded at the phone through my tears. I realized that there was nothing left for me to do but the most difficult thing of all: wait.

23

*V*ictoria Abril and a team from the French TV station TF1 came to visit us in May. She had raised more than €60,000 by appearing on chat shows the previous December, and we had received twenty-five hundred fan letters. We were thrilled, even if our tiny French office had no idea how to cope with such a success.

On that trip to Ghana the journalists made a documentary about Victoria's work with OAfrica, and we had a small fundraising dinner with the French community at the Novotel Hotel in Accra. The troubles in neighboring Côte d'Ivoire meant the French community in Ghana had suddenly swollen to double or triple its usual size. Since money at OAfrica was a perennial problem, Victoria's work was essential to our survival. Despite ARTs at $40 per patient a month instead of $400, the health bills kept mounting. We were caring for so many people with HIV, along with pregnant and nursing mothers.

Victoria is very clever and perceptive, and a close friend; it was such a relief to have her there. We talked about OAfrica, and about Sabrina and what her running away could mean. At this point it had been several months, and I still hadn't heard a word from her despite asking at the embassy, and all the teenagers. Victoria advised that I leave her be, saying that Sabrina would reach out to me in her own time. It was difficult advice to take, but I trusted her common sense.

With Victoria, I was also able to step back and look at the bigger picture for OAfrica, if only for a minute. We had moved on from just caring for orphans to caring for communities. Education, health, nutrition, and family planning: these were common development words that only make sense when you deal with abandoned babies on a daily basis and start to address how to prevent the poverty, ill health, and ignorance that create the situation in the first place. There were literally millions of women in Ghana who wanted contraception and protection from AIDS and could not get it; especially since the Bush administration had cut the funding for government or private campaigns based on condom use, preferring unrealistic abstinence programs. Every day we faced the challenge of knowing that a mother is a hundred times more likely to die in childbirth in Africa than in the developed world.

By the time of her visit I was ready to commit to the move to the countryside, and so we also visited the location I had in mind. I wanted her to buy in.

Finding the right location and the land had been a lovely adventure, *tro-tro*-ing around the surrounding rural communities and exploring. I eventually chose twenty-one acres of gently sloping land near a tiny mud-and-thatch village called Ayenyah, which looked utterly thrown together and of the earth, but was apparently a hundred years old. Unusually, it was a settler community; the people who lived there were of the Ewe tribe who originated in the Volta region, not from the local Shai tribe. I was in luck; the Ewe word for white people was *yevu*, not the hated *obruni*. I later learned that *yevu* meant "trickster dog" but, hey, it would keep me humble.

They had no electricity, but they did have one tap for water access. This meant that the village was linked to the mains, which was important for me. We had suffered so much from shortages in Famenya that water was my priority. The community comprised four neighboring villages, scattered with goats and chickens and umpteen nearly naked children that seemed to be just as carelessly strewn about. The nearest town was Dodowa, the sleepy district capital of the Dangme West District, fifty kilometers from Accra. The roads being what they were, that meant at least an hour-and-a-half commute, but I hoped we would not need to go into the capital too often.

The village was rural, characterized by no access to basic community services: electricity, health, education, or sanitation (there were no toilets whatsoever). There was no shop or even a chop bar, despite its being less than a mile off the main Accra road. Poverty and unemployment levels were high. In fact there was only one visible industry: a spluttering, medieval-looking mill for grinding corn and cassava. For the most part, people just worked on the rainfall-dependent maize and cassava farms, or on the nearby mango plantations.

For this reason, many of the men had emigrated to find work in the gold mines or in Accra. There were about 550 people in the village, of which almost half were children; the rest were mostly women. With no school and no church, Ayenyah seemed basically untouched by the twentieth century, let alone the twenty-first. Victoria agreed with me: it seemed like a place where we could put down roots.

In addition, we were touched by the fact that none of those kids went to school, since the nearest one was an hour's walk away. Almost every single person in that village was illiterate. In Accra you could easily find the diplomats, the United Nations staff, and the droves of volunteers; yet here in the bush, aid workers were unheard of. Even the Ghanaian administration seemed to have overlooked it. We knew we could change that. By the time Victoria left, my mind was made up; we would move here.

Someone else who had become important to me was very enthusiastic about moving: Fatima, a teenager who had been a cattle herder.

She believed we should have our own land too, and raise fat cows! She was eighteen, but in primary six, therefore six years behind at school. Often kids arrived with this kind of lag, and Marlowe's "home school" was there to bring them up to speed. Fatima had two younger brothers in tow, Abdul and Issah, and she was obsessively careful and loving of them. She was the head of the family, clearly. Two other siblings had not been picked up with her, and she worried about them all the time.

The dynamic headmistress at Famenya primary school had referred Fatima and her siblings to the police as she suspected child labor, due to the fact that the children attended school very sporadically. They came from a patrilineal tribe, the Fulani, who were transborder nomads and Muslims. In those societies when your father died, as hers had, you had no protection. Their mother had been banned from their uncle's house and the children had been kept there to tend cattle, effectively little more than slaves. Fatima was always anxious; she had an ulcer, and later caught pneumonia. Her family had installed in her a great fear of voodoo and black magic spells, as well as the virtues of different herbs.

Fatima could look at any cow shrewdly and tell you its value, but she knew nothing about modern life. She had never owned new clothes or a school bag or books. When she saw the library, she stood still in amazement with her eyes open wide. "Storybooks?" she asked me, her eyes shining.

"Yes, Fatima, you can come and read them anytime you want."

She could not believe there were books available at will, or food either, for that matter. Actually, she had never sat at a dinner table before. In the bush the vast herds of people just huddled over their bowls, always eating alone, so there was nothing like the cheerful communal meals at the house. Dinnertime became one of Fatima's favorite rituals.

When we showed Fatima her first film on my computer (we did not yet have a TV), she grabbed my hand tightly and became so immersed in the story that whenever the hero was about to walk into a trap, she would literally jump up and down pleading, "Mum, you have to tell him, he should not do that—it's dangerous!" She literally could not distinguish this lifelike moving picture from reality.

Her innocence was touching. We first became close when, as we shared a bathroom, I noticed she did not own a bra. I gave her one of mine, and she wore it and treasured it for years. I also initiated her into the mysteries of modern feminine hygiene. Traditionally Ghanaian women use pieces of torn-up cloth as sanitary protection. They are strung between their legs and suspended from the rows of beads they wear around their waists. Naturally she thought sanitary towels were a fantastic invention.

A few months after she arrived, her little brother Abdul was hospitalized at Korle-Bu with a massive cerebral hemorrhage. I knew that if we had not been in their lives, Abdul surely would not have survived. Before he had come to us, we learned that he had experienced epileptic episodes, which were attributed to sorcery. According to the local witch doctor, the cure was to live with him, drink herbal concoctions, and participate in rituals. Needless to say, the attacks only got worse. The witch doctor had concluded that Abdul was possessed, and submitted the child to gruesome exorcisms. When this story came out in bits and pieces over the years, I appreciated the fear and responsibility that Fatima had been carrying. Slowly she became my "eldest daughter" in the house. We needed each other. Life had been unkind to her, and I knew that hers was a life I could definitely save. A future I could assure. A family I could transform.

Hurt from Sabrina's disappearance, and still missing Johnny horribly, I was slow to let any of the other children become too close. I lived with them in the same house, like a loving auntie, but hadn't allowed myself to become emotionally involved with any one child. I had tried hard not to have any favorites, but Fatima changed that. I felt that through her, her younger siblings could benefit from my support. She had missed out on her childhood, caring for the rest of the family. The warrior inside me wanted to give her some of that care back.

The other child who gravitated toward me was Mensah, who was around fourteen. He was naturally caring and sensitive, and I suspected that he could sense my hurt and despair over Sabrina's defection, although I always tried to be brave in front of the children. Mensah began appearing and simply asking for chores to do. He was there to carry my basket, or go to get a photocopy. He was there to remove a mound of puppies or children from my bed. He was there to translate to the cook or fix a bicycle wheel. He was there to set up the TV when one was finally donated. He made himself indispensible. I trusted Mensah; over the years he too was to become my foster child.

There is no paperwork, even ten years later, to clarify or formalize the bond because we never felt the need. Yet these are my children, unmistakably. These two unrelated teens, Fatima and Mensah, both sought me out, and generously chose to give me a place and a role in their lives. I had no will then to adopt or take care of a child, since the drama with Johnny and Sabrina had left me all mashed up inside. But these two, out of the more than a hundred children and teens with whom I have shared a roof, did not give me a choice. They chose me and believed in me. As emotionally drained as I was, I could only hope that their belief might prove well founded.

It became clear to me that when we moved to Ayenyah, the young adults from Awutiase would not be moving with us. They needed things the countryside could not provide, like secondary and tertiary education, job opportunities, and mentoring and career choices.

Together we outlined what eventually became our young adults program.

Since my arrival in Ghana I had spent a lot of time listening to people. This, however, had not served me well at Awutiase, as I had been too respectful and circumspect to the point of closing my eyes (albeit for a short time) to human rights abuses. Now I tried to listen respectfully, but without being duped. The young adults needed mentoring, so I let them recruit their own leaders, whom I paid. They needed exposure, so we included lots of fun and educational excursions so they could get an idea of what was out there. They needed quality education, so we provided special tutoring to help them catch up from all the years of lousy education. They also needed to live independently within the community, not in an orphanage, so they could begin weaving the complex social networks that constitute an adult life.

OAfrica provided all of this, but not without problems. The young adults from Awutiase expected that every one of their needs would be provided for, whereas OAfrica's by now fully Ghanaian staff expected they would get summer jobs, internships, and the like, and not be totally dependent.

In a sense, it was the first of our programs to be outlined and carried out. This Young Adult Support Services program, or YASS as we call it now, still remains one of the most innovative and dynamic youth programs in the country. There are over three hundred graduates and seventy-seven currently on support. We focus on counseling, secondary and tertiary education, how to devise a business plan, and how to operate a small business.

The rest of the children, mostly babies and disabled and HIV-positive children, would have to move with us, as the rent on our house at Famenya was going to be increased. The rent advance (in Ghana you pay one or two years in advance, instead of monthly) was so huge that I knew I could build a large house in Ayenyah for the same price.

I was eager to avoid referrals to Korle-Bu, as that giant hospital was always overcrowded and ineffective. We were excited about rumors that Ghana would introduce a national health insurance system that would cover the cost of ART treatment. All of a sudden, we felt that we were not alone in trying to keep these children alive. The children we had put on ART on an experimental basis were making impressive progress, growing and gaining weight. A future for them now seemed possible; the worst days of the epidemic were surely behind us. I wanted them to grow up in the village with lots of fresh air, home-grown food, and space to run around. The idea of growing our own food and improving the diet was a huge motivation for the move.

The time had come for me to be "officially" introduced to the chief of the village. After all, this was Ghana, and things had to be done properly. The chief was an old man with a round face whose short stature was draped in twelve yards of lovely muted woven *kente* cloth. Ewe *kente*, I learned, was less brightly colored than the Ashanti version, but equally venerated.

I sat in his compound—three dilapidated mud structures and a palm-leaf awning—on plastic chairs (sourced from all over the village) with a few OAfrica staff and a group of his elders. As tradition demanded, there were two linguists; one for him and one for me. Traditionally thought of as a kind of demigod, a chief could never be addressed directly. *Don't cross your legs and don't use your left hand*, I reminded myself, since both were unacceptable gaffes. The elders all stood up and shook hands, left to right, I noted, the opposite of the Akans. The Ewes were patrilineal; a whole new culture for me. The linguists, as per the ritual, asked us our business and we handed over a couple of bottles of schnapps. Then we started talking. I said that we wanted to settle here with about sixty children, build homes for foster families, contribute to the community, and live with them.

I asked him what the community lacked, and what they wanted. In the beginning in Ghana, I had listened to long lists of requests because I felt guilty for all the wrong my ancestors had done here. A white person can feel perpetually guilt-ridden here; ancestral guilt and, more prosaically, for being able to buy a car, for going to a restaurant, for having shoes, for having choices. It is difficult to rise above that.

"We need a school," his son, an obviously ambitious middle-aged man who had been introduced as Jonathan, interrupted eagerly. "We have tried several times to build one, but we can never finish it. Let me show you."

We walked over to a large piece of land on the outskirts of the village. The mud foundations, using the rammed earth technique, were there all right, about knee height.

"What if," I wondered aloud, "the chief gives us the land, we build on the site, and then hand it over to you as a school?" There was a lot of translating and further talk, but eventually a conclusion was reached, and it was decided.

The villagers looked delighted. We drank to that, and there was more handshaking all around. We were in, and I had a plan. The twenty-one acres to be bought by the Missonis had not yet been linked to the water mains, and it would probably take several months for that to happen, since the paperwork in Ghana was notoriously complex. Why not move the children into temporary buildings that we could throw up quickly and that could eventually be given to the village as a school? This would enable me to move house quickly, while showing the villagers that I was serious.

A carpenter I'd met, Patrick Senyo, was a specialist in thatch. He said he could handle it, and in early 2005 the work began. Patrick and I turned out to have a very compatible vision. Working with him was a delight; only just literate, he was however hugely visual and very inspired. I had the ideas and he had the hands. He was an

Ewe and, thankfully, took over much of the communication between OAfrica and the chief's place. The villagers were happy since not only was the school being built, but they were also being paid for their labor to build it. Within four months Patrick had completed a beautiful compound to our specifications, for the price of a large car (or two years' rent advance).

We had run a design competition among the kids (child participation always being my war cry) and Beliratu won. She drew a huge summer hut surrounded by other smaller huts. This pattern echoed the arrangement of the huts in the polygamous Mamprusi tribal areas where she had been born.

This gave me another idea. I adored the frescoed mud houses in Bolgatanga, in northern Ghana, that featured heavily in the Brandt guidebook. Why not bring the house painters—the old women who painted the houses with dung, tar, chalk, and herbal juices in the dry season—down to Ayenyah to decorate the buildings? Heavily fueled by gin, the ancient old lady artists bent over their cauldrons to mix their dyes. They stamped our buildings with an unforgettable character all their own. This frescolike technique reinforced the walls and made them hard and resistant to rain and termites, as well as provided beautiful pieces of art you could live in. The women's designs were highly symbolic; they depicted cows and eyes for wealth, patterns to symbolize woven cloth for leadership, and sprigs of millet for fertility.

I enjoyed this time so much: designing, working in mud, being in the countryside, creating a healthy life and a refuge for the children. Since I had moved to Ghana, my creative side had been stifled under so much pain and loss and sickness and business that had consumed all of my energy. It was exhilarating to roam the village with my dogs, nodding at my soon-to-be neighbors, building a beautiful new home for the kids.

The site was also profoundly ecological: solar panels for energy, dry toilets with the waste being dried by the sun's heat, and use of sawdust for composting. I was delighted, and truly happy. All the kids were excited as we took them on site visits. Their exuberance was contagious. For once, despite the continued death threats, life seemed to smile.

*　*　*

However, Sabrina was on my mind. It seemed pretty clear from various sources that she was in Paris now. Finally she reached out via email. She told me that she had simply reported her passport stolen at the French embassy in Accra, and had been issued a new one. She had left for Paris at once. She was living there with her sister, the only person she knew well enough in Paris to crash with. As relieved I was to know she was safe, I was worried that she was being sucked into her birth family's struggles with the law, the social services, and life itself. Some memories do not fade with time but become more painful, like knives. Thus it was with me when I remembered how Sabrina's birth family had treated her. But I was in no position to advise her, as she had run away from me. I calmly asked her to let me know when she was ready to see me. For once, I gave up the struggle for control. Ghana had taught me a lot about letting go. Surprisingly, instead of falling apart, things with Sabrina actually started to get better from that moment on.

24

*O*ctober 2005. Suddenly it was the beginning of the dry season, and our lease in Famenya was up. OAfrica was three years old and ready for a proper home. We were days away from the epic move, but we still had no water at our lovely new site. Everyone was packed up and ready to go, but I knew I could not take the carers, staff, children, and babies to the village without running water. Phone calls by Mensah and visits by my staff to the Ghana Water Company had proved fruitless; a lot of promises, but nothing coming out of the brand spanking new tap proudly planted in the middle of our lovely mud-and-thatch compound. So I decided to go in person, in full regalia, and beg them to give us water.

I got into the direct *tro-tro* to Dodowa and they dropped me off close to the Water Company offices. There was a shortcut through the forest, the driver's mate assured me, indicating by waving his hand in some obscure direction toward the trees. In my impeccable outfit and highish heels, I tottered along through the massive jungle rather gingerly. I was not dressed for a forest detour. Eventually the forest path evolved into a paved road sloping upward toward where the Water Company office was apparently located. I would have liked to check that I was headed in the right direction, but there was no one else around.

I was angry at the delay, and under such pressure to get sixty kids and fifteen staff to Ayenyah the following morning. I was literally stomping my way down this deserted road in the middle of the jungle, mindless of my surroundings. I was going to get that water connected or else. I was busy being indignant and thinking bad thoughts about bureaucrats when suddenly, about five yards ahead of me, a brown and gray python as thick as my arm slid lazily off a ginormous tree by the roadside, plopping onto the tarmac and casually sliding across the road. Its length was a little longer than the total width of the road; so long that I did not see its tail-end appear on the tarmac on my right until his head had disappeared into the bush on my left.

I stopped stock-still. *That was one big snake.* But I reasoned it was late afternoon, and I had to get my water turned on. Who knew where that snake was now in the thick undergrowth? Behind me? In front? Waiting to pounce? He was so fast although he appeared to move indolently. Muttering, "Pythons have no venom," I waited a few minutes and then darted up the road as if I was being chased by all the devils in hell. When I arrived in the remote Water Company office, they were caught off-guard by the nicely dressed white lady, all alone and without a car, sweating and muttering incoherently about being chased by snakes. Taking pity on me, they immediately connected the water. All it took was a one-minute phone call from the boss, comfortably seated behind his big desk. Finally we could move to our new life.

Settling in took a while, as my vision of living off the grid and growing our own food didn't take off with the staff as I had hoped. Upwardly mobile Africans aspire to an urban life. The city offers hope, a better life; moving to the village was a step backward in their book. The children took a while to fit in with the villagers; there were even a lot of fights at first. But soon we started a very intense sports program that basically brought the kids from OAfrica and the kids from Ayenyah together. This program was later taken over by the Laureus Sport for Good Foundation, and with its life skills and HIV-prevention components, went a long way to easing the tensions. By then I had met a man who was to prove vital to OAfrica: Marcel Desailly, the Ghanaian-born French international football player.

"Who," I had asked Beth, "is the most well-known Ghanaian in the world?"

"Umm . . ." She looked at me worriedly. Was this a trick question? "Kofi Annan?" she asked.

Okay. The head of the United Nations. "Who else?"

"Marcel Desailly."

"Who?"

I had never heard of him, having given up following the sport when I moved away from football-crazed Barcelona when I was eighteen. She explained that he was one of the most decorated players in the world.

"Right," I said, "I'll call him." And I did; him and Kofi Annan. The odd thing is that they both said the same thing; they would have time for OAfrica when they retired. Being a football player, Marcel's retirement came first.

When I read that he had hung up his boots for good that season, I called him back. He had no time, he said, but we could meet on a plane. So we flew from Milan to Accra together as I was returning from pre-Christmas fundraising. We chatted the whole flight as fans flitted around taking photos. By the time I went through the airport VIP lounge exit with him in Accra, he had agreed to host a charity match that December 2005 to raise money for OAfrica. Managing celebrities was, after all, what I was known for. After that, he and his wife had a bunch of our children over to their luxurious house for swimming and pasta; and after that, there was no turning back. He has supported us ever since.

It was Marcel who hooked me up with Laureus, which has also supported us ever since. Marcel visited us in the village often, and that helped seal our standing in the community. Football, it seemed, was the way to Ayenyah's heart. However, education was to prove the way to its soul.

After a few months we kept our pledge to the villagers, and formed a school under a tree while we started to build a three-classroom block. The village children, who had roamed freely all their lives, were slightly taken aback at having to sit on benches all day. My heart went out to them. I felt like the evil force of modernization in Chinua Achebe's masterpiece *Things Fall Apart*. I loved the kids' wild village existence, but I thought that if one thing should be allowed to disrupt it, that was education. This way at least they stood a chance of being able to read Achebe for themselves one day.

Our small-scale OAfrica care facility for children with special needs or victims of abuse allowed us to research best practices. That in addition to the fledging school, the sports program, the fully staffed infirmary, and the permaculture farm was our life.

Slowly we all got used to it. The children got used to school, including the sitting still component, and the teachers could finally spend more time teaching than chasing the kids back into the classroom. The village parents got used to not having the free family labor that kids provided on the farm. And my staff got used to village life; chickens wandering in the kitchen, lanterns instead of electric light, and no shops. We *all* got used to the compost toilets I had insisted on. The ridiculous water shortages meant that water-based toilets just weren't an option. The dry compost toilets were perfect

in my opinion; there was a long drop, and you just sprinkled sawdust on the waste. There was no smell, and the by-product could be
used as compost for the trees on our farm.

My faith in this system was rewarded with a three-page article on
our toilets, "Komposttoiletten," in a scholarly German magazine. Toilets were a big deal in development, where waste disposal and water
wastage were burning issues. From that moment on, blond young
men in short shorts would turn up two or three times a year, ear-
nestly waving the magazine and asking to see our toilets. The OAfrica mothers thought it was hilarious. Traveling all the way to Africa
to look at our toilets? Did they not have toilets in their own country?

The children enjoyed the farm, which I was painstakingly
designing along permaculture lines, with a mixed orchard and
organic practices. They loved picking fruit, climbing trees, and their
favorite pastime (gulp), chasing snakes and scorpions. Whenever
one was spotted there would be excited shouts. In all these years
we've had only one snakebite, thank goodness.

One day the villagers turned up with a tiny monkey. He was a
baby orphan, way too young to survive, so I fed him drops of milk
from a syringe. The children baptized him "Monkiki," and he was
my constant companion for years; sitting on my shoulder or swinging from the rafters, making an uneasy truce with Puppy, Zara, and
Victor (my dogs).

Everyone appreciated the quiet—interrupted only by the weekly
drumming at fetish ceremonies in the village and the *gong-gong*, the
cymbal-banging denoting the town crier in charge of keeping all the
village up to date with important announcements from the chief—
the long nights, the days that ticked by according to the rhythm of
the seasons.

I loved the village life. I lived alone in a round mud hut in the
main OAfrica building. The next round hut served as my solar-power

office-cum-sitting room. When people came to visit they would have
to shove snoozing dogs off the sofa, and the heat often lay so heavily
across the village at midday that I would end up working at night. A
single bulb allowed me to read and research. The children wandered
in and out of that tiny circle of light and I showed them photos on the
screen, much to their delight. We would have little chats. Fatima and
Mensah were close by. With only sixty kids in our building, it felt like
one big family. There were fewer deaths and then, thankfully, no
deaths for a year, and then two, then three as the ARTs started working. Finally things became more peaceful.

Nearly two years after Kwame's departure, I had started seriously dating a Ghanaian photographer called Kweku. He was
younger than me, in his mid-twenties, which had really put me off
initially. But I realized that I needed a life outside of the endless,
urgent world of the charity and the children's imperatives. Our relationship was a release, and it was healing. He was artistic and creative, very sensitive and intelligent; different in every way to the
tougher types I had met in Ghana. He was modern, a free thinker,
and he did not seem to have one foot in the 1950s like many of the
adults I dealt with on a daily basis. He knew about pictures and
fashion, but also about Ghana; it was as if he was a bridge between
my old life and the new. Marcel teased me mercilessly about being a
cougar, but our precious if rare weekends away made life sparkle a
little brighter. I was grateful to Kweku, who was truly affectionate
and sensual. I felt like a whole person again in his arms. As a chief's
son, our relationship was frowned upon by his family, but we stayed
the course.

OAfrica was phasing out of running its programs in various private orphanages, which continued to be beset with difficulties. However, our youth program in Accra was up and running, and our
scholarship scheme had expanded to 280 children countrywide, most

of whom were in orphanages. But a stray email was about to change what we did, forever.

One day one of my Spanish board members sent me a file. It was called "A Last Resort: The Growing Concern about Children in Residential Care," published by the well-respected charity Save the Children. It was only twenty-three pages long, but it changed everything for me. Reading it was like a blow to my solar plexus. I clearly remember finishing the report and then walking down the long dry red-dust road to the village with the sun beating down on me, feeling dazed by the implications of what I had just read. It talked about how orphanages were actually bad for children, and should be a last resort. My eyes were opened; this resonated for me. I relived my memories of Awutiase, God's Grace, a horrible orphanage I had visited called Rastahome. As I walked into the orphanages we monitored I no longer saw a place of safety. Now I saw a place where children were not listened to, where they had been separated from their family, where their rights were being abused, where the belief system of the majority trampled on the rights of the minority.

This was an epiphany for me. With great clarity I saw what was wrong. I knew that most of the children in the institutions were not orphans; that they were there in the hope of getting food and education and rudimentary health care, because their families were too poor to take care of them. In fact in indigenous Ghana the concept of orphanhood did not even exist, because the extended family and clan networks were so strong. What I was seeing in the private orphanages, across the board, was a double deception: the families were deceived into giving up their children, and the donors were deceived into supporting children that they honestly believed were orphans. Some of the orphanages had no doubt been started with the best of intentions, like the pastor's at Obuasi, and just slid into abuse because, as the document clearly stated, the concept of shutting up abandoned children all together is intrinsically wrong. Other orphanages had been started by criminals who obviously saw children as money on legs: an asset, easy to transport, easy to sell, and with a ready market.

The journalist in me kicked in. I traveled to the only big Internet café in Accra and trawled the Internet for more information. I stumbled on "A Family Is for a Lifetime: A Discussion of the Need for Family Care for Children Impacted by HIV/AIDS." More of the same. Children need families; orphanages never provide love, only paid care. It was difficult for me to admit that I'd been mistaken. But suddenly I could see, as clear as daylight, that my ten-point plan was all wrong. I had to tear it up and start over.

I realized then that I only needed a one-point plan: *get kids out of orphanages and into families.* It was not only what I was reading of course; it was the nearly four years of experience in seven different orphanages, all with the same problems. Everything I was reading came alive, jumping off the page at me. I had actually seen it for myself, and had the proof blazed on my retinas. In all the orphanages I had visited there were corporal punishment, hygiene issues, overcrowding, nutrition deficiencies, and as I was beginning to realize, human rights abuses, sexual abuse, and identity issues.

The culture of a closed environment with strict rules of unquestioning obedience to the elders, and sanctioned forms of abuse such as beating children, makes it very easy for sexual predators to maneuver. As I read the words on the screen, I saw images: Emma starved because she was pregnant; little kids crying because they missed their mothers; babies neglected because the staff were uneducated and undercompensated; and, most terrifying of all, child-on-child sexual and physical abuse. Locking up damaged children in large groups would never be the solution.

Another document stated the effect of institutionalization on brain development in babies. This one was called "Designing

Research to Study the Effects of Institutionalization on Brain and Behavioral Development: The Bucharest Early Intervention Project." It was calculated that for every year of institutionalization there was a delay of three months in the babies' development. This delay could not be recovered, ever. I thought of Paa Kwesi, who could not talk; about Naa, who rocked herself to sleep violently; about the other self-harming cases I had seen at Osu. It became so clear to me. Most orphanages are unable to give a sufficient amount of personal attention to children, and yet the amount of one-on-one affection a child receives affects every aspect of their emotional and physical growth.

It dawned on me that orphanages were not the solution. Instead they were a huge part of the problem: a post-colonial foreign invention paternalistically imposed on a society even though the extended family existed and, even in the era of AIDS, could provide a resilient safety net. Sometimes it seemed that any product that was unsafe or out of date got shipped to Africa; so too was it with ideas. Orphanages hadn't existed in Western Europe since the time of *Oliver Twist*: why did they exist here? (And, I thought bitterly, they bore a striking resemblance to those in *Oliver Twist*.) Institutional care, I saw now, should be reserved only for children with significant emotional and behavioral problems who could not be managed at home or in the community. Or for children with severe disabilities who were dependent on technological support or specialized around-the-clock nursing. Or for children who came from abusive families.

Much of what we had started was good: the community services (infirmaries, birthing support, school support), the scholarships, and the young adult support services. These programs involved helping children and young adults in their own families. Now we had to design a new program; one that would give families who felt forced to abandon their children because of poverty a way of addressing the underlying causes of family separation.

I was faced with huge practical issues: obviously we would have to (gulp) close our own orphanage. How could we run an orphanage, however beautifully ecological and caring, when orphanages were obviously not the best places for children?

25

*I*t took me several weeks to digest the implications of this revelation, and then I discussed everything with Beth. I trusted her, and since she was effectively in charge of the whole of OAfrica outside Ghana, I knew that her reaction would give me a clue as to the kind of resistance I would see in the rest of the staff and donors. After the move from Awutiase and now the move to the new land, the last thing any of my board members wanted was more change. But I gritted my teeth; if this was what was right, then we would just have to do it. There was never going to be a right time for such a big change, and yet it had to be done.

I felt brave and frightened all at once. I knew that we would lose donors who were attached to the idea of a brick-and-mortar building they could visit, giving them a sense of control. They wanted to go to the building, see the kids, and make sure the money was being spent right. How would they feel if we (to paraphrase the words of one development theorist) "gave the money direct to families who needed it?"

Beth was shocked, as I had feared, but after a week or so she came around. She had been to Ghana, spoken to some of the kids, and now she too had read the research. She had been scared by accounts of my experience at Awutiase, and she had faith in my judgment. We devised a short communiqué called "Why Not Orphanages?"

It read:

- Orphanages separate children from family and community life, contributing to the breakdown of society.
- Children grow up feeling that they cannot form a lifelong attachment to a caregiver; something which every child needs.
- Orphanages increase the risk that a child's human rights will be violated; i.e., a child's right to privacy, identity (ethnic & religious), and opportunity is compromised.
- Changes in staffing, funding, and policy can result in inconsistency, and continuity of care can be compromised.
- Orphanages are expensive, and reach only a small number of children (the cost of operating an orphanage can be six times higher than the cost of caring for children in the community).
- Orphanages oftentimes start out as charities, but then develop into businesses at the expense of the children; i.e., donations and income are difficult to monitor, resulting in large-scale fraud.
- Care in an orphanage increases a child's risk of abuse because there is no single person that has overall responsibility for a particular child.
- Orphanages are oftentimes overcrowded, compromising sanitation and hygiene as well as development. Little individual stimulation is provided to children.

And then we told the donors. As I feared, we lost donors, and were faced with a mass of paperwork to change the mission in the three countries where we now had boards. I still stood firm that it had to be done because it was the right thing to do. So we did it. It was not until the following year that we officially started the process to close our orphanage, but we immediately changed our remit to "helping children to grow up in stable, safe, and permanent families." Our day-to-day activities changed too; from helping orphanages to helping them close down, and resettling kids in their families with birth certificates, scholarships, and cash transfers (a small stipend to the family, conditional on school attendance) to ensure they could stay there. It was no use giving scholarships if, for example, the kids had to stay home until after the yam harvest was sold because they could not afford the *tro-tro* fees to get to school. All our efforts now went into making sure these families were viable and safe.

It was difficult, but when I was discouraged I remembered my first weeks at Awutiase when everything seemed so new and foreign. I had been light-years away from understanding that any institutional orphanage, wherever it is, does children a disservice. When I saw 160 children with one "Maa and Dada" and a couple of helpers, I failed to understand that the whole system was wrong. After reading the research and contemplating my experience, I realized that what all children need is one permanent link of affection; a family of their own whether genetic or fostered or adopted. The only way to fix an orphanage is to empty it.

* * *

I started to ask the children about their families. We began having new conversations; conversations I hadn't known we needed to have. I had often heard the older kids talk longingly about their villages. Aware that I could be awakening painful memories, cautiously I began to ask about their families. I knew the children would be terrified of losing their scholarships or leaving the security of life with OAfrica. They would be afraid of change, so I approached the subject carefully, sometimes working around it without asking a direct question. In Ghana it can be hard to get the truth; because of the ubiquitous culture of politeness, even deference, children sometimes tell you what they think you want to hear, especially if they feel threatened. These children were already damaged, and I wanted to keep my pledge of safety to them.

In the quiet of the evening in the sanctuary of my little round mud office–sitting room, surrounded by sleeping dogs and with the monkey watching us from the rafters, the stories came pouring out. It turned out that, much to my joy, most of them did have family. The problem was that most of their families could not afford to take care of them. The more I heard from the children, the more excited I became. This was a window of opportunity, surely; some kind of support given to the families would allow them to keep their kids. Straightaway I was back on the *tro-tros*, visiting aunties and uncles, hearing stories about families, tribes, love, and loss.

In one of our first successful tracing attempts, I pulled into a tiny remote village on a bus with Reynold, who was sixteen. As he stepped off the bus, blinking in the sun after the long ride from Accra, a startling whoop cut through the air; a woman had recognized him as "the lost baby." Before I knew what was happening, a jubilant crowd of ululating women and kids encircled Reynold. The expression on his face after finally returning to his family after living in an orphanage, and before that on the street, had to be seen to be believed. Here, he belonged. That night there was feasting and dancing for his return, the village chief toasting me with local palm wine in an expression of appreciation. The experience was equally cathartic for me, but my mind was filled with questions.

Why was he in an orphanage in the first place when he was obviously loved and wanted by his relatives?

Why had he not returned on his own?

Why had his family not come looking for him?

What had to happen for him to live with his family?

A lot of tough questions had to be answered about resettlement, and I realized that I could not do this alone. The next morning I headed to Accra in the OAfrica van to visit the Department of Social Welfare. I had requested a meeting with the deputy minister of manpower. I felt a sense of urgency, and was eager to share the research and experiences I'd had.

Three hours later, as the morning gridlock gave way to the midday gridlock, we reached the minister's office. I waited for hour as the receptionist stared fixedly at a telenovela on TV in a corner. There was apparently no urgent work on that day. The minister seemed to loathe me on sight, most likely because I was white. *Reason enough*, I sympathized. The deputy director, however, listened to my spiel on closing down orphanages and invited me to come to the next meeting of the Orphans and Vulnerable Committee (OVC), which was charged with care reform.

At the committee meeting the follow week, in the boardroom of the ministry, I officially presented our new mission to a gathering of the twenty top NGOs, the Department of Social Welfare, and ministry personnel. I passionately outlined a vision for a system where children could be resettled from orphanages. The reaction was immediate; it seemed that half of the room was for and the other half against the concept. I was relieved to see that everyone was well aware of the controversy and the issues around orphanages. The proceedings were interrupted when the deputy minister burst in late, dressed in an intricate headdress and an impressive *kabba* and *slit*. As she hurriedly settled into her seat, she asked me to serve her tea. I sat motionless for a moment, not sure if I understood what was happening, and then it became clear. I was the youngest in the room and the only white person. I was too big for my boots, or "too known" as they say in Ghana, where the tolerance for self-importance is zero. I deserved to be taught a lesson. The room went silent as I got up from my chair and boiled the electric kettle, poured the tea, and set out the biscuits. Everyone watched in complete silence, and the tension was palpable. I served the deputy minister with a wooden smile and sank back into my seat.

The meeting was long and very bureaucratic; almost an hour was dedicated to correcting the minutes for the previous one. I was a bit lost among all the NGO-speak, but I did feel that they had the knowledge and the determination to change things. At the end of it rather than depleted, I felt exhilarated. A few days later I was delighted when I was informed that OAfrica was being considered for inclusion on the OVC Committee on a permanent basis.

I always did make a good cup of tea.

Save the Children did not have an office in Ghana but UNICEF did, and they were on the OVC Committee too. It was time to get much closer. The relationship between local UNICEF staff and the small NGOs they are directed to collaborate with (and fund) has often been a fraught one. Perhaps my favorite anecdote is the one told by Mali Nilsson, the wonderfully straightforward ex-head of Child Protection at UNICEF in Ghana. Unusually, Mali was an activist who had worked at Save the Children. She had participated in the United Nations Study on Violence against Children, so she knew what she was talking about, and I loved her. She was a big-boned Scandinavian with an easy laugh and an inclusive humor. She quickly got Social Welfare on her side, and the working relationship with them was easy and fruitful.

"Imagine a big house," she said, "with a big, handsome, well-groomed, strong guard dog. But the strong guard dog is asleep in his kennel—and the house is under attack."

"Okay . . ." I replied, not sure what she was getting at.

"And next to him there is a scruffy but simpatico little mutt, bark, bark, barking to wake the big dog up and alert everyone that the house is under attack," she continued as she started to smile. "The house is child protection, the guard dog is UNICEF, and the little mutt that is awake and vigilant—that is OAfrica."

Then Mali put her head back and roared with laughter.

One of these tracing excursions took place in the north of Ghana, where we were attempting to trace family for a HIV-positive orphan called Ramatu who had recovered spectacularly in our care. The Italian and Spanish country heads for OAfrica, Francesca and Carmen, along with Vida, Mensah, and I were involved in a horrific accident as the *tro-tro* turned over on a remote road. Francesca was badly scarred, and although I was not hurt I spent three unforgettably horrid days running from one ill-equipped hospital to another, trying to make sure everyone was all right. I carried a terrible trauma with me for years, and had to confront my new terror of roads every time I left the house. I started to believe there was a sword of Damocles over my head, and that at any time it could fall. This was intensified by the still-constant death threats on my email. It gave my relationship with Kweku a new intensity; a special poignancy. When death is close, we seek life, sex, and love. Kweku gave me precious reassurance, and our relationship became vital to me. Slowly we started discussing a future together. Battered by all the stressful personal circumstances, I hardly dared hope that here was something solid and true. But I considered it.

Next, OAfrica was able to do something incredible: we helped set up a public-private partnership with the government aimed at deinstitutionalization (closing down orphanages and settling children with their families), funded equally by OAfrica, UNICEF, and the government, called the Care Reform Initiative. OAfrica funded the training of orphanage owners and over 350 social workers. We sponsored

Department of Social Welfare teams into 149 orphanages in Ghana, and got data on every child in them. Then we constructed a database on all these children for use by DSW.

I wasn't surprised by our findings. As I had long suspected, child abandonment was much more common in the Akan regions of Ghana. The Akan are matrilineal, which means children belong to their mother and the mother's family. As opposed to European or American family systems where a woman marries into her husband's family and their children carry on the father's name, the Akan bloodline is traced through females. Under this traditional system the mother's brother would be responsible for the children, and usually mothers earned a living that could meet their family responsibilities. Research shows that more than 50 percent of Akan children have therefore never lived with their fathers.

However, urbanization and the resulting rural-to-urban migration have fundamentally changed the role that rural women play in their families. Today mothers whose income is based on the agrarian economy no longer own or control the means of production. Being often wholly responsible for the children, they are also less able to move the family to urban areas to find work. So they stay on the farms, scraping by in a traditional barter economy, while the men—who are responsible for their sisters' children but not their own, according to tradition—migrate to the cities and eventually earn more cash. That money rarely makes it back to his wife and children. In essence, Akan men who choose not to provide for their children in this new economy are sanctioned by tradition.

The increasing influence of Christianity in Ghana (71 percent of Ghanaians identify as Christians) is slowly changing the idea of the family structure among traditional Akans, but it will take at least a generation to transform an ancestral way of thinking. It is because of this that Ghana has such a high rate of child abandonment.

Mali called on Andrew Dunn, one of the biggest guns in child protection, to create the comprehensive multisectorial government of Ghana National Plan of Action for Orphans and Vulnerable Children, and OAfrica was an implementing partner. In fact we were the only private NGO to be named specifically in the plan. Over the next five years forty-eight orphanages were to be closed, and more than ten would be voluntarily dissolved. It was amazing; now we were making a real difference. The reality on the ground is that helping children is far, far harder than it looks. Anybody who is interested in philanthropy has heard of people who have good intentions but are easily misdirected; or heard stories of corrupt officials. I had grown from naïve volunteer to child activist to reformer in five short years, but this way of helping was finally sustainable and owned by the Ghanaian government itself.

The National Plan of Action for Orphans and Vulnerable Children still has a coordinating committee that meets every three months, and a regional committee that implements actions such as reforming foster care and adoption, closing orphanages, creating refuges, advocating and building awareness, and training social workers.

Working with the government has its own problems, though. Donors often worry about continuity. However, the reality is that people at the top of the various administrations can continue in their positions and continue to implement policy despite changes of government, ruling party, and president. The real problem is that the departments are incredibly underfunded and underresourced. When we started working with DSW, even the director had no computer. Obviously the government social workers, once trained, equipped, and sensitized, are best placed to do the job, as tracing children and their families and then resettling them requires cultural sensitivity and understanding of unwritten local customs. Social services implementation in Africa will only ever be as good as the social workers themselves, and they need support. In 2007 a government social worker who covered the whole of the northern region (roughly the size of South Carolina) was typically given $0.30 per month as transport money to visit children on his caseload throughout this vast area.

26

*A*s OAfrica focused on care reform, my personal life came back to the forefront of my mind. I continued to hear from Sabrina sporadically since we had moved to Ayenyah. At twenty-one, she had moved back to Barcelona. I was reassured to know she was finally, as an adult, emotionally and physically separated from her destructive birth family. Our conversations always ended up with Sabrina underlining this. The irony of my spending most of my waking hours reuniting kids in Ghana with their biological families, while warning my own daughter against hers, did not escape me. But there are families and families, and it was clear to me that each case has to be evaluated individually; there can be no one-size-fits-all rule.

* * *

On July 1, 2006, dressed simply in white and at age thirty-nine, I celebrated a traditional engagement with my long-standing boyfriend Kweku, who was working as a freelance filmmaker and photographer. I was determined that everything about the ceremony should be different to the nightmare of the last one. Beth and I giggled our way through it, involving the children in every aspect of it. Kweku and I were happy, and this ritual was true and precious. I finally moved out of the orphanage into our own little mud hut; I had been living in an orphanage of some sort for the past four years. I badly needed privacy, and to rediscover a kind of independent existence. It was lovely having our own little place, even if we had no light. More romantic, we thought.

Kweku and I traveled to Spain to spend some time with Sabrina. She seemed to be wild and running around with a bunch of druggies. I was cripplingly worried, but she seemed not to care. I forced myself not to intervene, knowing she would just flare up and disappear out of my life again. Sabrina isn't the kind of person you can tell what to do; she had to get there on her own. Still, it was so difficult to watch her, as beautiful, multitalented, and multilingual as she was, surround herself with misfits. *At least*, I kept reminding myself, *she's talking to me again.* I had to count my blessings. It seemed that I was not the enemy anymore, but I wasn't quite her friend either.

Bianca, the Australian volunteer who had so impressed me in 2003, had come back in August of 2007, giving me a bit more freedom. I was desperate to avoid being a one-man show. She had qualifications in finance, human resources, and development, now that she had finished school, which made her a natural choice to lead the teams in those areas. Her remit was that after her year or two was up, she should be able to hand it over to a totally Ghanaian team. We were progressing with the concept of closing down our own orphanage; slowly we were tracing families and finding homes. It was fascinating. I had been absolutely sure that it was the right thing to do in theory, but as I saw the reintegration working, I became convinced that we were doing what was best in practice too. We were well on the way to closing our orphanage.

One by one the children started to leave, being reinserted into their own families, villages, and tribes. Our main job as an organization became the tracing, support, and then monitoring of these families to ensure they were safe and permanent. We also trained parents; in Ghana there are strong family ties, but often there is very little adult-led development of the children in the families. Our parenting classes encouraged adults to actually spend quality time with the kids they took in. The children who were left in the orphanage were the ones that our full staff of Ghanaian social workers had established had no one alive or traceable, or else had abusive families.

Kweku and I agreed that we wanted to adopt, even though we were planning on doing an in vitro fertilization attempt, mainly to appease his family. One sunny lunchtime we sat down and looked at each child's situation, asking ourselves who was unlikely to be adopted by anyone else. We chose Ernest, a double orphan with no traceable family. He was also older; at six years old and with his chronic health problems, it was unlikely that he would find a permanent home.

We asked Ernest if he wanted to be our little boy, explaining that this involved leaving the OAfrica orphanage and moving into our house. We would be his mummy and daddy. "Yes," he said, "I do." Kweku and I gripped each other silently, and love swelled my heart. That day became his birthday, since we did not know his actual birth date. We started the celebration right away. Ernest and I had been together basically every day since he was two, so it wasn't a difficult transition. The bond of affection had always been there, but now we were three; now we were a family.

During those nightly sessions in my office at the nearly empty orphanage, I asked the few remaining children which of the orphanage mothers they would like to live with when finally the orphanage closed its door. In the same way we had asked them to draw the building before we built it, now we were asking them to choose their families.

What surprised me was that everyone knew instantly. "Ma Phyllis," said Rose, a fifteen-year-old with learning difficulties. Before coming to OAfrica, she had been used as a domestic slave.

"Ma Mary," said Aichatu, a refugee who had been raped by her own father.

"Ma Patricia," said Kobina, a Liberian boy who had been rescued from the clutches of a fetish priest about to sacrifice him in the forest.

In every case the attachment was there already. Well, in every case except one.

"I don't know," said Beliratu, the runaway girl from the north who was now about thirteen. Her legs had healed beautifully and, amazingly, she played on the under-seventeen regional volleyball team.

"No worries, Beliratu," I said. "We can talk again next week. But think about it, okay?"

"Okay." She gave me her magical smile as she dashed off to training.

The following week I asked her again, but she still did not know.

"Maybe . . . the cook?" she asked.

The cook was not a foster mother, I pointed out. I asked her if she didn't want to live with any of the other mothers, running through their names. "Nah." She shook her head and looked at me, giggling.

When I went home that night to the miniscule two-room hut where Kweku and I lived with Ernest, I told him about my encounter. Immediately he understood. "You want *us* to foster her?" he said skeptically.

"What do you think?" I asked, not answering his question quite yet.

Beliratu was not adoptable because she had a living mother, but she was not able to be resettled either. Her family had put her into what DSW called one of the "worst forms of child labor," and therefore she could not be returned to them. She was, sadly, destined to spend her life in foster care.

"Maybe you should ask her," I said. I wanted it to be his decision too.

The next day Kweku did just that, his long lanky form leaning against the mud wall as she looked up at him.

I watched from a distance, my heart in my throat.

"She said yes," Kweku said when he walked over to me, almost carelessly, as if it were the simplest conversation he'd ever had.

We laughed. Over the next few months we completed the fostering paperwork, and for all intents and purposes she too was our child, except that we could not travel abroad with her. *No problem,* I thought. *My life is here.*

The only thing pulling me to Europe was Sabrina. She was now twenty-two and pregnant, with no trace of the baby's father. She was determined to keep the baby, as she had always wanted children. In fact I thought the child might prove a stabilizing influence, and she also had a job running a restaurant. I spent some weeks with her during the pregnancy and in the early summer I took photos of her with her big belly, looking absurdly young. I was so frightened for her, but she absolutely loved being pregnant. She was radiating contentment and health, and it became easier to hope that this child would be a blessing.

On August 22, 2007, Marcos Ibrahim was born a little early. He had Sabrina's face, her eyes, and her skin. He was beautiful. To my eternal regret I missed his birth, as Kweku and I were due to get married the following week and my mother and many of my friends, including Carlo from my London days, had traveled to Ghana.

Instead of being next to Sabrina at the hospital, I had to stay home to look after our foreign guests and help to organize the proceedings. I had hoped that Marcos would be born a few weeks later so I could be there to welcome him.

Instead on September 1, 2007, a bunch of my friends came over from Europe and I married Kweku. It was a beautiful party despite the slow drizzle that unusually lasted all day. Ernest, our new son, stood by looking very proud. Fatima was my bridesmaid. We all wore black and white print, signifying joy. We bought outfits for the OAfrica kids, we donated twenty wooden benches to the school. We fed the whole village and all the children to celebrate our marriage.

Once the ceremony was over and before I could settle in with my new husband, I immediately flew off to Spain to meet Marcos, my first grandchild. When I saw Sabrina walk around the corner, proud and pretty with Marcos in her arms, I was overcome with emotion and hugged her tightly. Inside of me something was relieved. She would stay healthy for him; of that I was certain. The bond between them was so strong; I knew it was going to be the one thing that lifted her up. It was a very short trip, just to see the baby and make sure Sabrina was all right. I felt torn between my daughter and new grandchild in Spain, and my children, husband, and work in Ghana.

That fall was very difficult; the days were good sometimes, but the months were bad. Ernest was acting up, demonstrating a pee-vishness I had never seen before. One day he even bit Mensah quite badly, in the middle of a temper tantrum. I felt guilty about not helping Sabrina during the first months of motherhood. I was ill a lot of the time with an unexplained malarialike condition, feverish and weak. On top of all of that, living in our tiny mud hut with no light was uncomfortable and was putting pressure on Kweku and me. Beliratu was desperate to move in with us, but there was no room. If we took the two younger children out together, they would quarrel nonstop. Fatima was continually ill with a strange stomach ailment, and had to leave the prestigious boarding school we had been so proud to get her into. At eighteen, Mensah had decided to move closer to the city. My family felt all mixed up.

Slowly, I felt even Kweku slipping away from me. He seemed oblivious to his family, staying in bed for days on end. It was his black dog: a depression that came in cycles for no apparent reason. I knew nothing of depression, and found it chilling. I fixed my mind on the idea of building a bigger house that would bring everyone together around a massive kitchen table. I had not had a kitchen for six years, and I was really looking forward to it. The new purpose-built mud-and-thatch "extra-large" hut would solve all of our problems, I was sure. In the meantime I took Kweku's love and affection whenever he could offer it, and the rest of the time I threw myself into the building work. In July 2008 we finally moved in. It was quite isolated on the farm, about half a mile down a very rough track from the village, but we needed the space desperately. I was so convinced that my family needed a real home as soon as possible that I pooh-poohed warnings that it might be dangerous to be that inaccessible.

Two days after the move, Mali and I were involved in a terrible car accident when a UNICEF colleague's car turned over while we were both in the back. She went back to Scandinavia for treatment. Without her the relationship with UNICEF degenerated.

Although UNICEF funded some of our activities, they often did not turn up at their own sponsored programs that we had set up for them, and did not even share information. All of this was so puzzling to me and it was a sad experience, being sidelined by UNICEF, when we could have provided much-needed support. However, our relationship with the UNICEF-funded alternative care think tank, the Better Care Network in New York City, flourished. We were able to continue working on many local UNICEF projects too because the Department of Social Welfare insisted that we be included.

Throughout, our relationship with the government flourished, its staff often teaching us what was needed, and me frantically fund-raising to fund those initiatives. It was difficult for some donors to accept the funding of government social workers, as many Europeans still regarded African societies as being in need of foreign experts' advice. But I knew that the social workers were the only ones who could actually do the work. If social workers were as well funded in Africa as they are in rest of the world, they would do a great job: the problem is that no one prioritizes the funding.

* * *

In the following months when Kweku seemed to be a little better, I focused on the children. I tried my best to become a good Ghanaian mum. Of course there were a few hiccups. After all those years in an orphanage, when the food was prepared communally, I had become a bit rusty in the kitchen. There was no Western supermarket within less than a two-hour ride, and as we were so far from the main road, I went scavenging in the local towns once a week. Meat could only be bought in the abattoir, a wooden shack full of flies. It was filled with quarter-carcasses of tough Fulani cows laid out, hide, head, tail and all, across cement surfaces; decorated with piles of marrow bones, liver, and entrails. The abattoir was staffed by huge men in singlets, who shone with sweat and wielded big knives as they cracked the massive bones and weighed the meat on rusty scales. There were no recognizable cuts; just shapeless lumps of bloody red meat. Cat meat, dog meat, and goat meat were bought alive in the village. Rats and grass-cutters (guinea pigs) were bought smoked by the side of the road. The other protein option was snails, each as big as a small kitten. Locally there were no dairy products, except powdered milk and the oversweet processed yogurt sold as ice cream. Olive oil was considered medicinal, and was only available in the pharmacy where the pastors bought it to do their anointings in church.

The other problem was vegetables; the selection was very small, and only one variety of each seemed to exist. And there were hidden pitfalls. I learned, for example, that cocoyam leaves look and taste like spinach, but need to be boiled for a very long time because they contain arsenic. The first time, I did not cook them long enough, and we all ended up with swollen tongues after our dinner. Then came the realities of the irregular water flow in our jungle abode and the daunting task of going to the big Agormenya market, which was a huge swirling mass of big ladies in the red dust cloud with baskets of what seemed to be an extremely limited range of produce, mostly tubers and odiferous dried, smoked, or salted fish. Oh yes, and then there was the issue of our staple: tough and sinewy local chickens, live of course. Luckily, Beliratu took over the task of official chicken slaughterer, dispatching them in the morning before she went to school.

I started a vegetable patch, nostalgically hoping for the taste of home, and had a glut of giant arugula, basil, and eggplants, which we had to eat for every meal during two whole months, after everything else had shriveled up and died. I learned the hard way that in the tropics everything rots twice as fast as you think it could. Anything left outside of our big old-fashioned solar fridge oozed and suppurated in one afternoon. But despite these challenges, I was definitely settling into placid domesticity, even putting on weight. My heart and mind were invested in the children, Ayenyah, and our wonderful new house. Rooted, it seemed, at last. Until that December night when the tap flowed at midnight and, exhausted from flying home from the funeral for Paul, the man who had so kindly taken me into his family when my dad ran away, I forgot to lock the door.

27

I snapped awake, feeling the weight of a man on top of me. He was shrouded by the mosquito net, and trying to pull off my wedding ring. On my right, Kweku let out a short sharp cry. I came to in an instant, terrified and incredulous. They had crept up on us utterly silently.

The men—there were quite a few, it seemed—were barking at us nervously, in low voices. They were demanding, "Where is your money?"

My first thought was for Ernest and Beliratu; Fatima was sleeping over in the village that night. Had the brutes seen them? Did they even know the kids were sleeping in the house? Had they awakened them?

The men seemed young and very nervous: their movements were jerky. *Are they on drugs?* I wondered. *Or is it just adrenaline?* I could not make them out properly, as I didn't have my glasses. That haziness, that indistinctness in the darkness, was most terrifying of all.

Kweku collapsed to the floor and pleaded with them. He called them "sir." *That's right*, I thought dully. I'd read somewhere that meek

and acquiescent was the way to go in these situations if they happened, which of course they didn't. Not to people like us, who rescued children as our day job.

"Sorry, rasta, ehh," a thug said to him. "We don't like to harm a
rasta such as yourself. It be orders, it no be me oooooh."

Then I think he punched him, because Kweku cried out hard in
an oddly shrill voice.

I realized that it was fear that had changed his tone, or maybe it
was pain. They dragged him away, outside to the garden, and all I
could hear was him yelling loudly in the night, "Yes, sir. No, sir." I
realized that he was sending me a signal: be compliant. At the same
time, he was trying to make noise, to alert any hunters who might be
on our hill, the farmer in his house down the way. I could see the
sense in it, but I was terrified that the pitiful commotion he was making would wake the children. What would they do to Beliratu, just
thirteen, so fragile and slim, and Ernest? Suddenly Kweku's cries
stopped dead.

I realized with great clarity then that here on the hill, no one
would save us. We were on our own. They would kill us, and no one
would know until the staff arrived in the morning. Our only chance
was to get them to go to the village.

A savage blow to my spinal cord made me fall to my knees. The
man had a *langa-langa*, a kind of machete with a long flexible blade.
He struck me again, and then again, across my back. I fell to the
floor, grasping the bit of cloth I slept in and pulling it around me.
Facedown on the carpet, I tried to wiggle under the bed, but it was
too low. A last glancing blow fell on my neck, and I felt an electrical
shock go up and down my spine.

"Stop that!" came a curt command. The blows stopped.

Their leader gave me his hand. He helped me to stand, and I
sagged against the bed.

"Where is the money? he asked.

"I don't have any money, sir. It is in the office, in the village, sir. Please." I sighed the words, dragging the air through my aching thorax.

The *langa-langa* blade flew through the air again and landed on my shoulders.

He asked again, more harshly, "Where is the money, *white woman?*"

The hated "white woman," even now come to taunt me.

"I can't see . . . I can't show you . . . my specs," I mumbled.

"What? Find her specs!" he thundered. I sat dumbfounded as his men stopped rifling through our stuff and started a diligent search for my glasses, which were found after ten minutes, miraculously whole. The men were masked, and called each other "Charlie." I would never be able to recognize them, I realized. There were six of them, and they were thorough, organized; seemingly professional.

The whole thing reminded me of a B movie. Even as it was happening, it felt like *being* in a B movie, it was so unreal. I stood up straighter and looked around, as a tiny portion of my equanimity returned with my sight. I saw that the room was covered in a thick layer of papers; like a blanket of snow, everything was overlaid with my home office files.

Their torches shone dimly, and I could see that they all held knives or machetes, and guns. For a moment I thought that the guns were plastic, and that this was an unfunny trick. My dazed mind was still refusing to accept reality. There were an AK-47, a couple of blunt sawn-off shotguns, and even an old-timer's revolver that looked strangely out of place, like a leftover from a spaghetti western. The smallest guy had a rifle, similar to the ones the villagers used to hunt the antelopes that sought refuge in our garden.

I told them where things were, but they had already found everything we kept in the house: Kweku's filming equipment, the cash to pay his film crew, his Mac, our phones. We owned nothing more. I tried to explain this, with a lot of "Please, sir's" thrown in, pleading that everything was kept in the office, in the storeroom, and that untold riches were to be had in the container. *In the village.*

I got knocked around a bit more, but with less conviction, and then they tied the pillow slipcover over my mouth.

I watched as they ransacked my home some more. The man who appeared to be their leader walked over to me. He was close enough that I could smell his sweat as he nodded to the boy to untie my gag. That kindness, for some reason, overwhelmed me. In a conversational tone that seemed wildly ironic, considering the circumstances, he asked, "Where are you from?"

"Uh, I'm English, but I was born in Spain." The complicated reply rolled off my tongue as it always did, designed to halt further enquiry.

"I was in Spain once. They treated me . . ." he paused ". . . so badly."

I stayed silent.

"Why should I treat you any better? Why are you in Ghana? Heh?"

He seemed an educated man, but he sounded bitter. Silence seemed to be the best policy. I tried to shrink myself into nothing as I looked at my feet.

"Tell me why I'm here," he insisted.

What did he mean?

This did not seem like the time for existential dialogue, so I looked at him blankly. The cogs of my brain felt as if it they were literally moving through sludge.

Suddenly impatient, he asked, "Why do they want you gone? Why did they send me? Tell me. *You* tell *me.*"

This was a man who was obviously used to instant compliance. My neck hurt and I wanted to cry. More than anything right then, I wanted to know who "they" were.

"Yes, sir. Of course, sir," I replied in a conciliatory tone, stalling for time to come up with a reasonable response to his impossible question.

In that instant, I realized that this was my opportunity to talk myself out of rape, or worse.

"Okay. Let me explain, sir." I swallowed hard.

He snarled at his men to leave the room.

He rested his Kalashnikov comfortably across his thighs and settled down in the manner of listeners the world over. I wrapped my bit of sweaty cloth even tighter around me and explained why I was in Ghana; what I did, and the lives I had saved. I even told him that my dad had just died and how he wasn't really my dad, but was, *really*. How I had a stake in this country, in these lives.

By the time I stopped talking, it seemed that dawn was still far away, but the bite had gone out of him. I could feel it. He glanced up from fiddling with the gun across his knees and looked at me straight in the eye. He spoke quietly.

"If I had met you when I was a child, I would not be doing this job now."

There was silence. Even in my foggy state, I realized that was the best compliment I had ever received.

"Armed robbery?" I asked.

His reply was chilling. "Killing people," he replied softly.

"I'm sorry." I realize now that it was an odd thing to say to my attacker, but the balance of power between us had somehow changed.

He stood up abruptly, and suddenly I was really afraid. Guilt can make people do terrible things; I have seen that in my own life. My stomach contracted and my knees were trembling.

He called his men back in. The shortest one marched up to me, thrusting his pelvis at me, undoing his zipper. Closely followed by the man who had used the *langa-langa* to beat me. I shrank back from them, knowing this was it. My Scheherazade act was about to be judged.

"Master, make we rape am, now? Eh?" the boy asked excitedly.

"Foolish dog. We no be here for rape matter." The leader lunged at the boy with his gun and I screamed. Everything moved very fast from that moment. "Cut the cables," he barked.

Since we only had solar power, we did not have many electronics in the house. We only had a tiny ancient TV, a shortwave radio for the BBC Africa service, and laptop cords. I wondered what they would want with them.

The men used them to tie my hands tightly behind my back, the plastic cutting into my flesh.

"Get her shoes." The leader was oddly considerate. The boy put my flip-flops on the wrong feet and squeezed my thigh in the process. I suppressed my urge to kick him. I kept my head down and let myself be shoved around.

They marched me to our car. Squat and tinny, ugly and familiar, this was our way out of the nightmare. The boy ran behind holding the old TV. "Put that down," cried the leader, angry at being disobeyed, lunging out, waving his gun. "Heh, do think we be common thieves, or what? It only be the money and the woman we want."

Two of the men brought Kweku staggering over from the lawn near the clothesline. He was stripped to the waist and bloody. He looked terrified. When I saw him then, I cried for the first time. I was so relieved that he was alive.

Blubbering, coughing on snot and tears and sweat, I was pushed into the trunk of the car. They marched Kweku off somewhere unknown; to shoot him, I surmised wildly. No, I realized, they wanted him to get the car keys. Considering what a mess they had left the room in and the mess he was in, I have no idea how he found them. But it seemed to take only a second before they were back and pushing Kweku on top of me in the small space. They piled in the car and took off at top speed down the muddy rough steep track down the hillside. They must have been concerned that dawn was approaching. "Are you all right?" I was crying as I whispered to Kweku, my mouth crushed against his foot "We have to get away," I whispered to Kweku. "We have to wake the villagers!"

When we stopped in the village, I realized that we were among houses and hoped the engine had awakened people. I thought maybe it was nearly over. Surely the villagers would wake up, the watchman would see what was happening, and we would be rescued.

"Run away," I whispered to Kweku. I could see the whites of his eyes in the dark, and smell the fear on him as our broken bodies were crushed together in the trunk. "It's me they're after; you run away. Alert the village. Get to our children."

There were sounds of a scuffle, and then the trunk hatch was opened. They had pulled up in front of our office building. One of the thugs grabbed me, yanked me out, and put a gun to my head. They tied cloth over my mouth. As I was shoved forward, we passed our watchman who was curled over in an odd position, lying in the dirt. Was he dead? The hope seeped out of me again. The man walked me to the storeroom, the container, and the office. He arbitrarily hurt me, hitting me. He never took the gun from my temple. Was I a hostage now, in case anyone woke up?

"Where the keys, the money? Give me the keys. Where is the money?"

I didn't know where Kweku had been taken. No one seemed to wake up. By then I had basically collapsed in defeat, and they were holding me up as I led them to the office.

He threw me on the floor where he had dragged me to parrot the combination of the safe, now ungagged. I heard urgent voices. The gang in the room was huddled over the safe.

Now Kweku was right next to me again on the floor, still tied up, but also not gagged. We seemed to have become a bit of an after-thought. The office door was open. I suddenly realized the jet-black sky was clearing; there was gray dawn light outside. The birds were already making a racket. "Run, *run* . . ." I whispered.

Kweku wiggled to his feet and ran fast, his hands still tied together. He shouted at the top of his voice as soon as he got out the door. "Armed robbers! Armed robbers!" The robbers, alarmed, ran out the room and chased him. The room was empty, and I was alone. They seemed to have forgotten all about me. And then I heard it: the sound I had been waiting for all night; my whole life, it seemed like. I heard the sound of gunshots.

Surely they hadn't shot Kweku—or had they?

I had seen the man I loved race out the door. Bruised and bleed-ing, long skinny legs flapping, his arms akimbo, breaking free of the ties, and yelling at the top of his lungs as he raced into the cluster of mud huts that was our village. Then my view was blocked: gun-shots, car tires screeching, yelling, crying—pandemonium.

I dragged myself out the office door. They had taken our car, shot into the crowd, and gone. Fatima says she found me there, like that, in the dusty main square, in the predawn darkness. "Like Jesus," she says, on my knees, my skin shining with sweat and tears, bleeding all the way down my back; my hands now free, my eyes crazy in disbelief and confusion, clutching my cloth tight to my chest, wild-eyed.

"The children . . ." I began.

Fatima grasped what I wasn't able to say and took off like the wind back toward our house on the hillside. I followed, held up by Agbeko and David, two of the village boys who worked for my char-ity. I ran, stumbling, panting, barefoot by this point. Through the village I raced, gasping for air. Stop. Run again. Across the mango plantation; gasp, pant, my chest was bursting. Into our land, up the hill, my legs were burning, my breath short, I doubled over, stopped to breathe, nearly there . . . I ran as if possessed. I didn't know if Kweku was dead or alive; if the children had been knifed in their beds. How could they have slept through their father's screams, the ransacking, the car engine starting. The sound of our lives being violated. But somehow they did. Fatima only awakened Beliratu a few minutes before I clambered painfully up the porch stairs. Beliratu actually thought it was a practical joke until she saw me. Ernest did not wake up at all.

Kweku was fine, in the sense that he arrived thirty minutes later. The psychological wounds went deeper, and we would struggle with them for many months. But that dawn, exhaustion mercifully prevailed. We sponged the worst of the blood off each other as day broke, and by mutual accord went straight to bed until the police arrived.

I never slept well in that room again.

The next morning Ernest wandered into the kitchen in his pajamas, where I was sitting with the police. Wide-eyed, he asked me if I knew what had happened in the night. Wearily, tearfully I hugged him. "Yes, dear," I said.

"How did you know the tooth fairy came?" he asked, suddenly suspicious.

"Tooth fairy?" I looked at him vacantly.

"Yes, Mum, she gave me one cedi!"

I remembered then that long ago, in the evening before the attack, I had slipped a crumpled red one-cedi note under his pillow to commemorate the big gap in his front teeth. It seemed a lifetime ago.

This story has given us ammunition to tease Ernest forever, basically.

We moved into a hotel that day. A few days later the police had a suspect, then another and another. A day after that they were given bail and released. I was furious. I marched into the daub-and-wattle police station with its painted sign: GHANA POLICE SERVICE.

"Madame." The uniformed Criminal Investigation Department officer looked at me across the high wooden counter with the air of someone about to dispense bad news. He lowered his voice conspiratorially and spoke gently. "They were all bailed by the fetish priest at Somanya."

The village of Somanya was the epicenter of the mango-growing area, about twelve miles up the road.

That was when I realized that the law courts would never try the gang, and they would never be punished. The police were far too worried about the repercussions of messing with the fetish priest to even try to impose a semblance of justice. We live about three hours from the cradle of voodoo, or *vudun*, and most people here, whether cursorily Christian or Muslim, believe in *vudun* first and foremost. It is so woven into the culture—festivals, customs, and rituals—that it is part of what it is to be Ghanaian. This sense of superior spiritual power should be ignored only at your peril, as I had just learned.

With its superior powers of protection and retribution, everyone is terrified of incurring the priest's wrath, and in particular the wrath of priests like the one at Somanya. He practiced *juju*, an occult science, and made his living by putting spells on the credulous. He must have been hired by someone who did not like the work I was doing, closing orphanages. Someone who was making money through the orphanage racket. Or maybe just people after our supposed wealth. I realized then that I would never know.

The hated colonial masters' rulebook of law and order didn't stand a chance. The brutes were free and they would remain free, living a few miles down the road. To all intents and purposes they were our neighbors.

"Madame," the officer continued, pursing his lips and looking at me disapprovingly, "you should move to town . . . Or buy a gun," he added as he showed me out. I slid into the car Marcel had lent us, next to Kweku, bursting with anger and frustration. Later that day, the officer came to see me at the hotel to confirm that the men had jumped bail.

"But you were lucky," he said in a casual tone, "After they left you, they stopped a car and raped the woman who was driving." I gasped, felt my stomach contract, and suddenly felt connected to the unknown woman.

"You got off easy. Whatever you told them, it must have been a powerful story."

Epilogue

Ayenyah, May 2014

Next month it will be thirteen years since my first trip to Ghana. I'm still living in a tiny mud-and-thatch hut in Ayenyah, as our bush-fabulous house was burned to the ground by arsonists in February 2013. Again, as with the attack, we don't know who did it. I am still actively combating child traffickers operating out of illegal orphanages, so that is a possibility.

Of my five children, Sabrina has two boys of her own, lives in Paris, and is working in the fashion industry. She is a great mum to Marcos and Adam, and we continue to be very close. She has had the courage to deal with the demons in her past; she is, quite simply, amazing.

Fatima is as gorgeous and gentle as ever. She is finishing her degree in psychology, and recently got married to James. She has a lovely daughter called Skyla Lovatt-Smith, whose birth I attended.

Mensah has graduated from university and is planning for his masters degree. He wants to work in development. He has a fine questioning mind, and I'm very proud of him.

We were able to adopt Beliratu in the end. She is proudly study-ing business in Spain, and is still charming everyone with that irre-pressible smile.

Ernest, "my left knee," as they call the last born in the Dangme language, is finishing junior high. He is sitting next to me right now, doing his homework.

OAfrica has gone from strength to strength. Bianca is in charge now, having returned from almost four years at Save the Children Australia, where she was head of Africa and Asia. Apart from her, our whole program staff is Ghanaian. We serve over three hundred children and young adults directly, with a strong focus on special needs and abused children, especially those from institutions. Indi-rectly, through the Care Reform Initiative, we continue to advocate on behalf of the forty-five hundred children still estimated to live in orphanages in Ghana today. You can support us at oafrica.org. We need your help to finish the amazing work we have been able to achieve so far.

To successfully reach the children without appropriate care, the Ghanaian government must provide funding to their own Depart-ment of Social Welfare, in order to eliminate the need for orphan-ages by keeping children in their own families. Our dream is to support the reform of the social welfare system in Ghana to the point where we are not needed anymore. For the time being, a lot of chil-dren here still fall through the cracks, and we still have a role to play.

The big picture—United Nations, are you listening?—is to have child protection as a policy priority for all governments. Our cause has been hurt because child protection is not part of the millennium goals. It needs to be front and center of public and development policy all over the world. If the twentieth century was the one where women's rights began at last to be observed, let us hope that the twenty-first will be that of children's rights.

Me? I write and speak a lot on care reform, and in 2012 I was awarded the FACE Africa prize by a Liberian charity in New York. The same year, I also won the prestigious Prix Clarins de la Femme Dynamisante in Paris for my advocacy work in favor of deinstitutionalization.

And what of my passion, getting children out of orphanages and into families in Ghana? What of the forgotten children invisible behind the doors of residential homes used as hubs by traffickers and abusers?

In 2010 investigative journalist Anas Aremeyaw Anas released a film that was shot undercover. It documented incredible brutality and abuse at Osu Children's Home and the Remand Home. The deputy minister of manpower ordered a full investigation, and charged me with producing the reference materials for the committee. Later that year the National Plan of Action for Orphans and Vulnerable Children, the one that Mali and I had worked so hard on, was officially launched as a practical blueprint for reforming the sector. OAfrica was the only NGO named as an implementing partner. I was very proud.

Today the sector is well on the way to reform in Ghana; "Regulations for the Operation of Residential Homes" has been published by the government, and Ghana is preparing to sign the Hague Convention on International Adoption, which will tighten adoption regulations. In the meantime there is a moratorium on international adoptions. Some of the best international experts in the sector are working on a collaborative process with all stakeholders to produce regulations for adoption and foster care.

The new Ministry of Gender, Children and Social Protection has issued an ultimatum to operators of orphanages in the country to acquire licenses, or else face closure. It has already closed forty-eight orphanages since we launched the National Plan of Action. In

January 2014 the current minister for gender, children, and social protection in Ghana, an activist called Nana Oye Lithur, promised to close down all the illegal orphanages in Ghana over the next two years.

Awutiase is on that list.

Acknowledgments

*T*his book would certainly never have seen the light of day if not for my extraordinary agent, Elizabeth Evans at the Jean V. Naggar Literary Agency (JVNLA). She believed in the project from the word go and was much more determined to get it published than I was. (By the way, she is absolutely the most demanding editor I have ever worked with.) Elizabeth, I salute you. Thank you for pushing me so hard. Never change.

The wonderfully serene editorial director at Weinstein Books, Amanda Murray, and publishing director Georgina Levitt who chose my book out of literally hundreds of others, were unfailingly positive and great to work with. They brought me to my talented editor, the celebrated Leslie Wells, who was wonderfully encouraging and caring every step of the way, despite our tight schedule. She kindly coached me through the most difficult moments of creating this book. Leslie, thank you so much.

I would also very much like to thank Ruth Marshall, who became my friend through this book. She wrote the entire proposal, much of which made its way straight into the book untouched, as she is such a poetic and talented wordsmith. I'm extremely fond of the rest of the team, too: Jennifer Weltz, such a clever lady, and Tara Hart at JVNLA, and Kathleen Schmidt at Weinstein Books who have put so much of themselves into the promotion of this book.

I would like to homage Bonnie Lieberman, a legendary publisher at Wiley who saw the potential in my story and went out of her way to find me an agent. She invested in the book and thus made it a reality. Without Bonnie's kindness and savvy, the book would have stayed a daydream concocted by our mutual friend, Ryan Flahive, who had the original vision for this story as something that should be published. He put a lot of hard, entirely voluntary, work into the first draft of the proposal. Thank you, too, to the wonderfully spontaneous Michael van Gelderen, who came to lunch in Ghana and ended up financing the project.

I love all of you—this is actually your book.

I would like to acknowledge my life partner Nicolas Neufcourt, my lovely friend Regan Watson for the original material on Beliratu, Nana Brew Hammond for all the support from day one, Cori Deterding for the extensive feedback and editing, and Elizabeth Del Bourgo and Jonathan Hooker for precious input into the final manuscript.

The nice thing about writing your acknowledgments is that it makes you feel so grateful, giving personal meaning to the word *ubuntu,* "I am because we are." At different times in my life, when things were very hard, specific people reached out and lifted me up: Paul and Barbara McMahon, Serge Bakalian, Jonathan Hooker, Elizabeth Del Bourgo, Francis Hurtut, Jean Loup Sieff (RIP), Amy Short, Ramon Macía, Franca Sozzani, Victoria Abril, Marcel Desailly, Jamil Maraby, Hervé van der Straeten, Angela Missoni, Giancarlo Giammeti, Olivia Mariotti, Salvatore Ferragamo, Rossy de Palma, Isabelle Fromager, Anna Davenport, Katie Holmes, Frédéric Mitterrand, Christophe Robin, Martine de Menthon, and most recently

Eric Don-Arthur. Thank you for being an expression of pure kindness in my life. Without you I would have most probably given up.

I would not be the person I am today without my alternative family. Many of these people are in the book but because of space and narrative constraints, many are not. I would like to mention Alberto Heras, Jonathan McMahon, and Graham Kuhn, my brothers. Gerlinde Guelfenbein, Beth Del Bourgo, Regan Watson, Patricia Boving, and Armelle Saint-Mleux, my sisters. Charles-Henri Lobkowicz, Hervé van der Straeten, John Powell, Paul Duncan, Kofi Debrah, Remy Toussaint, Alan Tanksley, and Carlo Ducci, my besties. Anthony Allen for letting me go. Jonathan Hooker, as a respected guide and advisor. Anas Aremeyaw Anas, the master. Ramon Macía, Ed Asante, and Didier Hassan, who have protected me over and over way beyond the call of duty.

As for my boards and staff, there are so many wonderful and generous people involved in OAfrica, that it is impossible to list them all. In particular I would like to mention Margherita Maccapani Missoni, Rachel Roy, Anja Rutterman, Luca Magni, Sonia Barrajón, Sergio Volturo, Francesca Pinto, Ashley Allison Adam, Carmen Perez de la Cruz, Bianca Collier and Robert Dakwa, and the Bousquet-Chavanne family. Thank you for everything you do for OAfrica every day. Your karma is *immense!*

Most of all, I would like to thank the children whose desire to succeed despite their circumstances infused me with a warrior spirit and made me a new person. And for all those I was not able to mention, as the fire ripped through me, please forgive me.

Index

Keeping Children in Families

Children need families

Most of the children in "orphanages" in Ghana are not really orphans, but their parents and extended families find it difficult to care for them because of the burden of poverty, disease, and lack of social protection, and end up sending them to "orphanages" simply to ensure access to food and education.

What we do

OA helps families of children at risk of abandonment and gives them secure futures within their communities. Families are forever and even in the era of HIV/AIDS they provide a vital safety net for life—something an institution can never do.

We work to strengthen families and communities so they can care for their own children. We believe that poverty and ill health are not reasons for separating children from their families and that children living in institutions should be resettled as soon as possible through family tracing and reunification or fostering.

Our organization works to:

- Keep Families Together • Send Children to School
- Keep Mothers Alive • Protect Children by Transforming Systems

OAfrica depends on the generous donations of individuals and businesses to help us carry out our work in Africa. Thanks for your support!

To make a donation please visit: www.OAfrica.org

Contributions to Orphan Aid Africa, a tax-exempt organization under Section 501(c)(3) of the Internal Revenue Code, are deductible for computing income and estate taxes.